DONALD BROOK:

CONDUCTORS' GALLERY

SIR ADRIAN BOULT

CONDUCTORS' GALLERY

Biographical sketches of
well-known orchestral conductors
including notes on
the leading symphony orchestras,
and a short biography of
the late Sir Henry Wood

BY

DONALD BROOK

Biography Index Reprint Series

 BOOKS FOR LIBRARIES PRESS
FREEPORT, NEW YORK

First Published 1945

Second Edition (revised) 1946

Reprinted 1947

Reprinted 1971 by arrangement with
Barrie & Jenkins, Ltd.

INTERNATIONAL STANDARD BOOK NUMBER:
0-8369-8037-9

LIBRARY OF CONGRESS CATALOG CARD NUMBER:
70-136642

PRINTED IN THE UNITED STATES OF AMERICA

CONTENTS

PAGE

INTRODUCTION · 1

RICHARD AUSTIN

Frederic Austin — Early life — Opera — Bournemouth — E.N.S.A.
—Municipal orchestras—Regional system—Subsidies . . . 3

JOHN BARBIROLLI

Childhood — Royal Academy of Music — 'Cellist — Queen's Hall
Orchestra—Wartime—International String Quartet—Opera—Russia
—New York Philharmonic Symphony Orchestra—Sibelius—The
Hallé Orchestra—The younger players—Interpretation—A strict
master 9

SIR THOMAS BEECHAM

Boyhood—Rossall—Oxford—The Hallé Orchestra—Early experiences
—" Bankruptcy "—Imperial League of Opera—The Delius Festival
The New York Philharmonic Orchestra—The London Philharmonic
Orchestra—Sibelius Festival—BBC—America—Unique personality 16

SIR ADRIAN BOULT

A gentleman—Early days—Westminster School—Oxford—Leipzig—
Nikisch and Reger—Munich and Bayreuth—War service—London
Symphony Orchestra—" The Planets "—The Royal College of
Music—Musical pilgrimages—America—Bruno Walter—The City of
Birmingham Orchestra — Sir Walford Davies — BBC — The BBC
Symphony Orchestra—Brussels—Continental tour—Knighthood—
Coronation of King George VI—America—New York World Fair—
BBC in wartime—" The National Gallery of Music "—Purist—
Rhythm—Advice to young conductors—How to rehearse—Considera-
tion for the Orchestra—Respect for musicianship—The musical
renascence—Comfort of the audience—Modern music—Vaughan
Williams—Development of music—Personal notes . . . 21

WARWICK BRAITHWAITE

New Zealander—Scholarship—Youngest conductor in England—BBC
Musical Director—Cardiff Musical Society—National Orchestra of
Wales—Sadler's Wells Company—Scottish Orchestra—Modern music
—Scottish Audiences—Qualifications for conducting—Advice to
young musicians — Technique — Academic Influence — Women in
orchestras—Composer 28

CONDUCTORS' GALLERY

PAGE

BASIL CAMERON

Choirboy—Junior Clerk—York—Berlin—Queen's Hall Orchestra—
Torquay — War service — Hastings — America — The technique of
conducting 33

MOSCO CARNER

Vienna — Czechoslovakia — Danzig — England — Musicologist —
The conductor as a teacher—New Music—The younger school of
English composers—Mozart—Naturalization—Helen Pyke . . 35

ALBERT COATES

St. Petersburg — Nikisch — Leipzig — Opera — Scriabin — London
Symphony Orchestra—Sir Thomas Beecham—Leeds—World-wide
traveller — Composer — America — E.N.S.A. — The new audiences
—Russian audiences—The Soviet Regime—Contemporary music—
Kabalevsky—The freedom of Soviet composers—Cosmopolitan 40

LOUIS COHEN

A Northerner—Liverpool School of Music—War service—Royal
Manchester College of Music—The Hallé Orchestra—The Merseyside
Orchestra—Liverpool Philharmonic Society—Harrogate—Southport—
The northern audiences—The future of the musical profession 44

EDRIC CUNDELL

A Londoner—Horn students—Covent Garden—R.A.S.C.—Serbia—
Trinity College of Music—The Westminster Orchestra—The Stock
Exchange Orchestra—America—New Zealand—South Africa—The
Guildhall School of Music—London Philharmonic Orchestra—The
Royal Philharmonic Society — The trend of modern music — The
training of conductors—Composer—Artist 47

GIDEON FAGAN

A South African—Student days—" Hansel and Gretel "—Theatrical
experiences — " Diggenhof " — Film music — BBC Conductor —
Composer . . . . , . 51

ANATOLE FISTOULARI

Kiev—Infant prodigy—Touring in Russia—Germany—Chaliapin—
" Grand Opera Russe "—Colonne Orchestra—Paris—Monte Carlo—
Covent Garden—America—Soldier in the French Army—Cherbourg—
Flight to England—Anna Mahler—" Sorotchintsi Fair "—London
Philharmonic Orchestra—Impressions of British musical life . . 55

JULIUS HARRISON

Malvern—The Elgar Country—Childhood—Birmingham School of
Music—Sir Granville Bantock—Composer—Opera Conductor—Royal
Flying Corps—The Scottish Orchestra—Royal Academy of Music—
Hastings Municipal Orchestra—Worcestershire again—The BBC
Northern Orchestra — Compositions — Contemporary music — The
academic approach — Jazz—Conducting — Interpretation—Literary
activities—Personal notes 61

vi

CONTENTS

PAGE

ERNEST IRVING

Ealing Film Studios — Personality — Boyhood — Theatrical life —
Spain—Edward German—Royal Philharmonic Society—Sir Henry
Irving—Musical Director of the Ealing Film Studios—A Royal
audience—The development of film music—Criticism of the BBC—
Originality in contemporary music—Beauty in music—Perfection in
conducting—The new audiences   70

REGINALD JACQUES

C.E.M.A.—Early days—War service—Oxford—The Bach Choir—
Music Adviser to London County Council—The Jacques String
Orchestra—The origin and objects of C.E.M.A.—State support for
music—Industrial workers' appreciation of music—Concerts during
air-raids.   79

CONSTANT LAMBERT

A Londoner—Christ's Hospital—Early compositions—Journalist—
" The Rio Grande "—Vic Wells Ballet—Paris—Holland—BBC—
Unimaginative programmes—The new audiences—Neglect of Russian
and French music—Stereotyped programmes—The boom in music—
Ballet . . . . ,   85

MUIR MATHIESON

Childhood in Scotland—Royal College of Music—First film work—
Denham Studios—BBC—Queen Mary at Denham—Famous composers for the films—The ideal film music—Young composers wanted   88

HERBERT MENGES

Boyhood—Hove Town Hall—Royal College of Music—Brighton—
The Old Vic — Sadler's Wells Opera Company — The London
Rehearsal Orchestra — Opera in England — The future of English
opera—The need for competent administration in musical matters   93

MAURICE MILES

Cathedral choirboy—Royal Academy of Music—BBC Balance and
Control Department — Buxton — Bath — South America—Army—
BBC again—Neglect of contemporary composers—Music publishers
—" Buying " concerts—Young conductors . . ,   .   97

BOYD NEEL

Physician — Royal Naval College — Cambridge — St. George's
Hospital—The Boyd Neel String Orchestra—Recordings—Glynde-
bourne—Salzburg—Portugal—E.N.S.A.—State Opera—Zoning of
Orchestras—Ministry of Culture   100

PAGE

SIDNEY NEWMAN

Clifton College—Oxford—Music at Oxford—University Music Club—
Sir Donald Tovey — Royal College of Music — Tours abroad —
Newcastle—Edinburgh—Reid Symphony Orchestra—Value of the
amateurs—Musical standards—Wealth of song—Modern composers—
Newman on holiday 104

CLARENCE RAYBOULD

Schooldays—languages student—Birmingham and Midland Institute
—Sir Granville Bantock—Accompanist—Bachelor of Music—Army—
Beecham Opera Company—British National Opera Company—
Australia—Guildhall School of Music—BBC—Tours abroad—The
conducting cult—Qualifications for conducting—Modern tendency in
composition—Adaptation of the classics—Ballet—Music in radio
plays 111

KATHLEEN RIDDICK

Early days—Guildhall School of Music—Surrey String Players—
Manchester — Salzburg — London Women's String Orchestra —
C.E.M.A.—BBC 116

STANFORD ROBINSON

Leeds—Boy conductor—Starting from the bottom—Royal College
of Music—First day at the BBC—London Operatic Choir—London
Wireless Chorus—Deputy announcer—A tight spot—The National
Chorus—Sir Edward German—Stravinsky—Bach Cantatas—BBC
Theatre Orchestra — Marriage — Sir Thomas Beecham—Director, of
Opera—Trouble with the police—Blindfold conductor—Stockholm—
Italy—War—BBC Theatre Chorus—The future of studio opera—Size
of orchestras—Studios—Modern music—What the orchestra thinks—
Radio listeners—Money in orchestrating—Musical shows—Gardener 119

MALCOLM SARGENT

Native of Lincolnshire—Stamford School—Organist—Peterborough
Cathedral — War — Opera — Breakdown — Orchestral conductor—
Musical ambassador—Sweden—Portugal—Royal Choral Society—
Need for more first-class orchestras 130

ALEC SHERMAN

Londoner — Violinist — BBC Symphony Orchestra — New London
Orchestra—Dame Myra Hess—Royal audience—Ballet—A better
spirit in music—C.E.M.A. 135

CONTENTS

PAGE

HEATHCOTE STATHAM

Cathedral organist — Boyhood — St. Michael's College, Tenbury — Cambridge—Royal College of Music—Calcutta—Tenbury again— Southampton—Norwich Cathedral—Norwich Triennial Festival— Regional plan for symphony orchestras—Modern music—Cathedral fire 137

GUY WARRACK

A Scot—Winchester—Oxford—Royal College of Music—Sibelius— Handel Society — BBC — Music in Scotland — Musical journalism —Politics in music—Compositions . . , . . 140

GEORGE WELDON

Music in the Midlands — Schooldays — Royal College of Music— Hastings—Guest conductor—Birmingham—The " new " music— Foreign names—Motorist 143

IAN WHYTE

Another Scot—Boyhood—Student days—Lord Glentanar—BBC Composer—Music as spiritual propaganda—The great conductors— Opera and television—Advice to would-be conductors . . 146

LESLIE WOODGATE

London choirboy—Westminster—Royal College of Music—Organist— Composer — Carnegie Awards — BBC — Synthetic music — Choral singing — Wales — Modern music — Emotion in music — Musical cynicism — The other arts 148

SIR HENRY J. WOOD

AN APPRECIATION by Sir Adrian Boult 152

A SHORT BIOGRAPHY

I. Londoner—Boyhood—Royal Academy of Music—Amateur orchestras and choral societies — Musical pilgrimages— Opera 153

II. The First Prom—Making the programmes—New music— Princess Olga Ouroussoff — Windsor Castle — Queen Victoria — America — The " Fantasia on British Sea-songs " 156

III. Provincial activities — The London Symphony Orchestra— Max Reger—Exeter—Debussy—Tragedy . . . 162

IV. Knighthood— Elgar —Artist — Dame Ethel Smyth—Women in orchestras — Music in wartime — A Royal Visit — America again—First broadcast—BBC and the Proms— BBC Symphony Orchestra—South Africa—" Klenovsky " 163

ix

V. Jubilee Concert—War again—" Sir Henry Wood Jubilee
Fund "—Seventy-fifth Birthday—Companion of Honour
—The Jubilee of the Proms—Death 166

VI. The renascence of music — Opera — Subsidies — Ministry of
Culture?—State orchestras—Welfare of players—Young
composers—Foreign orchestras—The young conductor—
Modern singers—America—Music in the Empire—Film
music—Broadcast music 170

VII. Sir Henry's methods—London—Empire Meeting Hall for
music 174

APPENDIX

THE BBC SYMPHONY ORCHESTRA

Additional notes—The Orchestra in wartime—Bristol—News-letter—
Provincial tours—Sir Henry Wood Jubilee Concert—With the
Forces 176

THE LONDON PHILHARMONIC ORCHESTRA

Sir Thomas Beecham—Youth—Opera—Ballet—Tours abroad—
War—Liquidation—Re-establishment—J. B. Priestley—" Musical
Manifesto "—Jack Hylton—More trouble—Security—C.E.M.A. . 178

THE LONDON SYMPHONY ORCHESTRA

Hans Richter—Guest conductors—Sir Thomas Beecham—Work in
wartime—Air-raids—C.E.M.A. . . . 181

THE HALLE ORCHESTRA

Charles Hallé—Manchester—The Hallé Concerts Society—Richter—
Slump—BBC—John Barbirolli—Independence—The Free Trade
Hall 182

THE SCOTTISH ORCHESTRA

Foundations—Famous conductors—Glasgow Corporation—Sir Daniel
Stevenson—Lord Inverclyde—Plans for the future . . . 185

THE CITY OF BIRMINGHAM ORCHESTRA

Neville Chamberlain—Birmingham Corporation—Sir Adrian Boult—
Leslie Heward—A tribute—Work in the public schools—Future
plans 186

ILLUSTRATIONS

Sir Adrian Boult .	.	.	FRONTISPIECE	
Richard Austin .	.	.	FACING PAGE	6
John Barbirolli .	.	.	. ,,	7
Sir Thomas Beecham	.	.	. ,,	16
Sir Adrian Boult .	.	.	. ,,	17
Warwick Braithwaite	.	.	. ,,	32
Basil Cameron	.	.	. ,,	33
Mosco Carner	.	.	. ,,	36
Albert Coates	.	.	. ,,	37
Louis Cohen	.	.	. ,,	44
Edric Cundell	.	.	. ,,	45
Gideon Fagan	.	.	. ,,	56
Anatole Fistoulari	.	.	. ,,	57
Julius Harrison	.	.	. ,,	72
Ernest Irving	.	.	. ,,	73
Reginald Jacques .	.	.	. ,,	84
Constant Lambert .	.	.	. ,,	85
Muir Mathieson	.	.	. ,,	92
Herbert Menges	.	.	. ,,	93
Maurice Miles	.	.	. ,,	96
Boyd Neel	.	.	. ,,	97
Boyd Neel (Sketch)	.	.	. ,,	104
Sidney Newman .	.	.	. ,,	105
Clarence Raybould	.	.	. ,,	112
Kathleen Riddick .	.	.	. ,,	113
Stanford Robinson	.	.	. ,,	128
Malcolm Sargent .	.	.	. ,,	129
Alec Sherman	.	.	. ,,	136
Heathcote Statham	.	.	. ,,	137
Guy Warrack	.	.	. ,,	144
George Weldon	.	.	. ,,	145
Ian Whyte	.	.	. ,,	148
Leslie Woodgate .	.	.	. ,,	149
The Late Sir Henry Wood .	.	.	,,	156
Henry J. Wood in 1890	.	.	. ,,	157

The BBC Symphony Orchestra:
    First Violins .   .   .   FACING PAGE 176
    Second Violins .   .   .   ,,   176
    Violas
    'Cellos
    Flutes
    Double Bass
    Harp
    The BBC Symphony Orchestra with Sir Adrian Boult
    Oboes
    Clarinets
    Bassoons
    Horns
    Trumpets
    Trombones
    Tuba   .   FACING PAGE 177
    Timpani   .   .   .   .   ,,   177
The London Philharmonic Orchestra   .   ,,   184
The Liverpool Philharmonic Orchestra .   ,,   184
The Halle Orchestra
The Scottish Orchestra
The City of Birmingham Orchestra   FACING PAGE 185
The Boyd Neel Orchestra .   .   .   ,,   185

INTRODUCTION

※

THE remarkable wave of musical appreciation that has swept over the country during the past few years suggests that music is entering into the hearts of the British people.

At one time we deserved all the rude things that foreigners said about our musical life, because something like nine-tenths of the population made no attempt to understand and enjoy serious music. Symphony concerts were patronized only because it was " the thing to do." I have in mind a certain cathedral city where the Annual Concert was for years an outstanding event in the social calendar of *the quality*. The *best people*, dressed in slightly old-fashioned evening clothes, would arrive at the Assembly Rooms ten minutes after the concert had started, sit the whole evening trying to hide their boredom by making half-hearted efforts to look intelligent, and finally emerge assuring one another with stifled yawns that they had thoroughly enjoyed a *delateful* concert. While waiting for the "Carriages at Nine-thirty" one would hear the Honourable Mrs. Whatnot complain that the men who played the " bugle-things " were shockingly idle fellows: they had sat there half the evening doing nothing.

Now, everything has changed. We have seen the " respectable " world of property and class-conscious society crumble before our eyes. A devastating war has given us as realistic a glimpse of hell as we are likely to see on this side of the grave, and as a result, the younger generation and those middle-aged folk who are still on the sunny side of ninety are conscious of a strange craving for beauty. Perhaps it is a reaction to the depressing sight of bombed buildings or to the monotonous repetition of childish platitudes uttered by some of our politicians. Perhaps it is nature's way of indicating its disgust at the exploitation of the national emergency by those racketeers who would betray their brothers for rather less than thirty pieces of silver. I don't know. But there it is; this craving for the consolation and inspiration of the beautiful. It is making millions of people realise for the first time in their lives that music isn't a dull " highbrow " fetish, and that art and literature are something more than schoolroom topics.

I find that as people grow to love music, they become interested in the personalities of the men and women who make it, so I have written

1

these sketches in the hope that in their own little way my efforts will help to satisfy this healthy curiosity.

This is a book about conductors, chiefly those who are directing Britain's music at the present time, but it does not claim to be a complete guide to *all* of them, because one or two have been omitted through lack of space or for other reasons which need not be specified here. I might add, too, that the inclusion of several of the younger people who have not yet risen to eminence was heartily approved by their more distinguished contemporaries.

To avoid any possible misunderstanding, I should also make it quite clear that the length of each sketch has been determined simply and solely by the amount of biographical and other material made available to me, and *not*, of course, by the status of the individual concerned. As in my " Writers' Gallery," all questions of precedence have been avoided by arranging the sketches in alphabetical order.

Just one other point: I frequently meet musical enthusiasts who indulge in utterly irrational " conductor-worship." This seems quite harmless, I admit, but I sincerely hope that these sketches will not propagate this peculiar mania, because it is of no service to art. There is all the difference in the world between praise and adulation; admiration and apotheosis. If symptons of this mania are discovered, the reader should dose himself liberally with the sketches of composers and executants which I hope to publish in due course.

Finally, may I thank all those kind souls who have so willingly helped me in the collection of the material I have used in this book. It has been a joy to meet them, and I am most grateful.

DONALD BROOK.

LONDON,
Autumn, 1944.

THE news of the death of Sir Henry J. Wood reached me just as this book was going to press, and it was with a very heavy heart that I amended my script and recorded his passing from us. The last time I spoke to him was when my wife and I bade him farewell at the door of his London flat one afternoon early this year. He had been extremely kind to us, and in his lovable fatherly way had taken a great interest in this book. Little did we think that he was so near to the end : he seemed so full of life, and we both felt quite sure that he would live to see the new concert hall of his dreams. It is hard to realize that we shall never see him again.

D.B.

RICHARD AUSTIN

B EFORE I start to write about Richard Austin, I must refer briefly to his father, who will be known chiefly to my older readers as a baritone of opera fame and a composer of many delightful songs and works for piano and orchestra. In his earlier days, Frederic Austin was one of the finest baritones in England. He sang at great festivals all over the country; he was a principal in the Beecham Opera Company and later became the Artistic Director of the British National Opera Company. His compositions included the new version of " The Beggar's Opera," which was revived at the Lyric Theatre, Hammersmith, by Nigel Playfair in 1920. Austin's new harmonization and orchestration undoubtedly contributed to its great success: it ran for four years in town and was then taken on a tour of the provinces. Furthermore, it made possible the revival of " Polly," with which Frederic Austin was also associated.

His son Richard was born near Birkenhead on December 26th, 1903, and at school showed ability in drama as well as music. Incidentally, he went to the same school as Benjamin Britten, and quite recently conducted one of this promising young composer's works at a concert attended by their former headmaster.

Richard Austin became a student at the Royal College of Music and had the good fortune to come under Sir Adrian Boult and Dr. Malcolm Sargent occasionally for conducting. Of all the College activities, he seemed most attracted towards the opera class.

Soon after his twentieth birthday he spent two periods, each of six months, in Munich, and attended symphony concerts or the opera every night. His days were spent in intensive study, so that on his return to London he was able to accept an appointment as assistant instructor in the opera class at the Royal College of Music, where he conducted many of the students' performances.

· In due course he was engaged as chorus master and assistant conductor for the production of the ballad opera "Mr. Pepys," which was put on at the Everyman Theatre, Hampstead, by Raymond Massey. This led to several other theatrical engagements—chiefly as conductor of musical shows, light opera, etc., until he went as assistant to Adrian Boult for a season of opera given at the Victoria Rooms, Bristol, by

P. Napier Miles, the Gloucestershire composer. Soon after its commencement, Boult had to go to Egypt, and Richard Austin took over the conductorship.

While he was at Bristol, the local Rotary Club decided that the city needed more music, and formed a small orchestra to give concerts at the Glen Pavilion, inviting Austin to become its conductor. Thus at the age of twenty-five he got a professional orchestra of his own.

This little orchestra presented a remarkably good selection of light and classical works, and many excellent transcriptions, every evening of the week, including Sundays. It was from here that he made his first broadcast, as the BBC relayed his Friday evening performances for several months. In addition, he conducted the Bristol Symphony Orchestra on two or three occasions.

When the Carl Rosa Opera Company visited Bristol that year, they made him an offer to join them. He accepted, and in 1929 set out with them on a three years' tour. I should imagine that he has now conducted opera in almost every provincial theatre of any size in Britain. He certainly has plenty of tales to tell about his experiences. When I visited him recently he told me that they were once giving "Hansel and 'Gretel'' in a Sheffield theatre where the switches that controlled the mechanism of the scenery were in rather an exposed position. During the last act, somebody in the wings must have accidently brushed against them, for to everybody's amazement the gingerbread house suddenly shot up into the air, revealing a stage hand leaning against a prop and calmly sucking a pipe. The audience were highly amused, particularly when the man called out "Don't 'ee worry, she'll come down again.''

At the Lyceum, Austin was once conducting a performance of "Madame Butterfly'' in which the juvenile was not quite such a child as his make-up made him appear to be. A gushing lady happened to meet this "little boy'' behind the scenes and proffering a large box of chocolates, asked: "Would you like a chocolate, dear?'' The little chap blinked at her and then said in a deep bass voice: "Aye, thanks, but I'd rather 'ave a pint of bitter!''

As a musical director, Austin had by this time become quite well known in the theatrical world, and after his contract with the Carl Rosa Opera Company concluded with a tour in Ireland, he returned to London and conducted several successful musical shows.

In 1933 he joined the Metropolitan Opera Company as assistant to Albert Coates, their principal conductor. He had the pleasure of directing one performance of " The Flying Dutchman " and then the entire venture collapsed financially.

4

We find him next conducting "Hansel and Gretel" at the Cambridge Theatre, then as musical director at the Coliseum for " The Golden Toy," a fantasy on Schumann's music, featuring, among others, Peggy Ashcroft, Wilfrid Lawson, Nellie Wallace and Lupino Lane.

While he was there, he saw an advertisement for a musical director for the Bournemouth Municipal Orchestra, and at the last minute applied for the job. He was chosen out of a large number of applicants and started his new work in the same year. This meant learning a large repertoire for he was expected to give at least three concerts a week during the winter, and four or five a week in the summer. In addition to this, there was the great annual festival, when many famous conductors and artists were invited to take part.

For many years the orchestra had been built up by Sir Dan Godfrey, who had done an enormous amount of pioneer work to provide Bourne-mouth with good music. Although he was only thirty, Austin took over and continued the task so successfully that such eminent men as Sir Thomas Beecham, Sir Henry J. Wood, Nicolai Malko, Sir Hamilton Harty, Dr. Malcolm Sargent, John Barbirolli and Leslie Heward, were pleased to visit the city as guest conductors. Igor Stravinsky, the famous Russian composer, conducted at one festival, and brought his son, Sulimo, the well-known pianist.

Such distinguished artists as Cortot, Dame Myra Hess, Josef Hofmann, Rubenstein, Moiseiwitch, Albert Sammons, Solomon, Fener-mann, Lionel Tertis, Elizabeth Schumann and others, appeared in his programmes, and whole evenings were devoted to the works of famous contemporary composers. The weekly broadcasts from the Pavilion were continued for years.

Recognising the work that Richard Austin was doing to make Bournemouth famous for its music, Sir Henry Wood used his influence to help to get the size of the regular orchestra increased from forty-seven to sixty players.

*   *   *

The present war compelled the Bournemouth Corporation to make drastic economies in their expenditure on music, and the orchestra had to be cut down to thirty-five players. Austin accepted this as one of the inevitable sacrifices that have to be made in wartime, but vigorously opposed a later suggestion to reduce the orchestra still further to twenty-four members. It was when this second cut was made that he felt compelled to resign in protest, because it meant that the greater part of the repertoire had to be discarded. Little more than " teashop music " could be attempted with such a small ensemble.

On leaving Bournemouth, Austin spent some time at his country house in Berkshire, and then accepted his present appointment: Music Adviser to the Northern Command for E.N.S.A. His duties in this highly-interesting post are chiefly concerned with the encouragement of musical appreciation and music-making by the members of the forces, but he also arranges and frequently conducts concerts for factory workers in the great territory that lies between Northampton and Scotland, given with most of the great orchestras, including the London Philharmonic, London Symphony, Hallé and Liverpool Philharmonic. In the small amount of spare time he was available he keeps in touch with general concert work by acting as a guest conductor of most of the leading symphony orchestras from time to time. He is still a frequent broadcaster.

*   *   *

Richard Austin was married in 1935 to Miss Leily Howell, the well-known 'cellist. They met when she played the solo part in a concerto at Bournemouth soon after his appointment to the conductorship of the Municipal Orchestra, and they were married about five months later. Mrs. Austin still plays under her maiden name in concerts all over the country. She was born of Welsh parents in Chile, by the way, and received her musical education in Paris at the École Normale under Diran Alexanian.

Austin's favourite form of recreation is a patriotic one at the present time—farming! Although his work keeps him in the north of England most of the time—his headquarters are at York—he still retains the small farm around his Berkshire home, and when he is there he spends most of his leisure in an occupation that one would scarcely associate with a prominent musician. He is an enthusiastic pig-breeder! I must confess that I find it difficult to imagine him working in the vicinity of pig sties, but he assures me that it is great fun. I'll take his word for it, of course, but if he had not chosen music as a profession, I don't think he would have become a farmer. I have a feeling that he would have been an actor specializing in the sort of work one associates with Noel Coward.

*   *   *

When I discussed this book with him in his London flat, I suppose it was inevitable that the conversation should turn to the subject of municipal orchestras. In this country we have very few good orchestras at our seaside resorts—they can be numbered on the fingers of one hand—yet the value of a first-class orchestra in preserving the propriety of the place cannot be over-estimated. The attitude of most of the local

Bassano]

RICHARD AUSTIN

JOHN BARBIROLLI

authorities in the seaside towns is that whereas large sums of money can be spent upon public gardens without expecting any direct return, an orchestra must be regarded as a form of investment that must pay a cash dividend, otherwise it is a waste of the ratepayers' money. They entirely overlook the great cultural value of the music.

It is common knowledge that in peacetime, cheap, quick travel and holidays with pay combined to bring the amenities of our best seaside resorts within the means of the ordinary people; and that is just as it should be, of course. But it is also an equally well-known fact that every holiday town tries to preserve its amenities from the ravages of the type of hooligans who break beer bottles upon the sands, pick flowers in the public gardens, destroy the woods, indulge in drunken brawls in the streets and make themselves objectionable generally. Without being snobbish, it is necessary to preserve the "tone" of a resort.

From personal experience I know that the Bournemouth Municipal Orchestra, originally under Sir Dan Godfrey and afterwards under Richard Austin, did more than anything else to preserve the " respectability " of Bournemouth by attracting to the city the sort of people who were not likely to indulge in acts of vandalism or vulgarity. If the Orchestra had done no more than that it would have amply justified the very modest subsidy it received from the Corporation. But that was only part of its work. It made the Pavilion a centre of culture to which musical folk came from many miles around; it provided the residents with the best music for twelve months in the year; it brought Bournemouth to the notice of the whole country by broadcasting regular weekly concerts of considerable merit.

One can understand that a seaside orchestra would be expected to make the entertainment of the visitors its first consideration, but that doesn't mean " playing down " to the lowest level of public taste. In any case, those who persistently under-estimate the taste of the public by insisting that the " man in the street " wants to hear only musical rubbish, have been proved to be very much in the wrong. At Bournemouth, Richard Austin always resisted the influence of those who thought they could exploit the orchestra by turning it into a money-making concern for the production of worthless music. It would have meant a wicked waste of a fine ensemble.

I am emphasizing this here because I think it is a fact that must be borne in mind when we come to the restoration of the normal life of the seaside towns after the war. People will want holidays more than ever before, and a large section of the community will expect something more than dance bands and those funny old brass bands that used to play on the " Marine Parades."

Richard Austin believes that after the war there will be splendid opportunities for all the larger towns to maintain their own regular orchestras if they make the most of the musical revival we see to-day. If good music is made available, the people will come to hear it. Although he does not believe in " playing down," he is not in favour of " playing over the people's heads." His programmes at Bournemouth were always drawn up to include at least one or two items of good music that were of the easily-appreciated variety.

He considers that music's hope for the future lies in vigorous musical education in the schools, and this is already being proved by the preponderance of young people in the symphony concert audiences of to-day. He would like to see the regional musical societies preserved so that all the best orchestras are not State-subsidized organisations working from London. He feels that there is room for several more first-class provincial orchestras like the Hallé and Liverpool Philharmonic. At least half a dozen of our greater cities could create and maintain symphony orchestras if they adopted a regional system that would enable them to draw small subsidies from the smaller towns in their area in return for an annual series of concerts. The enthusiasm has now been aroused and we ought to make the most of it.

Richard Austin declares that there should be either Government subsidies or municipal grants to all the professional orchestras engaged in the provision of public concerts of educational value, otherwise the small towns will never hear them. He also contends that no orchestra should have less than sixty players.

He believes that the neglect of our contemporary composers by some of the large symphony orchestras is not due to indifference, but to box-office anxieties. Therefore, State subsidies to orchestras would greatly benefit and encourage our composers, because the musical organisations could then take the risk of performing unknown works.

JOHN BARBIROLLI

❧

JOHN BARBIROLLI comes of a musical family of Italian origin. His father was the leader of the Empire Theatre Orchestra, London, in the days when that house was famous for its ballet; and his grandfather was an orchestral violinist of some standing.

He was born in London on the 2nd December, 1899, and was educated at St. Clement Dane's School. The urge to conduct an orchestra was manifest in him since he was four years old; he can remember how his father used to take him to hear the L.C.C. band in Lincoln's Inn Fields, and how fascinated he was by the conductor. The band was of the type one finds on the pier at the smaller seaside resorts, but it seemed wonderful to Barbirolli, and he would go up on the bandstand after the concert and stand almost reverently on the conductor's rostrum.

He started learning the violin, but soon showed preference for the 'cello, and chose that instrument when, after winning a scholarship, he commenced his studies at Trinity College. He made his début as a 'cellist at the age of eleven when clad in a sailor's suit he played Goltermann's Concerto in A minor at a concert given by the students of Trinity College. The orchestra was a large unwieldy affair with a superfluity of certain instruments, while he played on a half-sized 'cello. It therefore caused a great deal of amusement when ' The Times ' music critic solemnly pronounced that though the 'cellist's tone was of beautiful quality, it was rather small !

He went to the Royal Academy of Music in 1912, making the 'cello his first study and the piano his second. Curiously enough he did not take conducting. In the same year he played the Saint-Saëns 'cello concerto on a three-quarter size instrument at the Queen's Hall in one of the Academy " end of term " concerts conducted by Alexander Mackenzie, the Principal at that time.

As a contributory cause of his success in childhood, Barbirolli speaks with gratitude of the great encouragement he received from his father, who took him about whenever he could to hear celebrities in every branch of the profession. He heard the fine singing of Santley, for instance, and at one memorable concert heard Saint-Saëns play the piano.

9   B

When I asked him more about his student days, he recalled with a chuckle the way he and some of his fellow students used to learn the chamber music of Ravel in secret because the works of that composer were *banned* by the authorities of the Royal Academy of Music as being too modernistic and fantastic for students! Even Debussy was looked upon with grave suspicion.

In passing, let me add a word about the other three students with whom Barbirolli played quartets at the Academy. The leader was W. Wolfinson, who is now leading the Stradivarius Quartet in America; the second fiddle was Joseph Shadwick, now leader of the Sadler's Wells Orchestra (though at the present time he is in the army); and the viola was F. Howard, who died a few years ago, but who was the first viola in the L.P.O. when that orchestra was founded by Sir Thomas Beecham. Barbirolli also played a great number of sonatas with Ethel Bartlett, who has also distinguished herself.

In 1916, when he was still only sixteen years of age, Barbirolli had the honour of being chosen by Sir Henry Wood for the Queen's Hall Orchestra. He was, of course, the youngest member of that notable body and played for two seasons before he went in the army. After giving his first public 'cello recital in the Aeolian Hall in June, 1917, he joined the Suffolk Regiment, and in a little while became an anti-gas instructor. The war ended before he reached the age of nineteen, so he did not go overseas.

After the armistice he found the musical world in a state of flux and did several odd jobs before he got his first appointment with the Russian Ballet at the Alhambra Theatre. He did not scorn the more humble engagements he had to accept to earn his living at that time because they provided additional experience and enabled him to retain his independence. Besides, they also made it possible for him to say that he has played in almost every sort of place—except the street!

When he finished at the Alhambra he played principal 'cello in a series of performances in which Pavlova appeared, and then joined the Beecham Orchestra at Covent Garden, gaining a great deal more operatic experience. He gave this up to join the International String Quartet, who, after touring this country, went to France, Holland, Belgium and Spain. The Quartet figured prominently in the first body of British musicians to play in Germany after the Great War: they performed several quartets at the Festival of English Music at Bad Homburg. From that time he did less orchestral playing and devoted himself instead to chamber music.

His first performance as a conductor was in 1924, when he founded the Barbirolli String Orchestra of twelve players, led by John Fry, who is now a professor at Trinity College, London. He gave his first concert with this orchestra after only one rehearsal: it was at the Marylebone Court House and they did works of such composers as Purcell and Bach, with Ethel Bartlett and John Goss as the soloists. It was a great success and led to his acceptance of many other engagements, including the conductorship of the Guild of Singers and Players and also of the Chenil Orchestra which gave frequent concerts in Chelsea.

John Goss was very interested in the music of Bernard Van Dieren and engaged Barbirolli to conduct a concert at the Wigmore Hall in which extracts from that composer's opera were played. Frederic Austin, who was then the head of the British National Opera Company, was in the audience, and was so impressed by Barbirolli's handling of the orchestra that he approached him after the concert and asked if he would like to conduct some of the British National operas. Barbirolli, who has always had opera in his bones, was overjoyed, and arranged to join the company that autumn (1926). He made his début at Newcastle with three operas in one week: " Romeo and Juliet," " Madame Butterfly " and " Aïda." Despite the fact that he had only an hour or two in which to rehearse each of these, he was an enormous success, and within a year was conducting at Covent Garden. The rapidity with which he distinguished himself as a conductor was staggering to some of the more staid members of the profession.

When the British National Opera Company collapsed, the Covent Garden Opera Company was founded for the purpose of touring the provinces, and Barbirolli was appointed Director of Music, and principal conductor. Among his many successes were the first English perform-ances in London of " Der Rosenkavalier " and " The Bartered Bride." At the same time he started doing general concert work as a guest conductor.

Sir Thomas Beecham was once taken ill before one of the London Symphony Orchestra's Monday night symphony concerts, and Barbirolli was invited to take his place. Casals was the soloist in the Hadyn concerto and was so impressed by the young conductor's interpretation during the rehearsal that he turned to the orchestra at the end and said: " Gentlemen, listen to him, he *knows!*" The performance also included Elgar's Symphony No. 2, which Barbirolli did not know. Un-dismayed, he learnt it from cover to cover in forty-eight hours and gave such a magnificent performance that on hearing from W. H. Reed that the symphony had been played so well, Elgar sent Barbirolli a letter of congratulation.

The year 1927 brought him an invitation to conduct the Royal Philharmonic Society, and also saw his rise to popularity as a guest conductor of such orchestras as the Hallé, London Philharmonic and the Scottish Orchestra.

Soon after his appointment as permanent conductor of the Scottish Orchestra in 1933 the Northern Philharmonic, Leeds, offered him a similar contract, and for three years he directed both with outstanding success. He also received an invitation from Sir John McEwen, the principal of the Royal Academy of Music, to take charge of the opera class at that institution whenever he could make himself available. This additional interest resulted in his production at the Scala Theatre of complete performances of such operas as " The Mastersingers " and " Falstaff."

He made a great impression when he visited Russia in 1935. The audiences there were particularly pleased by his handling of Russian music, and he was frequently referred to as " the Tschaikovsky conductor." He was also told that he had " much temperament " for conducting!

In 1936 the musical world was astonished by his sudden appointment to succeed Toscanini as conductor of the famous New York Philharmonic Symphony Orchestra. His outstanding ability was universally recognised, but few thought that he would leap to fame so dramatically at such an early age. His career had been watched carefully from New York, however, and he was invited to conduct for what really amounted to a trial period of ten weeks. During the sixth week he was offered a three years' contract as musical director.

To take over such a superb orchestra from a man like Toscanini was no easy task. The orchestra expected masterly direction, and the New York audiences were very critical. For the first six months the strain was very great, but Barbirolli proved his ability, and at the end of the period when Toscanini returned to conduct one of the concerts, he said: " John, my orchestra is just as I left it."

His contract was then renewed for a further two years, and in 1942 he had the honour of being at its helm when the orchestra celebrated its centenary. Thus Barbirolli earned the distinction of being the youngest conductor of note in charge of the oldest orchestra in the world. (The New York Philharmonic Symphony Orchestra is older than the Vienna Philharmonic Orchestra by several years.)

While he was in America he also had the pleasure of conducting the Chicago, Cincinatti, Los Angeles, Detroit, Seattle and Vancouver Symphony orchestras.

His recording of the Sibelius Symphony No. 2 made with the New York Philharmonic Symphony Orchestra was sent by the Finnish Legation in U.S.A. to Sibelius as a present for his seventieth birthday, and after a little while Barbirolli received a most enthusiastic letter which concluded :

"... I always feel more than happy when I know my works are in your masterful hands.

Your devoted admirer,

Jan Sibelius."

During 1942 Barbirolli became conscious of an overwhelming feeling of home-sickness. Britain had suffered greatly at the hands of the Nazi hooligans, and news from home was scanty and depressing. Suddenly, he received an invitation to come home to conduct several of our leading orchestras for a ten weeks' season, and with the encouragement of the First Lord of the Admiralty, Mr. A. V. Alexander, who made it possible, he set out one day from New York on a three-thousand-ton Norwegian freighter. After a most hazardous journey that lasted twenty-three days he landed at Liverpool.

During his ten weeks at home he conducted thirty-four concerts. most of which were given by the BBC Symphony Orchestra, the London Philharmonic Orchestra and the London Symphony Orchestra. The time passed all too quickly, and then he had to face the return journey on a four-thousand-ton banana boat. The convoy had a terrible time; three ships were sunk in four-and-a-half hours in one attack, and the nearest boat to the one in which Barbirolli was travelling went down in four minutes after being struck by a torpedo.

Back in New York he found it difficult to suppress the feeling that British music wanted him; he had been moved by the tremendous welcome he had received in this country, so when in 1943 he was asked if he would consider returning home again to reconstruct the Hallé Orchestra, he found it impossible to refuse.

He landed in May of that year, and had only one month in which to gather the orchestra together. In ordinary times this would have been quite a formidable task, but under wartime conditions, with many of the best men in the Forces, it required a tremendous effort. There was a nucleus of about thirty-six players, and he had to find another forty, but the undertaking was done to time and the full story of it will be found in the notes on the Hallé Orchestra at the end of this book. The success of his efforts may be judged by the following extract from a short article by Ralph Hill, which appeared in the ' Radio Times ' early this year (1944):

" That he has turned the Hallé Orchestra, which nine months ago consisted for the most part of young but inexperienced players, into one of the two finest orchestras in the country is a tribute to his energy, self-confidence and genius as a conductor."

As evidence of the great work he is now doing in this country, I cannot do better than to quote from a letter, dated February 10th, 1944, which he received from Arthur Bliss after a concert he had given with the BBC Symphony Orchestra on the previous day:

> " I must write to you at once and tell you what a magnificent performance you gave of the Fantastique Symphony yesterday. I listened to it at home with the score, and I do not remember ever hearing a performance so true to the spirit of it. In fact I felt I was really hearing it for the first time, and the impression remains very strong this morning. I hope you enjoyed the occasion as much as I know the orchestra must have done. With renewed congratulations."

This is typical of the sort of letter he receives. Here is an extract from another he had from Sir Arnold Bax, referring to his recent recording of that composer's Third Symphony with the Hallé Orchestra:

> " I thank you from my heart for all the devoted work you put into the recording of the Symphony—a work which will owe a great deal to you in the future. I am not talking with any exaggeration when I say I wish you could always conduct *all* my orchestral compositions, and I am delighted that you are to play that jeu d'esprit ' Work in Progress ' at its first performance. A thousand thanks my dear Tito."

*　　　*　　　*

Barbirolli is delighted with the remarkable revival of interest in music in this country. Music, he feels, is no longer regarded as a form of social activity to be indulged in chiefly by members of the " upper middle-class " wanting to display their evening clothes; it has now become a necessity to the masses who form the backbone of the nation.

The reception he has had in the Northern towns has been really amazing—he has vivid memories of the *furore* caused by the Hallé Orchestra in Hanley—and he hopes that as soon as possible after the war *all* towns will be provided with suitable, spacious concert halls in which the people can hear the finest music at reasonable prices.

He feels very strongly that the great orchestras of this country must not be compelled to make the box-office revenue their primary consideration: they must be subsidized somehow so that they can have plenty of rehearsals and give only a reasonable number of concerts. Under these conditions we can make our British orchestras as fine as any in the world. The Hallé Society is fully aware of the necessity for ample preparation of its concerts, and refuses to overwork its players by making them give six or eight concerts a week. When Barbirolli took the orchestra to Huddersfield and Leeds to give the first performance in those cities of Vaughan Williams' Symphony No. 5, for instance, he was allowed to call eight rehearsals.

The enthusiasm of the younger players to-day is another welcome sign of music's re-awakening. They are keen to do plenty of hard work, and to extend their repertoire. Nothing seems to discourage them.

Barbirolli would like nothing more than to dedicate himself to British music in the future, and he is determined to stand by the Hallé if they continue to give him the support he is getting at present.

With regard to opera, he believes that in this country it could only be restored to its proper place if those responsible for it followed the Hallé's shining example and planned boldly.

When I questioned him about the training of conductors he declared that in his opinion conducting cannot be taught. A man has to be " born " a conductor if he is to rise out of the ranks of mediocrity, and even then he must be prepared to rise in the hard school of practical experience.

On the subject of " interpretation " by conductors, he felt that the personality of the conductor is bound to show in his work, and that is as it should be, but he dislikes the methods of men who meddle with composers' work. Those who pretend to be " purists " often adopt their pose as an excuse for expressionless work. He was once accused of putting unnecessary accents in Beethoven's Eighth Symphony and in refuting the charge, he astonished his critic by sending him a complete list of all the accents indicated in the original score, and by pointing out those which are so often overlooked by conductors to-day.

Barbirolli is completely imbued with music; he puts his entire body and soul into his work. He is a remarkably vigorous conductor and has an uncanny way of drawing out the last ounce of energy from his players. Although he is small in stature, he is a strict master of his orchestra.

He has made some excellent transcriptions of the works of Henry Purcell and has used some themes of Pergolesi for a fine concerto for oboe which was first performed in 1936.

*   *   *

Barbirolli was married in 1939 to Miss Evelyn Rothwell, formerly the first oboe of the Scottish Orchestra. She was also prominently associated with the Busch Chamber Music Players and has made recordings of the Brandenburg Concertos and Suites of Bach in Brussels. For some time she was a member of the Queen's Hall Orchestra under Sir Henry Wood.

Barbirolli's recreations are reading and playing cricket.

SIR THOMAS BEECHAM

&

HAVING spent three or four years in America, Sir Thomas Beecham returned to England in the late autumn of 1944 to conduct a magnificent series of concerts with the London Philharmonic Orchestra and to make arrangements for their next American tour. My sketch of him will be comparatively brief, not because of his prolonged absence from this country, but because he has recently published the first volume of his autobiography, " The Mingled Chime," in which he tells his life story in far greater detail than I could attempt in this book.

I suppose everybody knows that Sir Thomas came from the wealthy family responsible for the manufacture of a certain patent medicine. He was born at St. Helens, Lancashire, on April 29th, 1879, and as a small boy wore pretty curls of which full advantage was taken by the more spiteful of the children with whom he associated. He went to a piano recital when he was six and was so fascinated by the music of Grieg that he made immediate demands to be given piano lessons. These were supplied forthwith by a local organist—a Mozart enthusiast, by the way—who also aroused his interest in opera.

When the family moved to Huyton he was sent to a private school in the vicinity, but he admits that he was thoroughly idle at this establishment. His interest in music, however, extended beyond all bounds when he began attending concerts and operas in Manchester and Liverpool. It was encouraged, too, by his father, who being very fond of music himself, spent substantial sums of money in enlarging his remarkable collection of musical boxes and other mechanical instruments. One of these was a colossal affair capable of emitting quite tolerable reproductions of the classics, and it proved to be very useful to Sir Thomas in his youth.

He found himself completely cut off from music when at the age of thirteen he was sent to Rossall, and for several months his reflections on public school life were not exactly sweet. Nevertheless, during the holidays, he made up for these periods of exile by spending every penny of his pocket money on operas and concerts. In 1897 he went up to Wadham College, Oxford, only to find that the purely academic life was both distasteful and futile to a man with his specific interests and intentions.

SIR THOMAS BEECHAM

SIR ADRIAN BOULT

His first experience as a conductor was gained when he formed an orchestral society at St. Helens, a mixture of amateurs and professionals, to give local concerts. But a far greater opportunity was soon to follow. He was barely twenty when his father engaged the Hallé Orchestra with its conductor, Hans Richter, for a special concert. At the last moment, Richter found that he could not attend, so Beecham immediately asked his father if he could conduct instead. Sir Joseph Beecham was profoundly shocked and would never have entertained the idea had not the leader of the Orchestra firmly refused to play under such a youth. This defiant attitude filled the eminent industrialist with such indignation that he forthwith suspended the leader and let his son take the concert, which he did quite satisfactorily!

Soon after this incident, Beecham had a dispute with his father, left home, and came to London. After a visit to Bayreuth, he became a pupil of Frederic Austin and Charles Wood, and by surprising the manager of a new opera company by his ability to play anything in " Faust " on the piano from memory, he got a job as joint conductor. For two months he toured various small towns in the London area with tolerable principals, a poor chorus and a truly dreadful orchestra.

Let me add that Beecham took his studies very seriously. He acquired a " working knowledge " of at least six orchestral instruments, including the trombone, which he learnt to play despite the bitterness it sowed in the hearts of all his neighbours. He continued his tours abroad year after year and gained a first-hand knowledge of the methods of the leading foreign conductors of the day.

One of his earliest London concerts was given at the Wigmore Hall with an orchestra of about forty players drawn from the Queen's Hall Orchestra. In 1907 he founded the New Symphony Orchestra, but more or less dissolved it two years later when he formed a larger ensemble. For this, he chose chiefly young players, including a violinist of twenty-three, whom he had found playing in the little orchestra at the Waldorf Hotel—Albert Sammons! It was at about this time that he first met Delius; the conducting of whose work afterwards became one of his specialities.

His first season at Covent Garden was in 1910, when he became joint conductor with Bruno Walter and Percy Pitt. Within twelve months he caused a minor sensation in the musical world by introducing to this country the famous Russian Ballet.

When the Great War broke out, Beecham was appalled at the meekness with which most of the musical organisations took it for granted that their activities would have to cease. He went to Manchester to the rescue of the Hallé Society, which was floundering without a conductor, and then having set it firmly on its feet again, returned to London to infuse new life into various societies here. At this juncture I had better record that Thomas Beecham succeeded to his father's title in 1916.

The return of peace brought on the dismal proceedings of his " bankruptcy." Even if I had the space to deal adequately with this, it would serve no useful purpose, because you will find the whole story in " The Mingled Chime "—and there are some illuminating details. Personally, I find it hard to restrain a feeling of disgust at some of the almost incredible remarks made in the court. Beecham relates that when it was pointed out that he had spent a very considerable part of his private fortune in providing good music for the edification of the British public, the learned judge remarked: " What's the good of ·that?" Later in the proceedings when a reference was made to the musical profession, another learned gentleman exclaimed: " You don't call music a profession, do you?"

After several years of comparative inactivity in the musical world, Sir Thomas reappeared in 1926 primarily as an orchestral conductor, and many people thought he had abandoned opera for ever. In the following year, however, he launched his great Imperial League of Opera. Within two years nearly forty thousand people subscribed, but despite this encouraging evidence of the public's interest, the venture never succeeded.

In 1929 Beecham gave the Delius Festival, which established him as the world's greatest exponent of that composer's work. Then followed more tours abroad, his acceptance of the conductorship of the New York Philharmonic Orchestra for a while, and his election as chief conductor of the Leeds Triennial Festival.

We now come to the London Philharmonic Orchestra which he founded in 1932, but the story of it will be found in the Appendix of this book, so I need not elaborate upon it here. The years that led up to the present war were not without difficulties, but Sir Thomas's achievements during that period were in themselves a tribute to his amazing ability as a conductor. His work in the sphere of opera received world-wide recognition, and the remarkably fine performances he gave with the Royal Philharmonic Society and the London Philharmonic Orchestra proved that he was no less capable on the concert platform. His Sibelius Festival in 1938, for instance, still remains indelible in the memories of thousands of music lovers.

His relations with the BBC were not of the happiest, chiefly because he was a severe critic of the Corporation's musical policy. He raised a storm of protest in the newspapers, for example, over an abridged version of Humperdinck's "Hansel and Gretel," which was broadcast one Christmas. This was typical of him, for he always kept a watchful eye upon anything that suggested official interference with artistic standards.

His own compositions have been few, but while he was in America recently, he wrote a Pianoforte Concerto in which he made use of several themes of Handel, and an interesting fifty-minute ballet entitled "The Great Elopement," which is based upon Sheridan's elopement with Miss Elizabeth Ann Linley, the beautiful daughter of Thomas Linley the composer: a theme which will make special appeal to those who are interested in the history of the English theatre.

Sir Thomas has strong views on the future of music in this country, and insists that there will have to be a radical change in our method of dealing with its problems. Post-war plans, he declares, will have to be made by people with post-war mentalities.

Broadcasting is still a dangerous subject to mention to him on this side of the Atlantic. "The BBC," he declares, "is a monopoly that would never be tolerated in America." The Government maintains its *status quo* because it wants a powerful institution that it can "put in its pocket for political purposes." In his opinion, it is evident that all control has been handed over to an imperfectly educated body of individuals. Criticism is useless, because we have no alternative to the BBC.

Sir Thomas stoutly defends the commercial broadcasting in America, and wishes we had a similar network here in Britain. "Over there," he says, "listeners hear the finest music broadcast by the greatest artists under ideal conditions; advertising is never allowed to spoil the programmes." As a contrast, in this country much of the broadcasting is done by second- and third-rate performers because the BBC, being far behind the times, cannot always afford to pay first-class artists.

Apart from that, Beecham believes that we shall need commercial broadcasting to stimulate our post-war trade. "We need a Government department with a spice of energy, goodwill, and an insight into American psychology." One of the very, very few British statesmen he admires is—Winston Churchill.

*   *   *

Beecham's amazing personality is quite unique in the world of music. His superciliousness might easily become offensive if it were not so cleverly relieved by his wit and unfailing sense of humour. He is fastidious from his buttoned boots upwards.

On the rostrum he follows no rules and cares not a jot about the "technique" of conducting. Few, if any, of his movements are considered; he " feels " the music and apparently trusts his intuition to convey his demands to his players. It is perhaps because of this sub-conscious process that his radiant personality is able to electrify the enthusiasm of those who play under him. It certainly never fails. He makes full use of his incredible memory, too, so that except in the case of the lesser-known compositions, a few glances at the score are all he needs.

Finally, his command of the English language enables him to express himself with an ease unknown to the average musician. He never minces matters. If he has a sharp criticism to make, he sees that it goes right home by the use of either a clever satire or a veritable torrent of invective, whichever is likely to have the greater effect.

SIR ADRIAN BOULT

❧

IF I may be permitted to say so, I think every music-lover in this
country should be profoundly thankful that the man who holds the
highest position as an executant in British music to-day is absolutely
unaffected and unspoilt by fame. Any other man with such ability,
experience, energy and power might easily have become a most tiresome
musical dictator, but in Sir Adrian Boult we find nothing whatever of
the vain, domineering, ill-tempered *maestro* who tramples upon the
souls of his players and seeks self-glorification even at the expense of
the composers whose work he desecrates. He is a gentleman in the best
sense of the word, and not as it is interpreted either in snobdom or in
the studios of my more radical or sweetly sophisticated friends.

He was born in Chester in 1889, son of a Liverpool business man,
and enjoyed the good fortune of having the entrée to high musical
circles, even during his schooldays. He still remembers the thrill he
felt when, at the age of sixteen, he sat next to Elgar at a social gathering
Sir Frederick Bridge was another famous musician whom he associates
with his boyhood, and as he went to the Queen's Hall every Sunday
and alternate Saturday from the age of twelve, he naturally became one
of Sir Henry Wood's most ardent and youthful admirers. The visits
of Debussy are still vivid in his memory.

He was educated at Westminster School, where he was rather
concious of his inability to distinguish himself at games, though he
was a good rifle shot and an enthusiastic member of the O.T.C. His
musical talent was generally recognised, but he was never allowed to
perform in public.

When he went up to Christ Church, Oxford, he found that Sir Hugh
Allen was the dominant personality in the University's musical circles,
and therefore regarded it as a great privilege when Sir Hugh allowed
him to act as his deputy from time to time. Boult was in almost everything connected with music at Oxford: he sang in the Bach Choir, took
part in the incidental music used in the productions of the O.U.D.S.,
sang in the chorus of the Greek plays, and rarely missed a concert, even
when he was merely a member of the audience.

He admits that he enjoyed Oxford, and although at one time he was
inclined to think that those years might have been better spent, he

feels now that they were well justified, because the experience of humanity, culture and tradition gained at the University was as valuable as the M.A. and Mus. Doc. degrees he acquired there.

Then he went to Leipzig and studied for a year at the Conservatorium under Nikisch and Max Reger. He also acted as accompanist to the principal singing professor, and sang in the choral society, a magnificent choir of about one hundred and fifty men and women and the boys of the church of St. Thomas. Nikisch conducted in a masterly manner that never failed to thrill its members.

Boult's fellow students were mostly Germans, Czechs and Poles, and it was significant that the pianists were by far the most brilliant. There were magnificent symphony concerts every week, but the opera was not quite so good as in Dresden, which he visited frequently in the course of his musical pilgrimages. He spent several memorable weeks in Munich and Bayreuth.

He was planning to visit Vienna and Moscow when shortly before the Great War, an illness upset all his arrangements. It also prevented him from enlisting when hostilities commenced, and he had to be content with a variety of less conspicuous forms of national service.

Actually, he was on the staff of Covent Garden as a musical assistant in 1914, but he resigned this position when he went to Liverpool to arrange a series of concerts in the theatre of the University Settlement, in which Lord Woolton was interested. Meanwhile, he spent many hours drilling raw recruits and giving secretarial assistance to a local general. Next we find him at the War Office acting as personal assistant to Lord Woolton in the task of controlling leather supplies.

Towards the end of the war—it was somewhere about March, 1918—he gave four orchestral concerts at the Queen's Hall with the London Symphony Orchestra. Among the items he chose was Vaughan Williams' ". London Symphony," which at that time was almost unknown. These concerts were an outstanding success, and drew the acclamation of every notable critic in London.

Three weeks before the signing of the Armistice, Holst visited him and said: " I'm going to Salonika next week, and Balfour Gardiner is giving me the Queen's Hall with an orchestra for a concert as a parting present. We're going to do ' The Planets,' and we want you to conduct." Boult showed his appreciation of this compliment by giving a truly wonderful performance of what many people regard as Holst's masterpiece.

Soon after this, Sir Hubert Parry died, and was succeeded at the Royal College of Music by Sir Hugh Allen, who invited Sir Adrian to take charge of the conductors' class. The invitation was accepted, and when he commenced his duties in 1919, he found himself in charge of what must have been one of the most talented classes the College has ever known. In it were such promising young men as the late Leslie Heward, Arthur Bliss, Armstrong Gibbs, Boris Ord, Scott Goddard, Constant Lambert and Gordon Jacob, and as one would imagine, enthusiasm ran very high.

Boult continued to make his musical pilgrimages abroad during the holidays, and it was at about this stage in his career that he made his first visit to America. Other tours took him to Barcelona, where he spent a month listening to Casals rehearsing his orchestra, and to Munich again " to worship at the feet of Bruno Walter!" Of the educational value of these travels there can be no doubt, but they also made him feel very impatient to get a good regular orchestra of his own.

He returned to England feeling decidedly restless and dissatisfied with his mode of life, so he started looking for a permanent conductorship. To his disappointment he found that no orchestra here seemed likely to be wanting a conductor for many years to come, so he decided to try his luck in Canada. He was just beginning to make plans to sail when the City of Birmingham Orchestra, then four years old, suddenly offered him an appointment. This was just the opportunity he wanted: the orchestra, enjoying a small municipal grant, was establishing a reputation with a six months' season of fifty concerts a year.

Typical of him is the thoroughness with which he set about his new work. He gave up his conductors' class at the College, retaining only the senior orchestra, which he took one day a week, and went to live in Birmingham determined to devote himself to the musical life of the Midlands. Looking back now he sees that those were happy days, for it was an interesting life with plenty of variety. He began taking his Orchestra round to all the public schools in that part of the country (full details may be found in the notes on the City of Birmingham Orchestra at the end of this book), and he got to know Sir Walford Davies by helping him with his festivals at Aberystwyth. During the summer he was free to continue his visits to musical centres abroad.

His first official connection with the BBC was in 1928, when he became a member of the Corporation's Music Advisory Committee. Two years later he was offered the position of Director of Music.

One of his first tasks was the organisation of the new BBC Symphony Orchestra, for up to that time the Corporation had possessed only studio orchestras. A hundred and twenty of the finest players in the country were selected and given a week of rehearsals in July, 1930. Then ninety of them played at the Queen's Hall for the ensuing Promenade season, and in October of that year the full orchestra made its début.

In 1934 Boult took the Orchestra to Brussels, and its success no doubt led to the continental tour of 1935, when it visited Paris. Zurich, Vienna and Budapest, playing a different concert in each city. They returned through Nazi Germany, and were surprised to find that although they had not arranged to play in that country, a most luxurious train had been sent to convey them across it.

Sir Adrian was knighted in 1937, and to tell you the truth, I had to look up the date in a reference book, because during my conversations with him he made no mention of the honour bestowed upon him in recognition of his great services to music. Incidentally, he took part in the Coronation of King George VI as conductor of the orchestral music given before the ceremony.

He visited America again in 1937, 1938 and 1939, and on the last occasion gave the first performance of Arthur Bliss's Piano Concerto at the New York World Fair, with Solomon as the soloist. Then came the Second World War, great changes in broadcasting, the evacuation of the BBC Symphony Orchestra to Bristol, and all the other vicissitudes which musicians have had to endure during the past five years. A few extra details will be found in my notes on the Orchestra in the Appendix of this book.

*   *   *

Sir Adrian regards himself as being impersonally in charge of the " National Gallery of Music " in this country, and he believes that it is his duty to " show all the pictures." That is why he performs all the music that he thinks ought to be done, whether he likes it personally or not. Actually, there is very little, if any, music which he dislikes, though there are a few compositions for which he prefers to engage a guest-conductor. (I hope nobody will read into this statement an implication that all the music performed by the BBC Symphony Orchestra under the baton of a guest conductor falls into this very small category!)

He is not interested in criticism; he takes any score and makes the best he can of it. " There is some modern music which I do not pretend to understand, but I take it, study it, and do everything within my power to interpret it as I believe the composer would wish it to sound." Then there is music in which he is interested, but towards which he feels quite impartial: Schönberg's Variations, for instance, which he neither likes nor dislikes.

He readily acknowledges his adherence to the " purist " school of thought in conducting. " I like to feel that I can get everything I want from the printed page. It is not a question of what we can do with a composition, but what we can get out of it. Who am I to try to improve upon Beethoven, for instance?"

24

Only in exceptional cases will he make the slightest alteration in the composer's scoring, in fact in the whole of Beethoven's works there are only about three places where Sir Adrian alters the orchestration, and then only very slightly. " I do a little less than Weingartner," he told me, " I don't adopt all the changes he recommended; and he was considered to be conservative. I *never* add an instrument."

He dislikes showmanship of any kind, and therefore never makes unnecessary gestures when he is conducting. Airs and graces and popular tricks to please the audience are abhorrent to him. Similarly, he will not tolerate all the extraneous marks of expression that scores are apt to accumulate from the hands of conductors bent upon colouring up the work of the long-suffering composer.

Rhythm is of the greatest importance to him; he goes to endless trouble to make his players feel the rhythmic swing of the music, particularly when the bar-lines tend to break this up.

In one of my discussions with Sir Adrian, I asked him if he would allow me to convey, through this sketch, his advice to young conductors. He agreed readily, and proceeded to emphasize, first, the necessity of getting a complete " bird's-eye " view of the work at the outset. This is where so many fail; they start at the first page and plod through it, stopping their players two or three times to correct wrong notes. Then they go on to the next page, trying to overcome difficulties here and there, and so on, until they come to the end of the first movement—if ever they do, in the time allowed for rehearsal. This, he contends, is quite wrong, for although they may have become acquainted with many of the difficulties in the music, they have failed to see the proper " shape " of the musical structure because they have been paying so much attention to its detail. It is absolutely essential that both the conductor and the players should have in their minds some sort of a picture—even if it is a sketchy one—of the contours of the piece; they should know where the emotional intensity increases and diminishes and how the music passes through different keys. Above all, they should become acquainted with the various themes, the sequence in which they are used, their contrast and balance.

For this reason, Sir Adrian recommends that the whole piece be read through, however roughly, right to the end two or three times at a considerable speed—faster than it is to be performed at the concert. While the players are getting their " sight " of the music, the conductor will be confirming his own mental picture of the work as a whole, and making notes, mentally or otherwise, so that after a single play-through at the proper speed, he can analyse it.

When making corrections, the conductor should plan his work so that certain sections of the orchestra are not obliged to sit about waiting while the others are being rehearsed. If, for instance, the strings require just a little attention, the woodwind a great deal, and the brass none at all, the brass should be allowed to leave the hall, the difficulties of the strings should be attended to next, and then finally, the conductor should work with the woodwind, having dismissed the strings.

Sir Adrian is always considering the feelings of his players. He avoids all unnecessary repetition at rehearsals, and by using the method I have just described, eliminates as far as possible the boredom that sets in when players have to sit patiently doing nothing while a few of their colleagues are being rehearsed. He will do almost anything to avoid tiring his players, particularly if they are to give the concert on the same day.

Perhaps the greatest advantage of his method of rehearsal is that there is no danger of the first part of a work being given a highly polished performance while the rest of it is scrambled through anyhow. In these days when rehearsals are few and often of short duration, we frequently hear programmes in which the conductor's favourite piece is beautifully played and the other items are just scamped.

Sir Adrian urges young conductors to have proper respect for the musicianship of their players, particularly if the latter are professionals with many years of experience behind them. " Never try to tell a man how to play his instrument : he knows far more about it than you do, and will immediately resent your effort. Instead, explain clearly what it is you want, and leave it to him to produce the desired tone, effect, or whatever it is. I frequently ask for a more mellow tone, or a harder tone, for instance, but I wouldn't dream of trying to tell a man like Aubrey Brain how to produce it!''

It must have been this that turned our conversation to the rather poor quality of tone one hears from the brass in some of our orchestras at the present time. Sir Adrian agreed that there was a tendency to spoil a climax by overblowing, but explained that this was easily done on the French instruments in general use in this country. He would not like to see them changed for German instruments, however, because a much wider range of expression could be obtained on them.

*   *   *

Sir Adrian believes that the present renascence in music will be maintained after the war because so many people have learnt to love great music and will not give it up. On the other hand, there might be a slump in attendance at public concerts unless the promoters pay more attention to the convenience of the people. They must give far more consideration to the comfort of the audiences, and should see that performances are held at more accommodating times, otherwise when people get the use of their cars again, they will not tolerate the inconveniences they endure at the present time.

Coming to contemporary music, Sir Adrian thought that our composers get a fair chance of being heard, and that they deserve it. Modern music, he said, will always be ahead of public taste, and therefore is bound to be puzzling to the majority of listeners. The composer of to-day is exploring new fields, and consequently some of his work is unintelligible to the masses.

He believes that in twenty years' time a Vaughan Williams slow movement will be treasured beyond anything that Delius wrote. "We have not yet learnt to appreciate Vaughan Williams properly, and I think the same might be said of the work of Arthur Bliss."

"On what lines do you think music will develop?" I asked. "Will quarter-tones come into general use in time?"

"Quarter-tones are only experimental, and I don't think they will be used much in the future. Vaughan Williams, Arthur Bliss and William Walton, for instance, can write great music without them. Besides, all the tunes and permutations of harmony are *not* exhausted. Personally, I think we might see more experiments with the modes— harmonic development seems to be moving in that direction."

"Do you think ugliness can be justified in music?"

"Occasionally in dramatic music," Sir Adrian replied, "but you must remember that the standard of ugliness is continually changing. There are many things I thought to be ugly when I was a boy which I now consider to be most beautiful. At first, William Walton's slow movements made no impression upon me, but now they are becoming beautiful to me. In rehearsal I have often noticed a chord in the work of Mozart which was considered ugly when it was first written."

*　　*　　*

Sir Adrian Boult was married in 1933 to Ann Mary Bowles, younger daughter of Capt. F. A. Bowles, R.N., J.P., of Sittingbourne, Kent, and has four step-children. Lady Boult was a member of the Bach Choir for many years, and is an excellent music critic. Their home is in Surrey, not very far from Guildford.

Sir Adrian's recreations are walking, cycling and swimming. At one time he was fond of shooting, but finds now that he never has time for this particular form of sport.

WARWICK BRAITHWAITE

※

W HEN last I saw Warwick Braithwaite he was contemplating a glass of sherry in " The Gluepot." For the benefit of those who are not acquainted with the habits of London musicians I had better explain that this is the favourite rendezvous of all who have had the honour of performing in the ill-fated Queen's Hall: to the uninitiated, it is merely The George," a pub in Mortimer Street. That was an evening in the early spring of this year—1944.

It struck me then that he could convince anybody at anytime that he was an Englishman, a Scot, an Irishman, an American, a Frenchman or even a Russian; but nobody would take him seriously if he declared himself to be a New Zealander. Yet that is precisely what he is: he was born in that distant Dominion in 1898, son of one of the first publishers and booksellers to settle there.

Braithwaite came to this country during the Great War and won a scholarship to the Royal Academy of Music, at which he studied composition under Frederick Corder and the piano under Mrs. Hedwig McEwen. After three industrious years as a student he joined a touring opera company, first as chorus-master and later as conductor. At that time by the way, he held the distinction of being the youngest professional conductor in Britain.

Then after a year with the British National Opera Company he was appointed by the BBC as Musical Director of their Cardiff station, a position which he held for nine years. While he was there he conducted the Cardiff Musical Society, a fine body of two hundred and fifty voices, giving four concerts a year and performing almost every important choral work in existence.

Chiefly through the efforts of such men as the late Sir Walford Davies, the National Orchestra of Wales was founded in 1927 with the support of the BBC. Warwick Braithwaite became its conductor. a d for several years this orchestra did magnificent work, but when certain reorganisations caused the BBC to withdraw its support, it had to be disbanded for financial reasons. During the last few months of its life, Braithwaite approached all the wealthy people he knew in Wales, seeking their financial support for a scheme that would enable Wales to retain its own National Orchestra. To his despair, he found that

28

not one of them would help him. The disappointment was made more bitter by the knowledge that the Welsh workers really *did* want their Orchestra, and were prepared to give of the little they possessed towards its maintenance. But the offerings of the mining communities, in those days very poor, were insufficient, and the Orchestra ceased to exist.

" I was heartbroken," Braithwaite told me, " because I knew that the Welsh, a people proud of their great musical traditions, needed the music we were giving. When I used to take the orchestra up into the mining towns and villages the reception we got was overwhelming. I have never in my life known such rapt attention and such thunderous applause. Even between the movements of a symphony, the people would sit or stand as if spellbound: not a murmur could be heard."

In 1931 Warwick Braithwaite joined the Sadler's Wells Company as a conductor of opera. He stayed with them until 1940, when he was appointed conductor of the Scottish Orchestra. From his earliest days he had been fascinated by opera, in fact he had made up his mind to become a conductor of opera when he was four years old! That was just after his father had taken him to a performance of "Lohengrin." Of the members of the company he had admired the conductor most of all, and on the way home had told his father that when he grew up he wanted to be like the man who waved the stick!

Braithwaite is sure that there will be a great revival of opera after the war. Every large city should have its own opera house, and the companies should be subsidized by the Government. The present shortage of suitable opera voices in this country is due, he thinks, to the absence of any steady demand for them. When the demand returns, we shall get the voices.

Just before he left the Sadler's Wells Company, he had a unique experience. He was rehearsing " Tosca " and taking good care that the " bells of Rome " were ringing out as they should, when two policemen appeared on the stage and told him that if he persisted in using the (tubular) bells, they would be obliged to take action, because all the people in the neighbourhood could hear them and were thinking that an invasion had started. It looked at first as if the bells of Rome would have to be silenced, but after negotiations with the police headquarters it was finally agreed that the bells could be used on the condition that two constables were present on every occasion in case anybody showed signs of panic!

Since he has been in charge of the Scottish Orchestra, Braithwaite has succeeded in extending its season from three to six months in each year. As a result, Glasgow is getting orchestral concerts of a standard never before achieved, chiefly because the instrumentalists have been playing together continuously under one conductor.

During the 1943-4 season, Braithwaite conducted one hundred and thirty-two major symphony concerts and eighteen children's concerts, and the Orchestra visited all the principal towns of Scotland. The enthusiasm of the audiences was most encouraging: the Caird Hall in Dundee (the largest hall in Great Britain, apart from the Albert Hall) was full for an orchestral concert for the first time in its history.

* * *

Warwick Braithwaite has very definite views on modern music. He will perform anything that *is* music, but flatly refuses to touch anything that consists of nothing but queer noises strung together by clever orchestration. He admires Walton, Moeran and Bliss, but he considers that Beethoven was the greatest composer the world has ever known, and thinks his sonatas should have been symphonies, chiefly because their slow movements are so masterly. After Beethoven, his preferences are for Sibelius and Tschaikovsky.

" What is your opinion of the taste of the Scottish audiences?" I asked.

" Whether it is modern or otherwise, the Scots appreciate all music that is *good*. They are very discriminating, and are not interested in empty, clever-clever stuff."

" Do you find that the greatest appreciation is shown by the younger people?"

" We get enormous numbers of young people at our concerts, but the great revival is not due exclusively to them. I have come across men of over sixty who have just recently developed an interest in music!"

The topic of our conversation turned—as it inevitably does whenever I talk to musicians for long—to the question of State or municipal subsidies for music.

" The Glasgow Corporation is now paying a grant to the Scottish Orchestra, and I can speak from experience when I say that some sort of subsidy is necessary. I should like the Corporation to take over the Scottish Orchestra entirely as far as its finances are concerned, so that we could be free from financial anxiety and give the people the music they want all the year round. We need subsidies because otherwise the musician can never feel secure. In peacetime his living was so precarious that parents were apt to look upon musical talent in their children as a curse."

Braithwaite has equally definite views on the qualifications for conducting: he maintains that a conductor should have a sound knowledge of the instruments in his orchestra and be able to play at least one or two of them tolerably well. As well as being an accomplished pianist, he himself can play the viola, horn, oboe, clarinet and timpani.

On the other hand, he favours no hard and fast rules on the technique of conducting. I asked him several questions on the sort of beat he gives, the use he makes of his left hand, and so forth, but his answer was: " I haven't the slightest idea. I like to let the music take possession of me so completely that the majority of my movements are made subconsciously. My only desire is to interpret the music as I feel it, and I'd turn upside down if I thought it would help to express something."

His advice to young musicians—professional or amateur—is: "Work hard at technique while you're young, because it won't come later. When you have acquired a good technique, regard it as nothing and concentrate upon expressing humanity through music. Technique is a thing you can forget about *when* you've got it."

" There is no short cut or royal road to success in music; it comes only by hard work—and the older you get the more work there is to do. I believe that music must be so wonderful that people are *bound* to come and listen to it."

Braithwaite has no great enthusiasm for the academic influence in music. He dislikes Doctors of Music with " paper " degrees—i.e., degrees for which no *practical* examination is made—who condemn great works solely because they appeal to the general public. Moreover, he has too often observed that a new composition scorned by the academics when it is first published is introduced by them into the curricula of their institutions twenty years later.

I don't know how the subject of women in orchestras was introduced, but I found that Braithwaite's feelings on it were a trifle mixed.

" Women make fine oboe players, but I'm not sure that I like them among the fiddles. They are too individualistic; they seem to be unable to sink their own personalities for the benefit of the whole. In the woodwind it doesn't matter so much because more individuality is required, but a sprinkling of women among your strings seems to spoil the team work."

" You would rather not have women in the orchestra, then?" I asked.

" Well, I'd hardly say that, but I think their place is more in the women's orchestra. I must say, they are splendid workers, earnest, keen and meticulously careful, but they don't seem to be able to take the long view of orchestral problems . . . . besides, their discipline is not as good as the men's."

Then I am afraid our conversation strayed into a diversity of by-ways, and we talked about America, which Braithwaite liked, and vested interests in music, which he did *not* like, until I realized that if I drank any more beer my journey down Regent Street to the Underground would be more precarious than the musician's living in peacetime, so I bade him farewell and departed.

*   *   *

Warwick Braithwaite, who was married in 1930 to Miss Lorna Davies, has two sons, Roderick, aged eleven, and Nicholas, aged four. His recreations are music and " having one " with his friends.

Shortly before the outbreak of war in 1939 he completed his opera " Pendragon." Although this has not yet been staged, several excerpts have been performed with great success at symphony concerts during the past four years. He has also written four Overtures, a String Quartet and a Symphony in E.

WARWICK BRAITHWAITE

BASIL CAMERON

BASIL CAMERON

❦

B ASIL CAMERON was born in Reading in 1885. As a child he took to
music with unusual facility. By the time he was seven he could
play the piano well, and had already started to learn the fiddle. He
was only eight when he earned his first fee—for playing second violin
in the "Elijah" at Tiverton, Devon, where he was a choirboy in the
Parish Church.

At the age of twelve he ran away from home and took a job as a
junior clerk. The next two years were spent in business, but then he
was persuaded to take up music professionally and went to York to
study under T. Tertius Noble, who was then the Organist of York
Minster. Later he was able to go to Berlin for lessons with Joachim,
and finally he completed his studies under Auer in London.

His first professional appointment was in the Queen's Hall Orchestra
under Sir Henry Wood, whose influence afterwards stirred in him the urge
to conduct. At that time, however, he put all his energy into improving
his technique as a violinist and he took a keen interest in chamber music;
in fact, he found that it gave him greater satisfaction to play in a string
quartet than in a full symphony orchestra or to do solo work.

Cameron maintains that the finest training a violinist can get is in
the string quartet, and incidentally, experience of that kind is also
extremely useful to those with aspirations to conduct, because it provides
such excellent opportunities to learn the secrets of perfect balance.

In 1912, the Corporation of Torquay opened their new Pavilion and
announced their intention of holding miniature Promenade concerts in
it. Basil Cameron applied for the conductorship, got it, and engaged
an orchestra of about thirty players. In his first year there he held a
Wagner Festival to celebrate the hundredth anniversary of that composer's birth. Considering that many of the older-established orchestras
and other musical organisations did nothing to mark the centenary, this
was no small achievement for a newly-established orchestra.

During the Great War Cameron served in the Kensington Battalion
of the London Regiment. He was wounded in August, 1918, and
brought home. After the Armistice he accepted several conducting
engagements of a short duration, and also tried directing one or two
of the cinema orchestras, but he disliked " messing good music about "

for the sake of the films, and in any case never felt the cinema to be his proper environment.

In 1923 he was engaged by the Hastings Corporation as Musical Director and for seven years conducted the winter concerts. During this period he spent the summer seasons directing the Harrogate Orchestra, and it is significant that many of the players under him in both of these towns are now in the leading symphony orchestras. In passing, I might also add that he first conducted the Royal Philharmonic Society in 1927.

Cameron went to America in 1930 and conducted the San Francisco Symphony Orchestra for two seasons. Then he had the honour of following Sir Thomas Beecham as conductor of the Seattle Symphony Orchestra, directing it for six seasons. While he was in the United States he broadcast frequently on ' nation-wide hook-ups.'

He returned to England in 1938 to conduct the Covent Garden Opera Company on a tour, and he continued his association with them until war broke out in the following year. Since then he has worked with all the principal symphony orchestras as a guest conductor; notably with the London Philharmonic during its more difficult days in the early part of the war. His chief activity in recent years, of course, has been in connection with the Promenade concerts, for which he has acted as assistant to Sir Henry Wood. In the 1943 season he undertook to conduct every concert during the first month at only four weeks' notice when Sir Henry was taken ill.

Although he likes guest-conducting, he feels that a conductor works best when he has his own regular orchestra. An interesting point which came out in a discussion I had with him recently at the Savage Club is that he has always regarded fencing as the best possible exercise a conductor can take. It helps him to acquire a perfect poise; it strengthens his wrists and promotes easy and graceful movement.

When I questioned him on the technique of conducting I found that he dislikes anything that suggests exhibitionism: he believes that the less there is of it the better, in fact, he would prefer both the orchestra and conductor to be out of the sight of the audience altogether. The proof of a good conductor, he declares, lies in his knowledge of the score, and that is why he himself spends at least forty or fifty hours in studying a new symphony before he attempts even to rehearse it.

MOSCO CARNER

❦

VIENNA was a musician's paradise when Dr. Mosco Carner was born there in 1904, for although the ordinary people were poor, music was in the air all day long, and that, to the Viennese, was all that mattered once the bare necessities of life had been provided.

His parents were Jews of partly Spanish origin, and very musical. His mother sang and his father played the flute. Mosco Carner was eight or nine when he started learning to play the piano, and as he showed unusual ability it was generally understood that he would become a professional pianist. Yet when he reached the age of fourteen, orchestral music made a far greater claim upon his attention, and from that time he lost no opportunity to study it.

When he entered the Neues Wiener Konservatorium, he chose the 'cello and piano as his instruments, and of course, took harmony, counterpoint, etc., in addition. For all that, as his general education progressed, other interests also attracted him, and he began to consider the advisability of making music his recreation and of embarking upon a medical career with mental diseases as his speciality. At eighteen, he found himself faced with the problem of deciding in favour of either music or medicine. He went for a walk, and within an hour had settled his course for the future: he stood outside Vienna University and decided to become a musician.

He continued at the Konservatorium, but also went to the University to study musicology. He took conducting first under Rudolph Nilius and Franz Schalk, and later under Robert Heger, who frequently visited this country before the war to conduct at Covent Garden. His doctorate was gained in 1928 for a thesis on Schumann.

The desire to conduct was stimulated by regular attendance at the opera in Vienna, which had been under the direction of Gustav Mahler, for whom Carner had the highest admiration. It is not surprising, then, to find that his first professional appointment was as assistant to the conductor of the opera class at the Konservatorium, but this evidently did not provide sufficient conducting for him, because he also founded an orchestra of his own, partly of professional musicians, which gave many concerts in the town. Occasionally, a programme would not be to the liking of his audience, and they would get up and walk out in the middle of it! One day when they grew particularly restless, he told the hall porter to lock all the doors to ensure that there could be no premature departures.

Austria was a poor country for many years after the Great War, and there were very few opportunities for young conductors to secure permanent appointments. The tendency among all the younger musicians was to seek work in Germany, but Carner found a post as an assistant conductor in the opera at Oppava in Czechoslovakia. He had all the odd jobs to do, of course; for instance, in " Der Freischütz " (Weber), he was posted in the " flies " to give signals to the "echo" singer above, who had to reiterate the number of bullets as they were counted by the singer on the stage. This was usually a simple task, but unfortunately one evening the stage singer miscounted, and despite frantic gestures on the part of Dr. Carner, the " echo " sounded one number in arrears as the bullets were counted !

From Oppava, Mosco Carner moved to Danzig, and in 1929 became the assistant conductor and chorus-master at the State Theatre. That was before Hitler rose to power, and the German residents in the Free City—they were a very large majority, by the way—were agreeably disposed, enthusiastic patrons of the opera. But the next few years brought great changes.

In spite of the ever-growing hostility towards the Jews, Dr. Carner still held his appointment when in 1933 he made a second visit to his relatives in England, having already spent a holiday in London in the previous year. While he was here he received a letter informing him that the Senate had no further use for his services. To this he replied drawing their attention to the twelve months' contract he held, but they refused to reinstate him, preferring to pay him a year's salary instead.

So he decided to stay in England, although the authorities would not give him permission to seek work. The only thing he could do was to write, and having already started to make a serious study of our language, he began contributing to various musical journals.

At first it was not at all easy to make a regular income in this manner, but he persevered, and in 1936 the ' Radio Times ' made him one of their regular contributors. In the following year he started a series of articles for ' The Listener.'

Then he became the London music correspondent of the ' Neue Frieie Presse ' and of the ' Prager Tagblatt.' These two appointments made it possible for him to go to a large number of concerts and to hear music of a type not performed to any extent in Germany: modern French, English and Russian compositions. All this experience was most valuable: it broadened his musical outlook considerably. In his earlier days he had thought little of English composers, for instance, but he soon completely revised his opinions, and became an admirer of Elgar, Walton, Delius, Vaughan Williams and Bliss.

36

MOSCO CARNER

ALBERT COATES

His first appearance as a conductor in this country was when in 1938 a committee was set up to give several concerts of the lesser-known works of Mozart by younger artists who had not yet become well-known. Dr. Carner conducted in this series with such success that he became noted for his superb handling of Mozart's music, and began to receive invitations to conduct all the leading orchestras, including the London Philharmonic, London Symphony and BBC Symphony Orchestras, both in London and in the provinces.

Continuing his literary work, he wrote " A Study of Twentieth Century Harmony," as a sequel to the volume of the same title by René Lenormand.

Reviewing this book in the 'Sunday Times,' Ernest Newman wrote: " Dr. Carner . . . . has not only a complete grasp of the subject, but an exceptional gift for making the most apparently abstruse things look simple, thanks to a lucidity of style that is rare among musical theorists." In ' The Monthly Musical Record ' Edmund Rubbra wrote: " This is one of the clearest expositions of the subject that I have read, especially is this so in the illuminating chapters on the harmonic systems of Schönberg and Hindemith."

I think it is also worth recording that Dr. Carner assisted in the compiling of " The Oxford Companion to Music," and wrote a biography of Dvorak for Novello's. He has also recently published a book of essays called " Of Men and Music."

Another interesting branch of his work has been his broadcast talks known as " The Music Lover's Calendar " and " Pictures in Music," though one of his most important activities for the BBC is quite unknown to the listener at home. I refer to the work he does in connection with the London Transcription Service, for which he writes scripts and sometimes makes gramophone records, which are sent to neutral and allied countries.

*　　　*　　　*

Dr. Carner believes that it is the conductor's task not merely to direct his orchestra, but to do everything within his power to assist in the musical education of the people. If all conductors were fully aware of their responsibilities in this direction they would exert a far greater influence upon the musical culture of this nation.

It would be a great advantage to the younger conductors if all the large cities could have their own municipal orchestras after the war, for then there would be far more scope for the younger men, who could act as assistant conductors. At the present time they find the greatest difficulty in getting experience with professional orchestras.

Although he is recognised as an authority on Mozart and Schubert,

Dr. Carner is one of the most active members of the Committee for the Promotion of New Music, which has for its objects the discovery of promising young composers, the hearing of their work, the introduction of it to concert-giving organisations, schools, etc., and the establishment of libraries of records and scores of it. He believes that it is our duty to see that the work of our modern composers gets a fair hearing.

Modern music, he feels, has now passed the experimental stage and is becoming more stabilized. Composers of to-day are more conscious of the reactions of the people, and consequently their work is becoming more intelligible to the masses. In contemporary music, Britain is now in the front rank.

" What about the Nazi influence on contemporary German music?" I asked.

" It has been detrimental in every way. The Nazi composers have been forced to abandon anything modern and intellectual, and therefore their development has been retarded. The Nazi Party favours crude, sentimental stuff in the old-fashioned romantic style."

" Do you approve of the Soviet influence, then?"

" Frankly, no. I don't think the State should be allowed to influence art in any way: it may, of course, encourage and stimulate it, but even the slightest form of control or influence would be bound to hinder the true development of art. The work of the Russian composers has somewhat deteriorated since the Soviets began to lay down rules for them: it has now to conform to an approved pattern."

" You would not welcome a Ministry of Fine Arts in this country then?"

" Such a Ministry could do excellent work provided that it had no power to dictate the actual style of the artists' work. Whether a composition is good or bad must be decided by the recognised, qualified critics and by the general musical public; not by the politicians."

" Which of our younger composers do you consider to be the most promising?" I continued.

" There are quite a number: Benjamin Britten, for instance, who has very fine technique; Michael Tippett, a rich personality; Lennox Berkeley, whose work has clarity and a definite purpose; and Humphrey Searle, a very young man with something of his own to say. There are many others, too, who might do a great deal in time."

" You don't think they are apt to spoil themselves by trying to be ' clever?' "

" It is the prerogative of youth to try to be clever!" Dr. Carner laughed. " They will settle down all right later on, and we shall see some very fine work from them."

" Can I formulate briefly your advice to young composers?"

' Well . . . . I simply advise them to study other composers as much as they can, but to concentrate entirely upon expressing *themselves* when they write."

"Why do you particularly like to conduct the works of Mozart?"

"For various reasons," Dr. Carner replied. "Mozart's music has ev_rything in it, in an objective form. You can let it speak for itself. If you make no conscious effort to control it, you get a more perfect picture than with the work of the romantic composers, which often requires dramatization on the part of the conductor."

" Shall we ever establish opera in this country?"

" I doubt it, unless the State is prepared to support it as in other countries. In that case, of course, it would flourish here just as well as anywhere else, though we should have to make a great effort to produce an English operatic voice, which we lack at the moment. I think that perhaps the climate here is unfavourable to singing."

* * *

Dr. Mosco Carner became a naturalized British subject in 1940. In January, 1944, he married Helen Pyke, the professional pianist, who tours the country as an accompanist in innumerable concerts organized by C.E.M.A. and E.N.S.A. Her chief activity at the present time is in connection with the Y.M.C.A. Army Education Scheme in Kent. Of the fourteen hundred concerts she has given, she has some vivid recollections, particularly of one at Dover when they were shelled for four hours by the German batteries on the other side of the Channel. I might also add that she has published a book of children's music entitled " Five Zoo Pictures."

Swimming is one of Dr. Carner's favourite recreations. He once swam across the Danube and back at its widest point, and where the current is exceedingly strong. The distance was about three miles.

He also enjoys walking, climbing—especially in Cumberland —and regular attendance at the theatre and cinema. He reads extensively musical and philosophical works and books by such authors as Somerset Maugham, H. G. Wells, Aldous Huxley and Hugh Walpole.

When conducting, his precise, restrained movements clearly reflect his gentle, sensitive character. He abhors " flashy " conducting and anything that suggests mere showmanship: he prefers to be quite unobtrusive. Rather less than the average in height, he never tries to dominate; you have only to show him that you respect the music he loves and his Schubertian features lighten up in one of the most friendly smiles imaginable.

ALBERT COATES

※

ALBERT COATES was born in St. Petersburg, now Leningrad, in 1882, a son of a Yorkshire business man who had settled there and married a Russian lady. He was educated in England, and intended to enter his father's business, but when he returned to St. Petersburg he found it difficult to interest himself in anything but music, so eventually he was given permission to go to Leipzig to study at the Conservatorium. He was twenty at the time, and had the good fortune to become a pupil of Nikisch for conducting, Klengel for the 'cello, and Teichmüller for the piano.

Nikisch soon became aware of his pupil's ability and before long appointed him as an assistant conductor and coach at the Leipzig Opera House. It was here that Coates conducted his first opera " The Tales of Hoffman," and gained the necessary experience to secure him the conductorship of the Elberfeld Opera House in 1906.

Two years later he became joint conductor with Schuch at Dresden, and after two seasons there went to Mannheim for a year. Then, in 1910, he was appointed Chief Conductor of the Imperial Opera House at St. Petersburg and stayed there until the Revolution, directing a rich and varied repertoire. By this time he had also become well known as a conductor of symphonic work, and was generally looked upon as one of the world's greatest exponents of Scriabin. He made his first professional visit to England in 1910 to conduct the London Symphony Orchestra, and returned in 1913 to share a season at Covent Garden with Nikisch.

His next visit to this country was in 1919 when he worked with Sir Thomas Beecham at Covent Garden, appeared again with the London Symphony Orchestra and did some fine performances with the Royal Philharmonic Society. Then began his association with the British National Opera Company, and the Leeds Festivals, which he conducted in 1922 and again in 1925.

For the past twenty years or so, Albert Coates has been travelling all over the world. We find him one year as a guest conductor of the New York Symphony Orchestra, the next year directing a special season of the Paris Opéra, then back in Russia, then at Covent Garden—until we wonder just where he belongs. But that is typical of him: he loves travelling, and a different orchestra every week would not disturb him in the least. So I hope I may be forgiven for not including in this sketch a catalogue of every important musical event in which he has figured.

How he has been able to find time to compose is a mystery to all musicians. His symphonic poem, " The Eagle," dedicated to Nikisch, was an outstanding feature of the 1925 Leeds Festival, and his two operas, " Samuel Pepys " and " Pickwick," aroused no small amount of interest in musical circles when they were first performed in 1929 and 1936 respectively. The former, by the way, was first given in German at Munich; the latter, in English, at Covent Garden.

From 1939 to March, 1944, Albert Coates spent the whole of his time in America, and musical folk in this country were just beginning to presume that he had settled for good in the States when he suddenly appeared in London to work for E.N.S.A.! But before I go on, I must mention one or two of his activities in America. He conducted a substantial number of the Hollywood Bowl Concerts, he appeared frequently with the South Carolina and Seattle Symphony orchestras, and at Hollywood arranged and directed the music of the Metro-Goldwyn-Mayer film, "Song of Russia," appearing in it also as a solo pianist. Shortly before his return to Britain he was associated with "Two Sisters and a Sailor," another M.G.M. film which will be released before this book is in print.

*   *   *

Albert Coates was married in 1910 to Madelon Holland, and has one daughter, Tamara, aged twenty-one.

When I met him a couple of months after his return to this country, he had already conducted a large number of concerts here under the auspices of E.N.S.A. He told me that our new audiences of enthusiastic young people reminded him of the musical renascence that took place in Russia some years ago. The " ordinary " man and woman in Britain is now learning to love music just as millions of the Russian workers did when their government began to provide music on a nation-wide scale. The only real difference is that most of our new audiences have been prepared by the radio, whereas in the more remote and poorer parts of Russia in those days there were millions who had never heard a symphony concert or seen an opera in their lives.

Some idea of what this means may be gathered from the fact that Coates once conducted before an audience who did not know how to clap! At the end of the concert they sat in silence smiling at the artists.

but making no effort to show their appreciation in the customary manner.
So at the next concert a few people had to be put in the audience here
and there to set an example. These "applause-promoters" did the
trick very nicely; in fact, the audience let their enthusiasm run away
with them and made a terrible din. The artists were delighted and
bowed in acknowledgment. Then, with one accord, the audience got
up and bowed back!

The people of the Soviet Union, Coates told me, are incredibly
enthusiastic about opera, yet he can remember the time when they were
so "raw" that they thought the coloratura soprano was laughing when
she sang her roulades and cadenzas. It was quite a common occurrence
to find the audience heartily joining in this "laughter": much to the
annoyance of the company! In one Russian village they couldn't understand why in "Carmen" the principals sang the solos all the way
through. During the second interval a local leader went up to the
conductor and said: "Why do you keep on bringing back the same
ladies and gentlemen to sing to us? We have heard their songs: now
let us hear what the others can do."

I asked Coates how he liked working under the Soviet régime. "At
first I disliked it," he confessed, "but gradually it improved, and now
I think it is wonderfully promising in every way. It is so much better
now that the Church has been cleaned up."

When we discussed contemporary music, I soon discovered that
Coates has the greatest admiration for the contemporary Russian school.
He thinks it is a great pity that we hear so little of their work in this
country: there are many really fine compositions that are practically
unknown to the English audiences. Kabalevsky, who is only thirty-six,
is one of the most promising of the Russian composers. A year or two
before the present war, Coates conducted the first performance of his
Second Symphony in Moscow, and as a result, the authorities gave
Kabalevsky the best opera libretto of the year to set to music.

It will be found that several of the biographees in this book believe
that the Soviet composers all write to a pattern. I mentioned this to
Coates, adding that it seemed to be the general impression in this
country, but he disagreed strongly, adding that as far as he was aware
there was no obligation of any kind on the part of Soviet composers
to write in an officially approved style. They are quite free to express
themselves in their own way, and merit rarely fails to find encouragement.

Coates is very impressed by the musicianship of our orchestral
players, particularly by their ability to learn new work quickly, but he
deplores our practice of giving concerts with so few rehearsals. In

America he was allowed to call five rehearsals for almost all the concerts he gave.

*   *   *

Albert Coates is tall and broad-shouldered, inclined to be stout, and very much the cosmopolitan. His hair, once black and striking, is now grey and genteel. One might easily mistake him now for a successful but still very energetic business man capable of playing merry hell at a board meeting.

As a conductor he excels in Russian music, where his vitality, strength, generosity and love of colour can be unleashed. Give him a programme in which there is plenty of emotion and warmth, and he is happy.

LOUIS COHEN

꙼꙲

Now I come to a conductor who originally made his name entirely in the north of England, but who is now becoming well known all over the country—Louis Cohen.

He was born in Liverpool in 1896, and as his father's favourite hobby was violin-making, it is not at all surprising that Louis could play the fiddle when he was very young. As a child he also sang alto in a choir, a fact which suggests that he was an unusually good sight-reader, because most boys find it quite difficult enough to read the soprano line without delving into the harmony beneath it!

Cohen made his first public appearance as a violinist in 1909, and was awarded a Corporation Scholarship at the Liverpool School of Music. Among his fellow students were members of the famous Goossens family. He also became an accomplished viola player and was only fifteen when he was engaged to play this instrument for a season of opera given in his native city by the Quinlan Opera Company. They were evidently very impressed by his ability because they offered him a contract to join them on a world tour, but he declined it, preferring to continue his studies.

In 1915 he joined the army and saw active service abroad as a gunner. Four years elapsed before he could return to music, and when finally he was demobilised, he went to the Royal Manchester College of Music to study the violin under Dr. Adolph Brodsky, and composition and harmony under Dr. Carrol and Dr. Keighley. He became a member of the Hallé Orchestra and played in the first violins under Sir Hamilton Harty for eleven years.

Cohen founded the Merseyside Chamber Music Players in 1923 and gave many concerts in Lancashire and North Wales, besides broadcasting from time to time. The success of this venture led him to establish the Merseyside Orchestra in 1929, chiefly to give Sunday concerts in Wallasey. Within three years he was able to increase the number of his players to forty-five and rename them "The Merseyside Symphony Orchestra." With the support of the Liverpool Corporation he gave a series of not less than twelve popular Sunday Symphony Concerts at St. George's Hall, Liverpool, every season until the outbreak of war in 1939, when the Liverpool Philharmonic Society took over the

J. E. Marsh]

LOUIS COHEN

EDRIC CUNDELL

personnel of this orchestra, augmented it to sixty players, and continued a similar series of Sunday concerts at the Philharmonic Hall. Mr. Cohen conducted the majority of these.

During the summer months of the years 1934-1939 he also worked at Harrogate as the Municipal Director of Music, giving a symphony concert with eminent artists, and a light classical concert, every week.

Another of Cohen's own organisations was the Merseyside Chamber Orchestra, which he founded in 1935 when the Liverpool Corporation invited him to give a series of chamber concerts in their Walker Art Gallery. Since that time he has given many excellent concerts of that type both in and around Liverpool.

During the present war his activities have ranged from directing summer concerts at Southport and symphony concerts in Liverpool to acting as a guest conductor of the Hallé, National and BBC Symphony Orchestras.

*   *   *

Louis Cohen can look back over some exciting years of music-making. There was the time, for instance, when at only a few hours' notice he was called upon to conduct in place of Sir Hamilton Harty, who had been suddenly taken ill. The programme included " Symphony Fantastique " (Berlioz) and " En Saga " (Sibelius). On another occasion he had the honour to conduct a huge orchestra of a hundred and fifty players at a concert given in aid of the Musicians' Benevolent Fund. You can imagine how impressive was the performance of Tschaikovsky's " Symphonie Pathétique."

He has no strong preferences for any particular type of music: the works of all schools appeal to him. He believes that our contemporary composers are getting a better chance of being heard nowadays, but that there is still a great deal to be done before they get the encouragement they deserve.

When I questioned him about the musical preferences of the northern audiences, he replied: " The answer depends entirely upon the sphere of music considered. The largest audiences are secured for Handel's ' Messiah,' which is invariably performed to full houses, and probably Elgar's ' Gerontius ' is the next most attractive. In purely orchestral music, Beethoven, Tschaikovsky, Dvorak and Elgar are the first four of the favourite composers."

He is confident that the present revival of interest in music will last, but thinks that it may take different forms in the future. For many years before this renascence took place, the enthusiasm for music in the north was very real. During the great " slump " he knew of an unemployed dock labourer who did without tobacco for a whole week so that he could obtain a ninepenny seat at a concert given by the Merseyside Symphony Orchestra. Incidentally, the man walked three miles to and from the concert, and considered his precious ninepence to have been very well spent.

Cohen is a little disappointed to find that although the demand for symphony concerts has grown tremendously during the past few years, the desire to hear chamber music has not increased in proportion. This, of course, might come later.

He was one of the first to advocate the provision of good music at first hand in factories and other places where large numbers of workers are gathered together, and to insist upon the necessity of giving school children talks on musical appreciation. He is now very anxious that music should play a more prominent part in adult education.

He feels strongly that qualified musicians should have a greater share in the shaping of musical policies both in the sphere of concert-giving and musical education. Furthermore, he contends that " the profession should take a far more active part in the working out of its musical vocation, in a manner similar to that which obtains in other professions."

His advice to young musicians is: " Whatever instrument you play or whatever line of music you take up, try to widen your knowledge of the art beyond your own particular course of study." This, he considers, is particularly important in view of the great changes and developments that are likely to take place after the war.

EDRIC CUNDELL

IF the management of one or two of our leading symphony orchestras had not sought him out, I think Edric Cundell would have been quite happy to have spent the rest of his days in academic seclusion at the Guildhall School of Music, of which he is now the Principal. But the first year of the present war brought unprecedented demands for symphony concerts; the great orchestras found themselves urgently in need of first-rate conductors with ample experience, and the result was that Edric Cundell's name soon became familiar on the programmes of the BBC, London Philharmonic and London Symphony orchestras.

He is a Londoner, born in 1893. His grandmother was an opera singer in Paris, and made such an impression upon Rossini with her remarkable voice that the great Italian composer pencilled in coloratura cadenzas on her music for her special benefit.

Cundell's parents were both very musical and must have felt gratified when their eleven year old son caused a sensation at his kindergarten school by playing Schubert's A-flat Impromptu with the assurance of a pianist twice his age. Throughout his school days he dreamed of music, and compensated his teachers for his lack of interest in general subjects by taking all the music prizes and performing at school concerts.

He had always been fascinated by orchestral instruments—the French horn especially—and when he left school he became a horn student under Borsdorf. With this instrument he won a scholarship to Trinity College of Music London, where he also studied the piano under Henry Bird.

When he was only nineteen years of age he was playing the horn in the opera at Covent Garden. The conductor in those days was Nikisch, and he distinctly remembers playing under this famous Hungarian conductor's direction in " The Ring."

Then came the Great War, and in 1915 Cundell volunteered for military service. He found himself in the army, and after a few months in the ranks obtained a commission in the R.A.S.C. Then he went to Salonica and with an English unit was attached to the Serbian army. For his initiative in one engagement he received the honour of the Serbian Order of the White Eagle.

During a lull in the operations in that country he wrote a symphonic poem called " Serbia," which he dedicated to King Alexander of Serbia, It was first performed by the Royal Orchestra in Salonica, but it was not heard in Britain until 1920 when Sir Henry Wood invited him to conduct it at a Promenade concert. Since then it has been performed and broadcast on several occasions both at home and abroad. It is interesting to note that Cundell wrote the entire work in a dug-out in about three days.

When he returned home after the Armistice he joined the teaching staff of Trinity College of Music, and also took private students for chamber music and the piano.

His next appearance at a Promenade concert was when he conducted the first performance of his setting of Robert Nicholls' poem, " Our Dead," with Gervase Elwes, for whom he had written it. At about this time he became the conductor of the Westminster Orchestra, a fine amateur ensemble. Another orchestra of this type, the Stock Exchange Orchestra, chose him as their musical director in 1924, the year in which he wrote his Symphony.

In the following year he went on an extensive examination tour for Trinity College, visiting chiefly towns in America and New Zealand. During his later tour of South Africa he conducted a series of concerts given by the Cape Town Orchestra. One of these was devoted to his own compositions, including " Serbia " and his Symphony, both of which were very well received.

Since that time, Edric Cundell's conducting has been 'rather spasmodic, though he has frequently broadcast, chiefly with his own chamber orchestra, which he founded some years ago. This small orchestra of twenty-four players was doing excellent work until the present war stopped its activity. One of the happiest memories of its members is of a concert they gave in Dublin with the Royal Dublin Society.

Cundell always took a keen interest in the Glyndebourne Festival Theatre, and during one season assisted in the coaching of the singers and players.

He was appointed to the Guildhall School of Music in 1938, and from that date has personally taken charge of the orchestra and opera class. The performance of Mozart's " Cosi fan Tútte " in 1939 was one of the best ever given in the history of the school; a great credit to all the students who took part in it.

During 1940 Edric Cundell conducted several concerts given by the London Philharmonic Orchestra, and the outcome of this was the invitation to take them on their Scottish tour in 1941. This was a great success, and since then he has toured with them in all parts of the country. In fact there are few towns of any size in Great Britain in which Cundell has not conducted the L.P.O.—the exceptions, I think, are Cardiff and Nottingham.

The BBC and London Symphony orchestras have also performed under his direction from time to time. In 1943, and again in 1944, he was chosen to conduct concerts given by the Royal Philharmonic Society.

* * *

Edric Cundell does not agree with those who say that serious music can never be made to pay in this country. He believes that if we had adequate concert halls our leading orchestras could pay their way without difficulty, though subsidies would, of course, be very helpful.

His views on modern music might be summarized in the statement that in his opinion the cacophonous style is giving way to something more orderly, grammatical and wholesome. " I think it is clear that the boomerang is returning; the restlessness of much of the music that has been written during the past twenty years is becoming a bore," he declares.

Cundell deplores the lack of emotion and poetry in much of the music that is being composed to-day. " Virtuosity in composition has been played out and proved wanting," he asserts. " The two vitalizing factors of the whole art of composition are melody and rhythm, and these cannot be superseded."

When I questioned him on the art of conducting, he said that there were far too many young men who wanted to start at the wrong end : they seemed to think that they should be allowed to inflict themselves upon professional orchestras at the very start of their career. He believes it to be essential that everybody aspiring to conduct should first go through an orchestra: they should be able to play at least one orchestral instrument, and should make their acquaintance with a large number of orchestral works from the players' point of view. They should learn the difficult job of making a poor orchestra sound good.

" Students of conducting often bewail the lack of opportunities to conduct orchestras," Cundell tells me. " My advice to them is: go out and organize amateur orchestras, choral societies and operatic societies for yourself. You will get no better experience anywhere."

* * *

Let me conclude with a note about Edric Cundell as a composer. As an indication of his ability, I would mention that he won a prize of a hundred pounds in the competition organized by the ' Daily Telegraph ' some years ago, with a string quartet.

Apart from the works I have already mentioned, he has written three orchestral suites, a Piano Concerto, a Symphonic Poem—"Deirdre," three quartets, a Rhapsody for viola and piano, and a "Hymn to Providence" for chorus and orchestra, in addition to numerous songs and minor choral works.

His most recent compositions are his unaccompanied Mass (words in Latin) and his Sextet for soprano, tenor and bass; violin, viola and 'cello, which was broadcast some time ago.

*   *   *

Cundell was married in 1920 to Miss Helen Harding Scott, of Thorpe, Norwich, who as a sculptress, has exhibited at the Royal Academy. They have one son and one daughter.

Like Sir Henry Wood, his chief recreation is sketching, and on the walls of his study at the Guildhall School of Music he has some fine specimens of his work in water-colours.

GIDEON FAGAN

❧

G IDEON FAGAN was born on November 3rd, 1904, at Somerset West,
Cape Province, South Africa, the youngest son of the late H. A.
Fagan, J.P., Mayor of Somerset Strand for a long period of years.

Educated first at the Somerset West High School and later at the
South African College School, Cape Town, Gideon Fagan's earliest
music lessons were with his brother, Johannes, a gifted composer and
pianist, who died in 1920, aged twenty-two. At ten years old Fagan
found opportunities to practise the organ in a local church, and from
the age of twelve he played for services in various parts of the Cape
Province. From 1916 to 1922 he studied at the South African College
of Music, Cape Town (harmony, counterpoint and composition under
Prof. W. H. Bell; the piano under Adolphe Hallis and later under Mrs.
Bell). His first experience of conducting was with the Students' String
Orchestra.

The rehearsals and performances of the Cape Tcwn Orchestra, under
Theo Wendt, were among his chief boyhood interests and at the age of
fifteen he obtained Wendt's permission to augment the percussion department at the weekly symphony concerts, thus receiving his first
opportunity to observe the workings of a professional orchestra from
within.

In 1922 he came to England and studied for four years at the Royal
College of Music—conducting under Sir Adrian Boult and Dr. Malcolm
Sargent, composition under Dr. Vaughan Williams, harmony and
counterpoint under Dr. C. H. Kitson, piano under Mr. Marmaduke
Barton, and tympani under Mr. Charles Turner. He conducted regularly
at College concerts, at several Patrons' Fund Rehearsals, and at the age
of eighteen a College production of " Hansel and Gretel " in the Parry
Opera Theatre. He acquired further practical knowledge of the players'
side of the orchestra by playing regularly in the percussion departments
of the College Orchestras and accepting casual professional engagements
as tympanist in and around London.

During a College vacation Fagan received an emergency call from
a musical comedy company which unexpectedly found itself minus a
conductor while touring the " smalls." Keen to get any kind of new
experience with the baton, he packed his bag, travelled to the back of

51

beyond and walked straight into a Monday morning rehearsal, blissfully unaware of the innumerable pitfalls that lie in wait in theatres for inexperienced enthusiasts. " Happily," he relates, " the first few minutes of rehearsal saw an episode which diverted attention from my own peccability. During a silent pause in the Overture the drummer crashed mercilessly on and when I managed to stop him I demanded that he should take the trouble to read his part. ' I don't read music,' the drummer replied. ' The bits and pieces I puts in has been enough for twenty-five years and tha'll have to put up with that or do without.' This attitude was supported by the local leader, whose bowler hat appeared to have been stuck on his head for the same number of years. I arranged a sort of start, stop, go-easy semaphore code, which worked only reasonably well, owing to the fact that either I or the drummer usually mistook the code at performances."

Upon completing his course at the College, Fagan returned to South Africa in 1926. He received invitations to appear as guest conductor with the Cape Town Orchestra in the City Hall, Cape Town, and when he decided in 1927 to return to England to seek wider musical experience, a committee formed for the occasion by professors of the University of Stellenbosch and the Conservatoire organized a farewell concert for him in the Recreations Hall, Stellenbosch, where he appeared in charge of the augmented Cape Town Orchestra before a large audience, many of whom were conveyed from outlying districts by special trains.

Back in London, aged twenty-two, ready for any adventures that might befall, he obtained a modest position as chorus master and assistant conductor, in a touring company giving " Rose Marie." A few months later he was appointed musical director of another company formed to tour with the same show, and he occupied this post for eighteen months, conducting over five hundred performances of the piece all over the British Isles. When a final tour was arranged on a twice nightly basis he decided to part company with the famous " Indian Love Call," and returned to London. Then followed a strenuous period of bread-earning by composing and arranging a great deal of light music in the South African vein for gramophone recording and broadcasting under the nom de plume " Diggenhof." Before long the BBC were employing Diggenhof the composer in their Variety Department and Fagan the conductor to appear as a guest with the BBC Orchestra!

Several more tours with theatrical companies took him to nearly all the theatres in this country, both large and small. He tells me that in some provincial theatres he met a standard of orchestral playing comparable with some of our best orchestras, but in many theatres in this country " the playing is a matter for the entire police force." He recalls one theatre at a famôus spa where the only brass instrument available was a solitary cornet. Seeking a remedy for the horrifying sounds that this man blew towards him from the far end of the orchestra pit, he made the player sit next to his rostrum and throughout this exasperating week guided him through his part almost bar by bar. One evening the player remarked, " Glad I ain't playin' this 'ere part for you next week, guv'nor. What with me a-playin' of it so near you this week, you'll be gettin' to know it backwards." At rehearsal in another theatre a tricky Overture to an operetta caused the principal violinist, a lady, to push her chair aside and stand up, exclaiming that in this position she hoped to be better able to cope with the technical difficulties. One by one her colleagues followed suit, until Fagan cut out the Overture to keep them in their seats.

From 1934 onwards he has assisted Ernest Irving at the Ealing Film Studios and deputized for him in various London theatres. An enjoyable episode was when Fagan conducted the Farjeon operetta, " The Two Bouquets," during its run at the Garrick. From 1936 to 1939 he combined with this work the musical directorship of FitzPatrick Pictures, Ltd., at the Sound City Studios, Shepperton, where he took charge of the music for James A. FitzPatrick, known chiefly by his " Travel talks," who came over from America to produce and direct twelve full-length pictures for Metro-Goldwyn-Mayer. Fagan composed incidental music for several of these productions, including " David Livingstone," the themes of which he used later for his Tone Poem, " Ilala." Written in 1941-2, this work had its first public performance at a Hallé concert in Manchester in December, 1942, under the composer's conductorship, and it has been broadcast repeatedly in the home and overseas programmes and by the South African Broadcasting Corporation.

In 1939 Gideon Fagan was appointed Conductor of the BBC Northern Orchestra by a selection committee headed by Sir Adrian Boult and the late Sir Hamilton Harty. The contract commenced on September 4th with a month at Broadcasting House, London, so that he could observe the workings of the BBC before taking up the post; but Hitler intervened and Fagan was forced to proceed straight to Manchester on the day war was declared and to take up his duties without any preamble or preparation. He tells me that during the long car journey to Manchester he reviewed his assets at that time—an intimate knowledge of some forty orchestral works, a working knowledge of perhaps another fifty, a hearsay or " gramophone " knowledge and nodding acquaintance with a hundred or so more—wondering what his first work would be. This proved to be nothing more formidable than the conducting of Frank Bridge's arrangement of the popular tune, " Sally in our Alley!"

For the first three months the work was shared by the late Eric Fogge, but after the death of that gifted musician Fagan had to look forward to doing all the conducting himself, with symphony concerts, light music and incidental music for plays, all forming part of a daily routine. The excitement of this varied and alluring prospect was, he tells me, slightly tempered by awe at having to perform to a large listening public, after one rehearsal, works of high complexity of which some were almost unknown to him. It was, however, a most valuable experience, which considerably expanded his repertoire.

Relinquishing the Manchester post in 1942, he returned to his home in London and shortly afterwards joined the International Ballet Company as guest conductor for a tour. He has since conducted frequently in the home and overseas programmes, chiefly the BBC Northern Orchestra and the BBC Orchestra, and recent public concerts have been with the City of Birmingham Orchestra and the BBC Orchestra.

*   *   *

When we went to see Gideon Fagan at his London house we were received by his charming wife. They first met in " Rose Marie," where she was known as Phyl Leslie, and married in 1928. Their two lively daughters—Terry, aged fourteen, and June, aged twelve—are passionately fond of animals of all species. They keep large numbers of rabbits, a cat, and a miniature aquarium, while they look forward hopefully to a withdrawal of their parents' ban on a garden full of monkeys, horses, and, if possible, an elephant.

*   *   *

Gideon Fagan's works include:—

1923. " I Had a Dove." Song; words by Keats. (Schott.)
1926. Nocturne for Woodwind and Strings. (Schott.)
1926-43. Eleven songs with Afrikaans words.
          Three songs with English words
1929. " The Harpies." Piano solo.
1931. Nocturne, transcription for violin and piano. (Schott.)
1942. Tone Poem, " Ilala." (Chester.)
1943. Afrikaans Folk-Tune Suite, commissioned by the BBC.
1944. Suite for Piano and Orchestra.

ANATOLE FISTOULARI

❧

W E cannot claim Anatole Fistoulari as a British musician, because he
has not yet become a naturalized subject, but he has been in London
for the last four years, and has figured prominently in our musical life.
Most of us had some great ambition in our childhood. In my own
case I wanted to become either a Cathedral organist or one of those
gentlemen who tear up our roads with pneumatic drills for reasons best
known to themselves. My reason, I think, was that in either capacity
I should be able to make a great deal of noise without being subject
to scathing reprimands from supercilious elder brothers and sisters. I
have achieved neither of these objectives; for although on one or two
occasions I have played a Cathedral organ, I have never found a Dean
and Chapter foolish enough to appoint me officially as an organist; and
I am not likely to become a navvy, because in that rôle I should be
worth rather less than sixpence a week to an employer.

Anatole Fistoulari, on the other hand, had even greater aspirations,
and fulfilled them at an incredibly early age. As soon as he could talk
in anything more than monosyllables, he informed his father quite
decisively that he had made up his mind to become the conductor of
an orchestra. The achievement of that ambition makes quite an
interesting story.

He was born in Kiev in 1907. His father, Gregor Fistoulari, who
afterwards became the Director of the Philharmonic College at St.
Petersbourg, now Leningrad, took him to all the operas and symphony
concerts given in the city, and was delighted to find that the boy had
inherited his father's great love of music. Anatole declared his ambition after one of these concerts, and added that he particularly
wanted to be able to conduct Tschaikovsky's " Symphonie Pathétique."
No doubt this caused some amusement, but it was not disregarded, and
care was taken to see that he was gradually initiated into the intricacies
of orchestral instruments, score reading, etc.

The little boy worked with astonishing assiduity and made such
rapid progress that soon after his seventh birthday his father called a
special orchestral rehearsal to test his ability. Everybody was so
delighted at his capability that he was offered an engagement to conduct
Tschaikovsky's " Symphonie Pathétique " at a charity concert given in

55

the Opera House at Kiev. To the amazement of everyone he took the orchestra right through the entire work from memory.

Thus he became an infant prodigy. The ability of even the most brilliant child to conduct an orchestra must always be a very contro-versial subject, but it is a fact that when he was still quite a boy, Anatole Fistoulari was conducting symphony concerts.

When he visited Odessa, his exceptional talent caused such a sensation that he was called upon to conduct a special programme given by the Orchestra of the Imperial Court of St. Petersbourg. Of the performance a well-known critic wrote: " Uncanny memory, extraordin-ary rhythmic sense and overpowering will, unknown in a child of his age, make him an entire master of the orchestra—these are the qualities that give a promise of this child becoming a truly great artist."

Much of Fistoulari's success was due to the wisdom and foresight of his father, who saw that he received the best possible training. When he started his tour of Russian cities his father personally took charge of his musical education, and thus he was afforded exceptional opportunities to learn under ideal conditions.

In 1920 he went to Bucharest, where soon after his arrival, Fistoulari, still only thirteen years of age, received an invitation to conduct " Samson and Delilah " at the Royal Opera House.

He then went to Germany, where he was soon offered engagements to conduct the State Opera Orchestra and the Blüthner Orchestra in Berlin. During this period he also visited Hamburg, Dresden and Holland, where his conducting of local orchestras received the acclamation of both Press and public.

Adolf Weismann, considered to be one of the most severe critics in Germany, wrote: " Fistoulari, the phenomenal child, possesses a great talent." At this time he came under the influence of Arthur Nikisch, who gave him valuable assistance and advice.

In 1933, Fistoulari, who was then twenty-five, met Chaliapin in Paris, and was chosen by him to conduct the " Grand Opera Russe " at the Châtelet Theatre, for he had already conducted over a hundred performances given by a smaller Russian opera company which had toured France, Belgium, Spain, Italy and parts of Germany. During the first rehearsal of " Boris Godounov," Chaliapin turned to a small gathering of Press representatives and exclaimed: " I have been singing ' Boris Godounov ' for forty-one years, but this is the first time I have said ' Bravo ' to the conductor at the first rehearsal."

Fistoulari worked with Chaliapin for the next three years. The " Grand Opera Russe " continued at the Châtelet Theatre until 1934, enjoying many great successes with its exceptionally talented cast,

GIDEON FAGAN

ANATOLE FISTOULARI

supported by the Colonne Orchestra and a brilliant Russian chorus. When finally the season closed, he conducted " The Barber of Seville " in the Theatre des Champs Elysées with a cast of artists from Scala de Milan, including Stabile, de Muro Lamante, Chaliapin and Valentina Vichnevska, accompanied by the Strarum Orchestra.

Fistoulari then conducted a series of concerts with the Pasdeloup Orchestra at the Opera Comique in Paris. During the interval of the first concert he received the following telegram :

" Dear Fistoulari,—I hope that these concerts will open for you a road to glory, which you merit by your great musical gift. I wish you the success of which I am certain.—Chaliapin."

After these concerts he went to Monte Carlo to conduct the Russian Ballet, for which he had been engaged by Leonide Massine. With the same company he came to London and conducted the London Symphony Orchestra at Drury Lane and the London Philharmonic Orchestra at Covent Garden.

With the Ballet de Monte Carlo he toured America for six months, appearing first at the Metropolitan Opera House, New York, and then visiting no less than sixty-five other cities. The company enjoyed the luxury of having a special train to take them and their equipment from place to place.

In New York, California, and other big cities, Fistoulari conducted several of the larger symphony orchestras, and was given a great welcome. He was very much impressed by the efficiency of the American musician, and by the lavishly equipped, spacious and comfortable concert halls.

Back in Europe, he appeared with the same company at the Maggio Fiorentino in Florence, where he was introduced to the Princess of Piedmont, who warmly congratulated him on a splendid performance.

His last appearance before the outbreak of the present war was with the Orchestra de la Société Philharmonic de Paris at the Palais de Chaillot. Here he played before the President, M. Albert Lebrun.

*   *   *

Fistoulari was still in Paris when war was declared, and although he was very depressed at the thought of giving up all his musical activities, he joined the French Army. In 1940, however, he was invalided out and in June found himself at Cherbourg when the Nazis were entering the city.

Having left all his possessions in Paris, he decided to escape to England, and after a perilous crossing, landed at Southampton at the time of the great evacuation from Dunkirk. He had no money whatever, but by selling his wrist-watch he was able to make his way to London in search of friends he had made during his previous visit to this country. Alas! the war had sent most of them out of the town and it was not at all easy to trace people who knew him. For those of us who had friends, homes and work in Britain, the summer of 1940 was indeed depressing, but how much more disheartening it must have seemed to Anatole Fistoulari. Unfortunately, his mother and father who had accompanied him on his last visit to Paris, were obliged to remain in France.

Yet it was in those dreary days that he first met Anna Mahler, daughter of Gustav Mahler, the celebrated Austrian composer, who died in Vienna in 1911. She, too, was a refugee, for she had escaped from Vienna two days after the Germans had entered the city. After eluding the Gestapo, she had travelled through Prague, Hungary, Italy and Switzerland to Paris, where she lived for a few months before coming to London in May, 1938. After a short engagement, they were married, and they now have a daughter, Marina, aged six months.

In August, 1941, Anatole Fistoulari met Mr. Jay Pomeroy, to whom he proposed a plan to put the opera, " Sorotchintsi Fair " (Mussorgsky), into production. Although at that time the fear of air raids prevented the public from giving their normal support to the theatre, Mr. Pomeroy agreed, and it was put on at the Savoy Theatre with the London Symphony Orchestra on October 6th, 1941. The proceeds at one of the early performances were in aid of Mrs. Churchill's Aid to Russia Fund. The cast included Daria Bayan, Oda Slobodskaya, Arsene Kirilloff, Ottakar Kraus and Parry Jones, and it was a colossal success.

After a successful tour of the provinces, " Sorotchintsi Fair " was brought back to London and put on at the Adelphi Theatre. In all, two hundred performances were given.

Anatole Fistoulari conducted his first symphony concert in this country in March, 1942, at His Majesty's Theatre, when Ida Haendel was the soloist. This led to a series of concerts at the Cambridge Theatre with the London Symphony Orchestra.

Another successful series of concerts was given with the London Philharmonic Orchestra, after which Mr. T. A. Russell, the Orchestra's Secretary and General Manager, told him that he had been chosen by the orchestra to become one of its regular conductors. With it he toured the provinces, giving remarkably well-attended concerts in all the larger cities and broadcasting from time to time.

At the age of thirty-six Anatole Fistoulari is now one of the most popular of the younger conductors we have in this country. He conducts mostly from memory, and has an exceptional gift of inspiring all his players with his own boundless enthusiasm. His success, I feel, is due to a great extent to his clear, unaffected beat: he has no use for frills and fussiness, and he never tries to " show off." He is popular because he always knows what he wants from his orchestra before he starts a rehearsal, and has faith in the musicianship of his players.

As I write, Fistoulari is giving regular concerts on Sunday afternoons at the Adelphi Theatre. He considers that our orchestras are excellent, and that the musicians compare favourably with any in the world. The interest and enthusiasm of the general public he considers to be a sign of nation-wide awakening to the beauty of music, and he is sure that now the masses have learnt to enjoy music, they will not give it up.

He has never forgotten the great kindness shown to him in this country when he arrived here in the blackest days of the war. "The English, they have been so good to me . . . . I appreciate their attitude so very much," he said when I met him recently.

Fistoulari believes that all our great orchestras should be subsidized by the State as they are in Russia, or by wealthy private individuals as in America; for the strain of performing sufficient concerts to pay their way is apt to tell upon the work of the instrumentalists. It would also be of great assistance to our younger musicians if they could be given State grants during their student days.

He thinks that the chief advantage the American orchestras have over ours is that they are able to afford at least double the number of rehearsals that we can call. ·One of our famous orchestras must give eight concerts a week in order to meet its liabilities, and Fistoulari fears that this often means inadequate rehearsals. He was very surprised when he was first invited to conduct a symphony concert in this country to see a look of genuine amazement on everybody's face when he suggested that there should be *three* rehearsals.

Although he naturally admires all the Russian composers, particularly Shostakovitch, whose Symphony No. 6 he introduced to this country on October 24th, 1943, he is always ready to acknowledge the merits of English composers. He particularly appreciates Purcell, Elgar, Bliss, Vaughan Williams and William Walton, and he believes that Benjamin Britten has a great future. An interesting point is that when he was in Germany, he heard a complete performance of Purcell's Dido and Aeneas," and he remembers that it was very well received.

He is inclined to think that there will be a great revival in opera in this country as soon as our musical organizations are better established financially. " It is such a pity that I see all the stalls taken away from your Opera House at Covent Garden. If there cannot be opera

we could give beautiful concerts there . . . . the acoustics are good . . . .
it should not be used as a dance hall.

He likes to see both orchestra and audience in evening dress, because
it has a psychological effect upon the performance. He also believes
that our great orchestras will in the future figure more prominently in
the best type of films: his only anxiety being that the reproduction in
some of our cinemas tends to distort the music. The mechanism is often
maladjusted with the result that grotesque amplification spoils all the
beauty of the tone.

*   *   *

Fistoulari lives in a spacious flat in Kensington, which is furnished
artistically in a light, modern style. He spends much of his time in
study when he is not with his orchestra. He is an accomplished pianist,
but does not care to give recitals in public. Madame Fistoulari tells
me that when he is not working at music, his favourite recreation is—
going to symphony concerts! He always enjoys hearing orchestras under
other conductors, and invariably stays until the end even when he is
not impressed by the performance. He likes to read, but his radiogram
is always a temptation to him. In peacetime he likes to drive his car
through the countryside, and he is very fond of spending an hour or
two in a motor-boat. His English is excellent, but it is not without
traces of a Russian accent.

Madame Fistoulari is liberally endowed with that cultured charm
peculiar to the Viennese. She is a highly skilled sculptress, her exhibit
at the World Exhibition in Paris in 1937 having been awarded the
Grand Prix. She is naturally fond of music, but is very modest about
her skill as a musician.

I hope Anatole Fistoulari will not be tempted to go permanently
to America when the war is over, as many of our more promising
musicians have done in the past. They were not to blame, of course,
because the decay of musical life in this country between the two world
wars was enough to dishearten the most stalwart of our young artists.
But now the future is bright, and we need the enthusiasm of youth.

JULIUS HARRISON

THE little train rattled slowly into Malvern Link station half an hour late with an air of resignation to the vulgar restrictions of the time-table. In this genteel resort they never hurry. The gracious country around them seems to make everybody so placidly happy that a leisurely affability pervades everywhere.

As we drove to his house, Julius Harrison, grey-haired, red-faced, and clad in a tweed jacket, grey flannels and sandals, explained what it meant to live on the " wrong " side of the railway. The Best People, it seems, live on the " right " side—on the slopes of one of the lovely hills—and do not as a rule visit those whom the Great Western Railway has cut off from the *élite*. Ruminating on this, he chuckled quietly. Social distinctions mean little or nothing to him.

It was a glorious afternoon in early summer, and we decided to forget about books and music for a while and to take tea up on one of the hills. Half an hour later we were sitting about a thousand feet above sea level, surveying the Severn valley on one side and a glorious panorama of dreamy hills on the other.

There is something indescribably enchanting about the " Elgar country." As you look around, the pastoral scene is gentle and friendly and the hills have a benevolent, ageless dignity that must surely have inspired the fine *Nobilmente* passages in the work of our great Worcester-shire composer. As we sat there we agreed that if a man had music in his soul, he could not fail to find a means of expressing it when living in that part of the country.

" I am very much affected by the beauty of our Worcestershire countryside, and by its close association with some of the great events in our national history," Harrison told me. " To me, as with many other Worcestershire folk, this county seems to be the very heart of England, and there is a song and a melody in each one of its lovely hills, valleys, meadows and brooks."

*　　*　　*

Those who have read my "Writers' Gallery" will recall that Francis Brett Young, the famous Worcestershire author, was born at Hales Owen in 1884. Julius Harrison, whose compositions express in music much of the emotion and colour that Brett Young portrays in his books, was born at Stourport, not far away, just one year later.

Harrison, whose maternal grandfather was a native of Heidelburg and an able song-writer, was educated at Queen Elizabeth's School, Hartlebury, near Kidderminster. His parents were both good musicians, and, as one would imagine, gave him an excellent grounding in music at an early age. As soon as he reached proficiency as a pianist, they encouraged him to learn the violin and the organ, and raised no objection when in a moment of exuberant enthusiasm he decided to take up the French horn as well. His brothers and sisters, however, were not quite as encouraging, for, knowing nothing of the great difficulties encountered in playing that instrument, they were apt to put on a long-suffering expression and sigh "Oh, heavens, there's Julius with his hooter again!"

In the year 1900, when he took the Cambridge Local examination, he was the first in the United Kingdom in music in the Junior list. Twelve months later he won the same distinction in the Senior list, and in 1902 secured a Worcestershire County Council Scholarship worth a hundred and fifty pounds, which enabled him to go to the Birmingham School of Music, where he studied under Sir Granville Bantock. He took harmony, counterpoint and composition, and added to his practical accomplishments by studying the woodwind instruments—notably the clarinet.

One of his earliest memories of the Birmingham School of Music is of the time when, as a lad of seventeen, he played the timpani in Gluck's " Orpheus and Eurydice " under Bantock. In his youthful eagerness he played the Overture at double the proper speed, and finished just as the rest of the orchestra were half way through!

His father's greatest desire was that he should one day become a Cathedral organist—I think we can see here the influence of the Three Choirs Festivals—and frequently reproached him for not devoting more time to the organ; but the boy's real love was for composition—and it always has been. One of his first works to be performed in Birmingham was a remarkable Prelude and Double Fugue for two pianos, written in 1905. In the same year he wrote a " Ballade " for strings, three piano pieces: Rhapsody, Intermezzo and Capriccio, and six songs, all of which indicated the particular style which he had begun to develop: rich chromatic passages and short, but very pleasant excursions into the more remote keys being the most prominent characteristics. The " Ballade," by the way, was performed in Worcester, Llandudno, West Bromwich, Croydon and Stourport soon after it was composed.

In 1907 he won the fifty-guinea prize offered by the Norwich Triennial Festival Committee for a cantata, "Cleopatra," which was
performed under Sir Henry Wood at the 1908 Festival.

*   *   *

Now I must leave his compositions for a moment and go back a
few years to record that at the age of sixteen, he was appointed organist
and choirmaster of Areley Kings Church, near Stourport. Five years
later he took up a similar post at Hartlebury Church, but in 1908 came
to London to accept the conductorship of the Dulwich Philharmonic
Society, a good choir and orchestra, which gave four concerts annually
at the Crystal Palace. This was his first engagement as a conductor
and with teaching, assignments to correct pianola rolls and the usual
sporadic work that helps to support general musicians, he was able to
earn a modest living.

In 1912 he was appointed pianist or *maestro al piano* at Covent
Garden, and played under such great conductors as Nikisch and Richter,
gaining a sound knowledge of German opera. Then he went to Bayreuth
to hear " The Ring," and met Siegfried Wagner.

Two years later the Royal Opera Syndicate at Covent Garden sent
him to Paris to rehearse the Colonne Orchestra in "Parsifal," "Tristan"
and "The Mastersingers" for a German season to be given by the Covent
Garden Company and the Boston Opera Company of America under
Nikisch and Weingartner.

His ability as a conductor was soon recognised by the Beecham
Opera Company, which he joined in 1915. It is significant, too, that
the first opera he conducted was " Lohengrin " at Covent Garden in
1913: not an easy task for a young man.

Harrison joined the Royal Flying Corps in 1916 as a member of
the ground staff, and had the good fortune to be stationed near London.
This allowed him to continue conducting for the Beecham Company
from time to time, and he recalls how on an October evening in 1917 he
was directing " Tristan " (for the thirteenth time!) when a bomb
was dropped on Covent Garden market opposite.

On another occasion he was being examined in camp by the medical
officer when an orderly announced that he was wanted on the telephone.
Wearing nothing at all he went to answer it, and heard Beecham's
manager at the other end calmly asking if he could conduct " Tosca "
at Drury Lane on the following evening!

After the war he became joint conductor of the Scottish Orchestra
with Sir Landon Ronald, retaining the position until 1923, although in
the previous year he had accepted a position as a conductor with the

British National Opera Company, which entailed touring as well as regular duties at Covent Garden.

From 1924 to 1929 he was the Director of the Opera Class at the Royal Academy of Music, a period in which he began broadcasting. He also became associated with the Leeds Symphony Orchestra and the Bradford Permanent Orchestra.

Before we come to the next stage of his career I would like to emphasize the extent of the work that Julius Harrison has done in the world of opera, because most of my younger readers will regard him almost entirely as a concert conductor and composer. Some idea of his experience may be gained from the fact that he has directed well over forty different operas, including many of the lesser-known ones, and such old favourites as " Pagliacci " on more than fifty-five occasions!

It was in 1930 that Julius Harrison succeeded Basil Cameron as Director of Music to the Hastings Corporation. He threw himself with tremendous energy into his new work, and the White Rock Pavilion, a model concert hall as far as comfort and acoustics are concerned, became a centre of musical culture supported by an ever-growing band of enthusiastic music-lovers as well as the summer visitors. If Harrison and his orchestra erred at all, it was on the side of over-generosity: no less than twelve concerts a week were given, frequently with such distinguished guest-artists as Paderewski, Rachmaninoff, Beecham, Heifetz and Cortot—to mention only a few; and when the BBC began to broadcast the orchestra regularly, they received letters of appreciation from all over the world. Harrison had the help of an assistant conductor at this time, of course. They did fine work, too, with the Hastings Choral Union, whose singing compared favourably with many of the larger choral societies in other parts of the country. Beethoven's Choral Symphony was a regular feature in their programmes.

Even when war broke out in 1939, the Hastings Muncipal Orchestra continued with their work, and it was not until May, 1940, that the threat to our southern shores made it necessary to disband the orchestra temporarily. Characteristically, they finished with a grand flourish: a magnificent Tschaikovsky Centenary Festival, on which, incidentally, they made a substantial profit for the Hastings Corporation.

With no reason to remain in Hastings, Julius Harrison then returned to his native Worcestershire with the intention of settling down to a quiet life of composition. But the BBC were already seeking his services as a conductor, and he agreed to undertake regular work with their Northern Orchestra. As I write, he is still broadcasting frequently with that body of players and conducting concerts with the Hallé and Liverpool Philharmonic Orchestras.

*   *   *

It would be impossible to portray Julius Harrison without telling you more about his activities as a composer, for as much as he likes conducting, the urge to write music still predominates within him.

His famous " Worcestershire Suite," composed in 1919, consists of four pieces, " The Shrawley Round," " Redstone Rock," " Pershore Plums " and " The Ledbury Parson." The inscription from " The Vision of Piers Plowman " (William Langland) reads:

> " On a May morning on Malvern Hills,
> A marvel befel me—sure from Faery it came—
> . . . I rested me on a broad bank;
> And as I lay and leaned and looked into the waters
> I dreamed marvellously (of)
> A fair field full of folk."

But why did Harrison call his beautiful slow movement "Pershore Plums "? The answer is because he feels that plums can be far more beautiful than grapes, which have often inspired other people to write verse and music in the past. Plums can be much richer in bloom and their colour is usually much more varied.

Now look at a much later work, his Rhapsody for Violin and Orchestra, " Bredon Hill." Here, again, the Worcestershire countryside has inspired him, for he can see Bredon Hill from his bedroom window. Soon after he took his present house at Malvern, the presence of this hill made him feel an overwhelming desire to express in music the thought behind the following lines from A. E. Housman's exquisite poem, " In Summertime on Bredon ":

> " Here of a Sunday morning
> My love and I would lie,
> And see the coloured counties,
> And hear the larks so high
> About us in the sky . . . ."

Those who know Elgar's " Severn Suite " will no doubt compare it with this Rhapsody of Julius Harrison's to see how differently two composers will react to what is more or less the same inspiration. I ought to add that Elgar and Harrison frequently exchanged views about the " smell of the Severn " in music.

Worcestershire is again portrayed in his Three Sketches for Piano, " Severn Country." They are " Dance in the Cherry Orchard," seen at Ribbesford; " Twilight on the River," seen at Bewdley; and " Far Forest."

65

Julius Harrison once wished to preserve the memory of a most enjoyable holiday he spent in Cornwall with his wife and children, so he wrote his " Cornish Holiday Sketches " for String Orchestra and wove into it all the little tunes that the various members of his family had been humming and playing on tin whistles at the time! It is surprising what a jolly composition this has made.

Among his many other works we find " Autumn Landscape " for String Orchestra; " Widdicombe Fair," a Humoresque for String Quartet or String Orchestra; " Rhapsody," a setting of Walt Whitman's poem, " On the Beach at Night," for Baritone or Contralto and Orchestra; and " Marching Along," a song for Tenor or Baritone, which has been made very popular by its use in the BBC Vaudeville programmes on Saturday evenings.

Other compositions of his are settings of " Merciless Beauty," a roundel by Chaucer, and " Requiem of Archangels for the World," a poem by Herbert Trench; but as I write he is working upon a magnificent Mass, which I think will be one of the loveliest compositions of its type written in modern times. He played parts of it to me when I visited him, and I was particularly impressed by its depth of feeling. Moreover, its " under-parts " (alto, tenor and bass) were rich in flowing melodic outlines that would delight the members of any choir accustomed to singing music of a high standard.

*　　　*　　　*

Julius Harrison was married first in 1913 to Miss Mary Eddison, and for the second time in 1929 to Miss Dorothie Helen Day, whom he met at the Royal Academy of Music when he was in charge of the Opera Class, for she was a student there at the time. His daughter, Pamela, is now married to Flying Officer F. D. Hughes, D.F.C., a nephew of the late Irish composer, Herbert Hughes.

Colin Julius Harrison, aged seven, is tremendously proud of his father; in fact, at the conclusion of a concert given by the London Symphony Orchestra in Bristol, the little lad jumped up, turned round from his seat and addressed the audience: "You see that man what conducted? THAT'S MY DADDY!"

*　　　*　　　*

During my visit to Malvern we discussed modern music at length. To give a complete statement of Julius Harrison's views on the subject would take more space than I can allow in this book, but here is a brief résumé.

Although he recognises that the trend of modern music is towards complexity, he firmly believes that music can no more do without the diatonic scales and harmonies than painters can do without the primary colours. "The trend of film music, which is used only incidentally to the picture itself, is towards nothing but a series of clashing dissonances, and I cannot help feeling that this trend is largely responsible for the general abuse of the art of music affecting some composers of even symphonic reputations."

"Rhythm for its own sake," Mr. Harrison continued, "is not worth developing any more than an attempt to develop our language by a greater insistence on consonants and a partial exclusion of vowel sounds. I hold rhythm to be an integral part of music only in its relation to the other parts—melody and harmony. You cannot develop music by developing one part of it at the expense of another."

He repudiates the assertion made by one or two modern composers that melody is "played out." Some of our contemporary composers are inclined to neglect melody, he feels, but it is no more played out than poetry is played out; yet those who still believe in melody are often considered to be old-fashioned. At the same time, nobody could dislike the purely academic approach to music more than Julius Harrison, for he once wrote a strong article in ' The Musical Times ' deploring pedantry in musical examinations. In it he declared that certain examiners' crabbed and unintelligent interpretation of the laws of music tended to produce among candidates for degrees an utter atrophy of the inner musical sense, baneful in the extreme. He accused the " old pundits " of wanting the candidates to reduce their musicianship and to stick to the dry-as-dust formulæ of their art in order to get a degree, and proceeded to show how a candidate for the degree of Bachelor of Music had been " blue-pencilled " for using a progression so " modern and ungrammatical " that it was identical with one that had been employed by J. S. Bach! He now notes with some satisfaction that things are a little more progressive these days.

Julius Harrison detests jazz as much as he hates the dance band leaders who delight in guying the classics. When Jack Hylton tried to " de-bunk " classical music in one of the daily papers, Harrison replied with a vigorous letter, of which the following is an extract :

> " Mr. Hylton's erudite analysis of the old and new music should give the Editor of Grove's ' Dictionary of Music and Musicians ' furiously to think. Since the orchestra as we knew it is dead, it is time that all these verbose articles on the one-time great orchestral composers should be sternly blue-pencilled, and that Mr. Hylton . . . should be asked to take this section in hand on more up-to-date lines.
>
> " Beginning with his own magnificent phrase ' Life has a new rhythm,' Mr. Hylton could then describe to us how the ' new music ' is related to modern life in all its best phases—to

the craze for speed that kills 150 people every week, to the craze for noise that is nearer Bedlam every year, to the craze for " ennoblement " of the human voice as exemplified in the crooner, and to the craze for the utter debasement of noble brass instruments playing into mutes, hats, caps, nooks, crannies, holes and corners. And finally, I beg of Mr. Hylton to spare at least one volume to an analysis of the phrase used by all jazz musicians, ' putting the dirt in,' for I understand that this is the popular designation of all the ' new ' orchestration effects so dear to the heart of Mr. Hylton."

When Debroy Somers arranged his " Operas in. Rhythm," it was Julius Harrison who led the attack with :

" This pot-pourri is a sickening travesty in jazz rhythm of the main melodies from ' Carmen ' and ' Faust,' in which not even that loveliest of all love songs, the ' Flower Song ' from Bizet's masterpiece, is spared the degradation of being vilified in fox-trot style. Bizet and Gounod being dead, and their copyrights having expired, those of us who love and revere the masterpieces of music must, under present laws, stand idly by while this monstrous vandalism proceeds apace to satisfy the appetite of that Moloch, jazz."

*   *   *

When we discussed the art of conducting, Harrison told me that he is mainly self-taught, and that he favours no particular school of thought on the subject. " I am unable to appreciate the ' prima donna ' school who put their own personalities in front of the immortal personalities of those whose work they conduct. *Sic transit* . . . . yes, the conductors (myself included), but *never* the great masters of the symphony."

In classical music he always endeavours to read nothing into it which the composer has not implicitly expressed, but at the same time he believes that highly-coloured modern music can take on as many tints as you care to put in—within reason; and therefore one's interpretation of this type of music can have a rhapsodic flexibility which would be as wrong in the interpretation of classical music as it would be to paint over a masterpiece by Leonardo da Vinci with the vivid colours of a Van Gogh or Gauguin.

Personally, he has no world-wide ambitions in music. " I am torn between a desire for activity with my colleagues and a deep-seated desire to have the time to compose the music I feel within me."

To conclude his comments upon conducting: he insists that a conductor must have a working knowledge of the instruments in his orchestra. He has never for a moment regretted the time he spent in learning to play the various instruments mentioned previously, although, of course, he does not pretend to be able to play anything in the wind department with any degree of proficiency.

* * *

One of Julius Harrison's major accomplishments is undoubtedly his splendid book, " Brahms and his Four Symphonies." It is both biographical and critical, and includes a very fine analysis of each of the symphonies. Sir Henry Wood said: " The plan of the book is so excellent and the analysis so masterly and so lucidly explained that its success and its appeal to the layman and the professional musician is assured. We have had nothing like it since the early days of Parry and Hadow. Words quite fail me to express the delight and pleasure this fine book has given me, and I hope to read it and refer to it many times."

* * *

Finally, a few personal notes. The deepest-impressions I had of Julius Harrison were of his complete sincerity and artistic perception. He prefers a simple life and is never happier than when he is at home at Malvern setting down upon manuscript paper the emotions stirred in him by the people, countryside, books and paintings he loves. Moreover, he never forgets that much of his happiness is due to the devotion of his talented wife, who associates herself with all his interests. He reads chiefly poetry, biography and history.

He finds that he can work best in the morning when his mind is free of extraneous incidents, so he goes to his study immediately after breakfast, and if you happen to be staying with him you find yourself frequently called in to pass judgment upon odd fragments of music which he will play upon his grand piano or sing in a voice that automatically drops an octave as it ascends past middle C.

The Harrisons have no dog, and the explanation is, I think, that a former canine pet was rather too much of a critic of his master's compositions. One effort which had evidently offended his doggy ears was discovered on the floor—chewed up into very small pieces.

ERNEST IRVING

ツ

Now in case you are getting tired of my narrative, we will have a little diversion. Perhaps you will grab your hat, coat and umbrella and come with me to Ealing.

No, I'm afraid we can't take a taxi, because all the cabs you see tearing about this part of London are going to "the dogs." If you had an urgent appointment with Mr. Winston Churchill, or if you had to be at Victoria, St. Bartholomew's Hospital or the lunatic asylum within fifteen minutes you'd be unlucky, because the taxi-men know only of one highly-profitable destination: the dogs. So we travel in a nice red L.P.T.B. omnibus which will drop us (literally, if the driver is in a dirty mood) at Ealing Green.

Ernest Irving has a studio adjacent to the Ealing Film Studios of which he is the Musical Director: it's the sort of place I've been seeking for months. As we enter we find ourselves confronted with a large notice in the bloodiest of scarlet lettering:

> DANGER
> Man at Work

We ignore this, of course, and push our way into a large, pleasant room in which every piece of furniture from the Hagspiel grand down to the humblest footstool groans beneath a heterogeneous mass of music, magazines, books, photographs and newspapers. In one corner, like a shrine standing aloof from all that is worldly, is a chess table with a beautiful set of pieces in scarlet and white ivory. (Irving was for many years the Chess Editor of the ' Illustrated London News.')

We find a tallish, greyish figure sitting in an armchair talking— as he always is—on the telephone:

"No, my dear chap, it went tum-tum, pom-pom, teedle-teedle, dum-dum, wallop! Just like that. It was like . . . ."

We sit patiently while he pours out analogies culled from Shakespeare, Homer, Virgil, Ovid, Sophocles, Euripides and Cicero. After about ten minutes of this we agree that it would be quite impossible to " interview " such a character, and are just preparing to sneak out and have one at the local (just across the road) when he rings off and engages us in a battle of wits that brings both of us to the verge of a nervous breakdown.

He wins six-love, so we just sit back in our chairs and, having explained our mission, let him talk.

" I was born at Godalming, Surrey, in 1878. In the choir at seven, learning the piano from the Town Clerk's sister at eight, copying the chants at nine, studying the organ at ten, Harmony (Stainer!) at eleven, counterpoint (Goss!!) at twelve under Dr. Webb, and then a musical hiatus, till at eighteen, distaste for the profession selected for me caused a complete domestic disruption and the necessity of turning to practical account a somewhat sketchy musical training and an evil propensity for writing light verse.

" My first adventure was a complete failure: conducting what was then called a musical burlesque, "Villiano the Vicious or the Gay Princess," for Walter Osborne, a well known operatic baritone. I discovered that the band at Maidenhead was not too good, and that it is difficult to distinguish ladies apart when they are made up. Second attempt, writing and conducting a pantomime at Grimsby, was abruptly finished by fisticuffs with the manager, who, though knocked out, would obviously have been unfertile when he recovered consciousness. Third attempt, writing and conducting a comic opera called ' Lads Ashore, produced a stormy voyage lasting three weeks until the venture went firmly on to the rocks at Newport, Mon., from which spot the two principal comedians had to walk home to Liverpool. Tired of Hakluyt, I got a resident appointment as musical director for the 'Music and Arts Corporation' in Duke-street, Adelphi, where my duties were to teach anything musical to anybody who should come along. A young lady pianist did come along for tuition and made things difficult, since she played much better than the musical director. One of the managers of the Corporation wrote a comedy for Willie Edouin, called ' The J.P.,' for which I wrote the incidental music, and very bad it was, too. I had plenty of spare time for the Opera gallery, the Queen's Hall, the Oval, and the Vienna Café, where all the chess professionals used to meet on Sunday nights to fleece the amateurs.

" Up to now life had been very exciting and illuminating, but not at all profitable. So followed more touring experience with third-rate opera and second-rate musical comedies, which took me to all corners of Great Britain and Ireland, and gave me spare time to walk about fifty thousand miles to see all the mountains, lakes and beauty spots of these 'blessed Isles,' acquiring also an intimate acquaintance with the intricacies of the King's Gambit.

"The first musical excitement arrived with a season in Madrid at the Comedia, under the patronage of the King and Queen of Spain, where about twenty musical plays were performed in three months— 'The Geisha,' 'The Greek Slave,' 'A Country Girl,' 'Miss Hook of Holland,' 'The Circus Girl,' 'The Gaiety Girl,' 'The Shop Girl,' 'The Blue Moon,' 'The Dairymaids,' 'Tom Jones,' 'The Girl Behind the Counter,' 'The Runaway Girl,' and others. The orchestra was from the Spanish opera, so the language had to be 'learnt' on the boat, and the whole thing might be described as a musical phantasmagoria. A typical day's work was: chorus rehearsal ('Greek Slave'), 10 a.m.; Principals ('Geisha'), 12 noon; Orchestra ('Miss Hook of Holland'), 2.30; Dress Rehearsal ('The Blue Moon'), 4.30; Performance ('The Shop Girl') at 9.30, if the audience had arrived, which was unlikely in that country of unpunctuality; and as the intervals were each of about 45 minutes, the thing usually finished about 1.30 a.m. Thursdays off were useful to see bullfights, explore the city, visit a Zarzuela, get a hot bath (very difficult) or chase up curios in the second-hand shops. There was a week to spare at the end of the run, so I walked back most of the way to Vigo."

(The telephone rings again, and we are treated to a juicy diatribe on somebody's "interpretation" of a Brahms symphony, and two wicked little stories about an eminent conductor who shall be nameless.)

"'Tom Jones' brought me into touch with Edward German, an association which was to prove of the utmost benefit to me. Pleased with the precision with which I had condensed that score so that it could be played by small provincial orchestras, German insisted that I should be engaged to conduct 'Merrie England' when Walter Passmore and the Savoy Company took it on tour. Meanwhile, I had adapted and supplemented the score of a continental operetta called 'The Sweet Girl' for a management that just previously had sacked me for incompetence at the instance of a hostile stage-manager. The management offered a fifty pound prize for a song for its leading lady, and I won it under a pseudonym, the award being innocently made by my old enemy who had been appointed judge. I am not a vengeful man, but that was a pleasant 'come back!'

"The last night of the tour of 'Merrie England' brought another stroke of luck. George Edwardes, monarch of the musical theatres, had come to the Coronet Theatre, Notting Hill, to see an artist. He was struck by the accuracy and intelligence of the chorus singing, and sent for me during the interval. Thrilled to the marrow, I chased up the

Photo by Clifford Stelfox from a portrait in oils by Gladys Vasey]

JULIUS HARRISON

ERNEST IRVING

spiral staircase to his box, knocked at the door, and, bidden to enter, fell down three steps and landed on hands and knees before the great man's chair. ' Don't kneel,' said Edwardes. ' I want you to conduct ' The Dollar Princess ' for me, and that is no job for a courtier.'

" Touring was pleasant in those days, and the Edwardes' companies were fêted wherever they went, while the evenings were pleasantly spent with the music of Leo Fall and Franz Lehar. Another successful fight (this time with a fiddler who wouldn't watch the beat) got me the sack again, and I went out for a time with another company of ' The Dollar Princess ' run by Robert Macdonald and T. B. Young (who had been the manager of Edwardes' company). Eventually back to London to conduct ' Toto ' at the Duke of York's and manœuvre a return to the Edwardes's management with ' The Happy Day.' The ' old man ' himself was taking a cure in Germany and died in internment. Then came an invitation from Howard Carr to conduct ' The Lilac Domino ' at the Empire, which led to membership of the Savage Club and friendship with Norman O'Neill and Herman Finck. Pleasant work was now plentiful, and Finck planned to make me ' the Finck of Paris ' by appointing me musical director of the new Mogador Theatre, which opened between the Armistice and Versailles with a revue starring Jack Hulbert, Gwennie Brogden and Maurice Chevalier. When President Wilson departed, the audience went too, and Finck's plan having luckily proved abortive, I returned to England to conduct ' Mary Rose,' ' Kismet ' and several other plays for Norman O'Neill. O'Neill was treasurer of the Royal Philharmonic Society, and got me on to the managing committee by exercising Sir Alexander Mackenzie's casting vote, with an idea of reorganising the Society's orchestra and tackling the ' deputy system,' which at that time made concert ensemble-playing so ragged and unpleasing. On that committee I have remained ever since and am now working under Keith Douglas to help steer the old society (aet. 132) through this war, as under Mewburn Levien in the last war."

(The 'phone rings again and we hear in the distance the gargantuan laugh of Gideon Fagan. Then we get analogies from Socrates and Thucydides and a stunning anecdote.)

" To come back to the theatre, I should like to say I learned nearly all I know about dramatic values from Seymour Hicks, who derived his inspiration direct from Henry Irving. I am not, by the way, related to Sir Henry Irving, whose name, indeed, was Brodribb, but when I conducted the music at the' Daily Telegraph ' Irving Centenary performance, I was officially ' adopted ' by Lawrence Irving, Sir Henry's grandson, to avoid explanatory re-iteration. I served many short engagements at the Palace, Coliseum, Aldwych, Lyceum, etc., with Sir Seymour Hicks, of whose genius I am a profound admirer; being always careful not to stay too long at a time and so bore my mercurial friend and patron. Then came the association with Sir Nigel Playfair, and Frederic Austin's music, ' The Beggars' Opera,' ' Polly ' (two masterpieces) and a season of the Regent's Theatre with a bad play by Arnold Bennett. I found time to play in the International Chess Congress at Westminster, finishing fifth in the First Class.

'' Somewhere about now, William Boosey invited me to conduct Clutsam's ' Lilac Time,' which is founded, as everybody knows, on the tunes of Schubert; and this I was destined to do for six hundred and seventy-five performances in company with Clara Butterworth, Charles (Courtice) Pounds, Percy Heming and Edmund Gwenn. My most abiding memory of this is that one of the brass players wore the same indiarubber shirt-front throughout the entire run and then left it on the peg in the band-room for the next dress-shirtless player.

'' Some work for André Charlot followed, including ' Dédé ' at the Garrick with Gertie Lawrence and Joe Coyne: and the beginning of a long association with Sir Barry Jackson, composing and conducting music for the Malvern Festivals and his seasons at the Queen's, Haymarket and Court theatres. Meanwhile, in 1927, Charles Cochran engaged me to direct a very bad musical comedy from Chicago called ' Castles in the Air,' which proved appropriately impermanent, but led to my first (and last) revue job, Noel Coward's amusing opus ' This Year of Grace,' at the London Pavilion, with Maisie Gay, Jessie Matthews and Sonnie Hale. This, though it had its moments, was a bore to conduct, the only entertainment for the conductor being the piano improvisations by the pianist, none other than the redoubtable ' Hutch '! Then came a job to write the music for Basil Dean's production of ' Beau Geste ' at His Majesty's. for which I imported a lot of ' clarions ' to get the correct French military atmosphere.

'' This led eventually to my present engagement at Ealing Studios, which were built for Dean by the Courtaulds.

'' After ' This Year of Grace ' followed a joyous episode: comprising the music for ' The Circle of Chalk,' a lovely old Chinese play Englished by James Laver, and put on at the New Theatre. Dean could only afford a hundred pounds a week for the orchestra, which was composed as follows: Conductor (playing harmonium), Cor Anglais, muted Harp, E flat Trumpet, E flat Clarinet, Piccolo, Viola, 'Cello tuned up an octave, Leslie Bridgewater playing Bass Oboe, Marimba and Xylophone with the greatest versatility; and three percussion players with three tympani, eight small drums, ocarina glockenspiel, horseshoes, marbles in boxes, jews-harps, woodblocks and, in fact,. most things that one could hit to make a note. Anna May Wong very nearly made a success of this, and some of the songs still live, being occasionally broadcast with a more Christian orchestration. This was done while on sick-leave from Cochran, who now called me back to the Pavilion to conduct a Cole Porter revue, a summons which both parties soon had cause to regret. Freed by my failure satisfactorily to interpret dance band music, I joined Edward Laurillard to conduct that strangely popular musical comedy, ' The Student Prince,' at the Piccadilly Theatre, and the revival of ' The Maid of the Mountains ' at the Hippodrome. Then came the most enjoyable of all my engagements, Sir Barry Jackson's last revival of Boughton's faery opera ' The Immortal Hour " at the Queen's Theatre, with most of the original cast and a perfect choir and orchestra.

" Back to operetta, Tauber's first appearance in England, at Drury Lane Theatre, in ' The Land of Smiles,' renewing an old acquaintance with that wizard of light music, Franz Lehar. I went down to Dover to meet Tauber, the pomp of whose arrival was severely discounted by another passenger on the boat, the tragic figure of an earlier patron, King Alfonso, who had just abdicated the throne of Spain. I next directed Anne Croft's revival of ' The Chocolate Soldier ' at the Shaftesbury, and then ' The Dubarry ' at His Majesty's, with the beautiful and ill-fated Anny Ahlers, a strange psychic figure whose untimely death robbed the theatre of a great artist. The death by accident of another great friend, Norman O'Neill, led to my taking over Sir Oswald Stoll's Shakespearean season at the Alhambra, and afterwards at the Manchester Hippodrome, writing and conducting the music for ' Twelfth Night ' and ' The Merry Wives.' Meanwhile, film work for Dean, at first intermittent, had become more continuous, and I signed a definite contract with Ealing Studios, starting off with an enormous ' do ' at midnight in Hyde Park with the Welsh Guards' Band and about a thousand actors (amateur and professional) for a scene in Galsworthy's ' Escape.'

" Since then I have directed the music for some eighty films, composing the music for about twenty. They include eight Gracie Fields, six George Formby and four Will Hay productions, the Mozart film, ' Whom the Gods Love,' ' Proud Valley ' (with Robeson), ' San Demetrio,' ' They Came to a City,' ' Greek Testament,' ' The Halfway House,' ' High Command ' and ' Next of Kin ' (with William Walton's music).

" An enjoyable episode was ' The Great Mr. Handel,' made at Denham for Mr. Rank by permission of Ealing Directors. In an effort to recapture the authentic sound of Georgian strings, I persuaded the London Philharmonic Orchestra to scrap all their wires and put on gut.

" In between films, I managed to provide the scores for ' The Two Bouquets ' (Ambassadors and Garrick theatres) and ' An Elephant in Arcady ' (Kingsway and Savoy) to the libretti of Eleanor and Herbert Farjeon, and to conduct Priestley's ' Johnson Over Jordan,' which had a thrilling pore-opening musical climax composed by Benjamin Britten. Another interlude was to conduct Mozart's ' Figaro ' and ' Cosi fan Tútte ' for my old friend Sydney Carroll who was then running the Regents Park Open Air Theatre. An orchestra pit to hold forty players was dug in the turf by a reluctant L.C.C. gardener, and on the first night a tempest filled it to the brim with water, driving the company, orchestra and audience into a large tent, where Mozart's masterpiece was carried through to a damp finale in weather conditions like those which flooded out the composer's funeral procession.

" During the intervals of my film work, I have found time to score several ballets for the International Company, including ' Everyman,' in which the use of Richard Strauss's ' Symphonic Poems ' brought down the ire of ' The Times,' and Delibes' masterpiece, ' Coppelia,' which I conducted myself at the Savoy.

" Other special occasions have been the ' Daily Telegraph's ' Henry Irving Centenary performance, two King George's Pension Fund concerts and the tremendous affair given by the Government at the India Office to President Lebrun just before the war. The courtyard in Whitehall was roofed over, and in it gathered Their Majesties the King and Queen, all the Royal Family, the Cabinet and most of Debrett. Sir Seymour Hicks and many famous artists played to an audience blazing with diamonds and gold lace, backed by a symphony orchestra of fifty-five, the band of the Grenadier Guards, the silver trumpets of the Life Guards, the pipers of the Welsh Guards, the BBC Choir and a gaggle of eight harps."

Presentation to the Royal Circle completed what Irving describes as a most exciting evening, and he hopes to be asked to conduct another such concert when we again welcome the French President in London.

* * *

We have by this time recovered our nerve sufficiently to ask him a few questions, so the monologue now becomes a dialogue.

MYSELF: Can you see any great possibilities in the development of film music, and can anything be done to control the appalling reproduction of music in some of the cinemas?

IRVING: It is only commercial considerations that prevent perfect sound-track recording, but there is no object in concentrating on the quality of film music when its reproduction is butchered by a mechanic. Each cinema should have a musician in charge of projection, equipped with a full score and full authority.

MYSELF: Do you think we shall ever see the greater operas made into films?

IRVING: The action of an opera is too slow for filming, though it may be that we shall see some day an amplified and jet-propelled libretto for " The Ring." I should like to see what Mr. Pascal would do with Wotan.

MYSELF: Can you summarize your criticisms of the BBC?

IRVING: Music has a very great deal for which to thank the BBC, which has taught the uncultured public that a symphony is not so deadly as hyoscyamine, nor so painful as mumps. It is able to give unlimited rehearsals to new works, and thereby encourage young composers to write impossible parts. It maintains a large stall-fed symphony orchestra, hoping to demonstrate by its efficiency that permanence is the highest orchestral virtue. Its bureaucratic organisation makes rather for heavy precision, rather than for originality of thought, and soon knocks the " promise " out of the promising young conductor. But, above all, it can spend fifteen hundred pounds on a concert that brings in only seven hundred and fifty pounds, which, if galling to its pay-as-you-go competitors, is pleasant for the recipients of such bounty. It is, of course, much easier to form an accurate appreciation of the BBC from outside than from underneath the steamroller.

MYSELF: Do you detect any marked originality in the work of our younger contemporary composers that promises any great development in music?

IRVING: There is a noticeable tendency to avoid romanticism and to scrap treacly harmony in favour of muscular counterpoint: but remembering there was once a man called Bach, I should hesitate to call this originality.

MYSELF: Should the expression of beauty be the primary object of the composer?

IRVING: Beauty lies in the eye of the beholder. I once heard a woman call Schiehallion " an ugly brute!"

MYSELF: Should ugliness be depicted in music?

IRVING: I can see no reason against it. The Zoo has its mandrill, Hyde Park its Albert Memorial, Dickens his Bill Sikes and Squeers, Shakespeare his Caliban and Iago.

MYSELF: How far is a conductor justified in superimposing his own personality on the music he directs?

IRVING: Not at all.

MYSELF: In what directions do you think a conductor should strive for perfection?

IRVING: Reduction of the waistline, development of brain, assiduity of study, patience at rehearsal, gratitude for the miracle of men who magically manipulate wood and hair and gut and brass while bending their wills to the baton's caprice, and enabling the conductor to pose as Proteus.

MYSELF: Do you think . . . .

IRVING: (interrupting):

Ten minutes to closing time! Are we going over for that pint of bitter?

There is now a scramble for hats and coats in which reams of manuscript paper fly in all directions, and then we follow this Musical Shaw across the road to the local.

MYSELF: I'll give you the last word in this sketch.

IRVING: There is a wonderful new audience of young people who without any critical criteria have become familiar with classical music and find in it a marvellous new source of spiritual enjoyment. It is time they were taught that there are other composers than Beethoven and Tschaikowsky. What delights await them when they learn to love and appreciate the purity and subtlety of Mozart, the logical beauty of Bach and the grandeur and rich scholarship of Brahms! If only they would form an association to hammer at the box office managements demanding " Show us the others, teach us more," who knows what might happen to the musical world?

REGINALD JACQUES

༝

I F you ever meet a musician whose enthusiasm strikes you like a
tornado, he will be Dr. Reginald Jacques. I have never in my life
felt the need of a double whisky and soda as much as when I spent
an hour in discussion with him one morning early this year. He left me
literally gasping for breath. A more dynamic personality would be
almost impossible to find, and that, of course, is why he is the Director
of Music to C.E.M.A. (the Council for the Encouragement of Music and
the Arts.)[1]

He was born at Ashby-de-la-Zouch, Leicestershire, on January 13th,
1894, and was educated at the local grammar school. As a child he
showed outstanding musical ability, and when he was only fifteen years
of age he was appointed organist and choirmaster of St. Luke's Church,
Sheffield. Soon after the outbreak of war in 1914 he joined up and went
abroad with the Second Battalion of the West Yorkshire Regiment. He
fought in' France and Flanders, and after an engagement in which he
was seriously wounded, he was sent home. When the hospital ship
arrived at Southampton he was given the choice of two destinations:
a hospital at Newcastle or one at Oxford. His choice of the latter altered
the whole course of his life.

Although he was a patient for five years he was allowed to move
about after he had spent a year in bed, and this enabled him to continue
with his studies. He matriculated and then went to Queen's College,
Oxford, of which he was appointed organist and Director of Music in
1926. He took degrees in English Literature and Music and subsequently became a Supernumerary Fellow. He was also the director of
the Eaglesfield Music Society and the Oxford Orchestral Society. He
made an extensive study of choral work and in addition gained something
of a reputation as a singer with an excellent baritone voice.

In 1929, while he was still at Oxford, he married Miss Thora Beatrice
de Vries Wells, of Ealing. They have one son.

He was appointed to the conductorship of the Bach Choir in 1932,
and in the years that followed found himself so much in demand in
London that in 1936 he decided to leave Oxford. In the same year he
succeeded Sir Percy Buck as Music Adviser to the London County
Council, and was elected a Fellow and Professor of the Royal College of

---

[1] Dr. Jacques resigned his position with C.E.M.A. in the spring of 1945 shortly
before the Council was renamed " The Arts Council of Great Britain."

Music, where he conducted the Choral Class. At the College his experience and exceptional ability as a choir trainer caused him to be regarded as a high authority on choral singing, and led to the publication of his text-book " Voice Training in Schools," which is one of the best of its kind.

In 1937 he accepted the position of Director of Music at Reading University, but was obliged to relinquish it in the year that followed owing to ill-health.

During his six years' association with the London County Council he was responsible for the building up of an extensive programme of children's concerts. He still takes the keenest interest in this class of work, and broadcasts regularly in programmes for the schools.

Of all his activities his preference is for conducting. His own orchestra, the Jacques String Orchestra, and the Bach Choir take up most of the time that he can spare from his duties with C.E.M.A., yet every week he seems to be able to squeeze in a few extra engagements with other bodies requiring his help. In the past he has also broadcast frequently with the BBC Orchestra and the BBC Singers. He has conducted and adjudicated at the more important festivals all over England and has even found time to tour Northern Ireland! Add to this his activities as a lecturer at vacation courses and other educational institutions, and you will have some idea of the busy life he leads.

*   *   *

When the war broke out in 1939, Dr. Jacques, who was at that time busy arranging a series of children's concerts, was told that his work would have to stop because it would be dangerous to bring together large numbers of children in theatres and concert halls. But this did not deter him. He immediately planned to take an orchestra around with him and give the concerts in the schools. The maintenance grant was therefore continued, and he has now given over four hundred wartime concerts to children in the schools without a single mishap.

He became interested in the work of C.E.M.A. early in 1940, and for two years he gave his services as a voluntary organiser. It was not until the Council felt that the appointment of an official Director of Music could no longer be postponed that Dr. Jacques became a regular member of its staff.

Before I go on, let me tell you something of the origin and objects of C.E.M.A. The first few months of the present war brought about an overwhelming demand for music, drama and other cultural recreations just when the black-out and fear of air-raids caused the suppression of much of the work of our artists, musicians and actors. Millions of people were unable to take part in the cultural activities they had enjoyed in peacetime, so in December, 1939, Lord De La Warr, then President of the Board of Education, approached the Pilgrim Trust and suggested the formation of an organization to encourage the development of art, music and drama under war conditions. " The Trustees made an immediate offer of twenty-five thousand pounds for this purpose, and C.E.M.A. came into existence at the beginning of January, 1940. Three months later the Treasury made an offer of a pound for pound grant; and in March, 1942, the Pilgrim Trustees, having seen their offspring well on the way to maturity, retired, leaving C.E.M.A. as an official body, administering a Treasury grant, with the members of its Council appointed by the President of the Board of Education and with Lord Keynes as Chairman. Since then, three Advisory Panels for music, drama and art have been added to the Council."

C.E.M.A. is concerned not only with the maintenance of the highest standard of art, but also with the task of bringing it to the people. Sir Stanley Marchant is the Chairman of the Music Panel, and with his guidance " C.E.M.A. has made itself responsible for the provision of concerts as a direct part of the war effort. These are held in factory canteens, workers' hostels, rest centres for the homeless after air-raids, Y.M.C.A. clubs, centres for American and foreign troops and for members of the Allied Merchant Navies, and also in village halls, churches, and in small towns where transport conditions have isolated the inhabitants and thrown them back on their own resources. The artists are drawn from special panels, built up by C.E.M.A. at head-quarters and in the provinces, and are paid flat-rate fees—the same for everyone. The work they do is recognised as National Service by the Ministry of Labour."

I should like to quote a few more paragraphs from a short C.E.M.A. manifesto sent to me by Dr. Jacques:

" In many places these pioneer concerts have awakened a demand for a regular supply of music. Where this has happened, the Council encourages the local people to organize their own series of concerts, for which artists generally receive their normal fees, which the Council is prepared to guarantee. Some of these concerts are held at lunch-time in the art galleries of the larger provincial towns and represent an extension of the successful series inaugurated by Dame Myra Hess at the National Gallery shortly after the outbreak of war.

" The Council has made it possible for established chamber music clubs to obtain through their headquarters, the National Federation of Music Societies, a guarantee against loss on a year's programme of concerts. The increase in the number of chamber music clubs taking advantage of this insurance scheme has been most marked.

" The Council is associated with a number of symphony, chamber and string orchestras of national reputation. Financial arrangements of varying kind and degree are made with each orchestra to assist its work; and it is hoped that in association with the Council these orchestras will find it possible to maintain the best possible working conditions for their players, to limit the number of concerts so that there is sufficient time for rehearsals and rest, to provide opportunities for new conductors, new soloists and new works, and generally to improve the standard of performance. It is, of course, the Council's special aim to encourage the orchestras to perform in places which, mainly for reasons connected with the war, have been cut off from the enjoyment of ' live ' music.

" The Council is also assisting an experiment, which is being carried out by the Musicians' Union through its Committee for the Promotion of New Music, to give composers the chance of having new orchestral works rehearsed and performed in public."

In the short space I have available I cannot attempt to describe the work that is being done in drama and art, but it is interesting to note that the Sadler's Wells Opera Company, the Sadler's Wells Ballet Company, the Ballets Jooss and the Ballet Rambert are associating themselves with the work of C.E.M.A. The work has now extended to Northern Ireland, where thousands of factory workers are enjoying the work of this great organization.

*   *   *

Dr. Jacques believes that the work of C.E.M.A. is the most wonderful thing that has ever happened in music. At last the State is backing art, not merely for art's sake, but for its value in the lives of the people. Whereas the Government now subsidizes our finest orchestras only for specific concerts, Dr. Jacques hopes that by the time this book is in print the State will give full support to all their musical activities.

This would not mean that such bodies as the London Philharmonic Orchestra, the London Symphony Orchestra and the Hallé Orchestra would come under Government control; on the contrary, they would still enjoy the freedom of self-government, but as long as they did work of educational value to the community they would receive financial help. This, of course, would mean that there would be the finest concerts at prices that all could afford to pay.

Dr. Jacques is insistent upon the need of adequate concert halls in all those towns which do not already possess them. In London, at least three new halls are required, each holding about three thousand people, and at least two more to hold about one thousand. They should be civic halls belonging to the people and not subject to the restrictions of private interests. He considers the Liverpool Philharmonic Hall to be the finest concert hall in Britain: its acoustics are perfect and it is eminently suitable in every way for symphony concerts. All the big orchestras should visit these halls in a circuit, and all the other musical organizations in the country should see that their activities are noted in the newly instituted ' Concert Calendar ' so that no overlapping takes place. The secretaries of the leading orchestras are already collaborating by meeting once every three months under the auspices of C.E.M.A. to discuss points of common interest.

Reginald Jacques is very hopeful for the future because the people have now learnt to appreciate the value of music, and to love it. " If on the grounds of economy any attempt is made to cut out music after the war, there will be an infernal row " he says. Music is now part of the life of the people: they like a good tune, and for that reason we must not be scornful of the more popular classics which have done so much to make converts to music.

" The notion that the ordinary people do not as a rule appreciate good music is just nonsense. They might not be enthusiastic about good music performed by bad artists, or bad music performed by good artists; but when they hear the best music by the best artists, they always listen intently and enjoy it." Dr. Jacques has happy memories of concerts he has given to the very " toughest " sort of industrial workers in heavy industry. At every performance there was tremendous applause and requests for more. It was at a concert of this nature that he played Bach to burly great men of the navvy type! What is even more surprising is that they demanded an encore.

One of his favourite practices is to play Bach's " Air on the G String " without previously announcing it. After the applause subsides he informs the audience, much to their astonishment, that they have been listening to a composition by J. S. Bach. The result is that they generally ask for more, whereas had he told them beforehand that he was going to play music by Bach they would have shown their disapproval in no uncertain manner. He finds that he can make them appreciate anything from Vivaldi to Bartók; though Mozart, Dvorák and Tchaikovsky generally draw the greatest applause.

The C.E.M.A. musicians frequently exposed themselves to great personal danger in their efforts to take music to the people of the towns that were suffering from aerial attack. Dr. Jacques recalls that during the severe raids of 1941 they gave many concerts in the larger air-raid shelters. On one occasion they were unable to take the piano down into the shelter, and the pianist raised no objection when he was asked to play the instrument halfway down the stairs while the soloist sang at the bottom.

Air-raids frequently took place during the concerts, and on one evening the artists emerged to find that their cab had been blown from one side of the street to the other. However, the driver soon had the vehicle in running order and calmly drove them on through the raid to the next concert.

Dr. Jacques is very gratified by the wonderful renascence of string music. C.E.M.A.'s grants to the string orchestras have enabled them to appear in the most remote parts of the country. At one village the inhabitants had never seen an orchestra in their lives, and were highly interested when he explained the function of some of the instruments they had heard on the wireless. His popularity is due, no doubt, to his genial personality and tremendous enthusiasm, but behind this there is his thoroughly sound knowledge of his work. His interpretation of Bach is particularly inspiring, but he has also taken keen interest in folk music, of which he has published several excellent arrangements.

REGINALD JACQUES

CONSTANT LAMBERT

CONSTANT LAMBERT

❦

THAT Constant Lambert should have distinguished himself in the world of Ballet is not surprising when one considers that he was brought up in an environment dominated more by art than music. His father was G. W. Lambert, A.R.A., the painter, and his brother Maurice has now risen to eminence as a sculptor.

Born in London in 1905 and educated at Christ's Hospital, Constant Lambert did not fully appreciate what music meant to him until a prolonged illness cut him off from all the other and more usual schoolboy pursuits. He tells me that this illness affected the entire course of his life, because while he was indisposed he had little else but music and books to occupy his attention. His piano was such a joy and consolation to him that he resolved to become a professional pianist, and at the age of seventeen he entered the Royal College of Music.

He had begun to compose when he was about sixteen, and the encouragement he received at the College—not only from the staff, but from the other enthusiastic students around him—stimulated him to write a considerable amount in his youth. He has now withdrawn most of his early works because he regards them as immature, but they must certainly have shown outstanding merit, for he was only twenty when Serge Diaghileff commissioned him to write a ballet for his famous Russian Ballet. Incidentally, he was the first English composer to be honoured in this manner. The result was " Romeo and Juliet," which was first produced at Monte Carlo in 1926 and put on in London soon after. He followed this with another ballet, " Pomona," which was given its first performance in Buenos Aires in 1927.

This promising start to his musical career did not pave an easy way to prosperity however, and he had to do a variety of odd musical jobs to pay his way in those days. Free-lance journalism in musical subjects was one of the methods he chose to augment his income, and in time he became a regular contributor to ' Figaro,' ' The New Statesman and Nation,' and the ' Sunday Referee.' His book, " Music Ho! A Study of Music in Decline," was published in 1934.

One of his most notable successes was his setting for chorus, pianoforte and orchestra, of Sacheverell Sitwell's poem, " The Rio Grande." It was first performed in Manchester on December 12th, 1929, and was heard in the Queen's Hall, London, on the following day, when an excellent performance was given by Sir Hamilton Harty and the Hallé Orchestra.

His " Music for Orchestra " was first played at Oxford in 1931, and then nearly five years elapsed before he produced " Summer's Last Will and Testament," with words from Thomas Nashe's comedy. The latter made its debut when it was played in the Queen's Hall by the BBC Symphony Orchestra under his own direction in January, 1936 One of his latest works is the ballet " Horoscope."

It was not until he was appointed Musical Director of the Vic-Wells Ballet that he finally established his reputation as an authority on ballet. He took the Company to Paris for the 1937 Exhibition, and in 1939 appeared with them before the King and Queen at a special gala performance. The Ballet was reaching a high standard of perfection when war broke out and imposed great difficulties upon the Company. Nevertheless, it was not long before they were touring the provinces again—without an orchestra, and relying entirely upon two pianos, one of which Lambert had to play himself! They were in Holland on a propaganda tour when the Germans overran the country in 1940, and they had to fly for their lives.

In his association with the BBC he has always specialized in programmes of contemporary and ballet music, and it is only in the last two or three years that he has done symphonic work. Recently, too, he has toured with the London Philharmonic Orchestra, and worked with E.N.S.A. in the provision of symphony concerts for factory workers.

*   *   *

Constant Lambert considers that the present routine of concert-giving is stultifying the art of music, for although he appreciates that the more popular works of Tschaikowsy and Beethoven have often to be used to draw the public, he can see no reason why the vast number of lesser-known compositions should not be mixed in with the popular music. The leading symphony orchestras should have a much larger and more varied repertoire.

It is interesting to note that far more modern and unusual works can be played in concerts given to factory workers than in the programmes played to the more sophisticated audiences in London. Constant Lambert finds that the "new" audiences appreciate anything that possesses vitality and colour.

He insists that we should do far more of the earlier works, because most people's knowledge of music starts with Beethoven, and the bulk of the music written before his time is unknown to them. There is also a tremendous amount of fine Russian and French music that has never been performed in this country. The neglect of this—as of the works of many of our contemporary composers—is probably due to the lack of time for adequate rehearsal in the arrangements of most of our orchestras to-day. The programmes we get now are becoming far too stereotyped: *must* we always have one symphony and one piano concerto? Lambert would like to see far more programmes made up of attractive smaller works.

The present boom in music will subside, he thinks, and therefore after the war we must be far more enterprising, choosing our programmes with greater care and thought for the audiences. People tolerate inferior work now because the war has restricted their other forms of entertainment and recreation; but as soon as conditions revert to normal, as soon as people get the use of their cars again for week-ends in the country, only first-class concerts will attract them.

The tremendous interest now being shown in ballet is more likely to continue because the English Ballet is now as firmly established as the Russian (which evolved from the Italian, by the way). Moreover, it now has a much more general following, whereas before the war it was patronized chiefly by an exclusive " highbrow " audience. But even in this sphere, untiring efforts must be made to improve the standard continually, since there is always the danger that the novelty will wear off and that the " new " audiences will look elsewhere.

MUIR MATHIESON

❦

WE walked down St. Martin's Lane one spring afternoon just as London's City workers were preparing for their usual Battle of the Underground.

" I thought we'd have a cup of tea somewhere " I suggested.

" Tea?" Muir Mathieson echoed faintly with a look of sheer horror in his eyes, " you . . . you don't expect me to drink *tea* at this time of the afternoon?"

We led him as quickly as possible to one of the pubs which for some mysterious reason are allowed to open half an hour earlier than their neighbours, and sat him down in front of a pint of bitter. He took a gulp and sighed heavily.

" If you'd seen as many feet of film as I have to-day, you'd understand why I need this " he murmured with another sigh.

Then he sat back, made a futile effort to smooth down his shock of turbulent hair, and behind a cloud of cigarette smoke told us of the progress he had made in introducing the work of Britain's greatest composers to the film industry.

Most of his life-story I had to dig out of two of his scrapbooks. It starts in Stirling, where he was born in 1911, son of a well-known Scottish etcher and painter. In his childhood his ambition was to become an artist like his father, but when he began to study the piano with Philip Halstead in Glasgow, music made a stronger appeal, and under the guidance of his mother, an accomplished violinist, he acquired a useful knowledge of stringed instruments.

By the time he was thirteen he could play the violin, viola and 'cello, and it was not long before he had a children's orchestra of his own. The success with which he managed this little group of a score of players—not one was over sixteen years of age—may be judged by the fact that several of their concerts were broadcast from Glasgow. The training of these youthful musicians was not an easy task : at first he had to write special music himself because some of them could not play more than a dozen notes!

His parents never allowed him to pose as a boy prodigy: they preferred that he should become a practical musician. They saw, too, that his diligence was rewarded, and he is proud to claim that his first pair of football boots was earned by accompanying his mother on the piano.

When his school days drew to a close he wanted to go to Edinburgh University, but a distinguished musician persuaded his parents to send him to London to become one of Arthur Benjamin's pupils. This they did, and in due course he had no difficulty in winning the Leverhulme and Julian Clifford scholarships to the Royal College of Music, so that he came under Dr. Malcolm Sargent for conducting and was able to continue studying the piano with Arthur Benjamin.

He was still at the Royal College of Music when he made a contract with London Film Productions to act as assistant to Kurt Schroeder whom he later succeeded. That he should have received this offer at such an early age was perhaps due to the success with which he conducted College concerts and various amateur operatic societies. He had also been associated with a little film called "Wharves and Strays," for which Arthur Benjamin had written the music. At that time, opera made an irresistible appeal to him, but the possibility of securing a remunerative appointment with an opera company seemed rather remote, so he welcomed the chance of entering the film industry because it seemed to be a fairly good substitute.

He also became Dr. Malcolm Sargent's assistant for the "Hiawatha" productions at the Albert Hall, and he will never forget how at one of these Sargent felt unwell, and after the first act asked him to take over. He had never read the score beyond the second act, and all through the first interval he had to scan the rest of it while people were rushing about frantically telephoning for another conductor. Soon after the third act had commenced, however, the telephoning stopped, because it had been decided that he could be entrusted with the job of directing the performance through to the end. None of those responsible for this decision knew that he was reading the score at sight!

When London Film Productions opened their splendid new studios at Denham, Alexander Korda saw that Mathieson was put in charge of the music. When he took on this important job, Muir Mathieson made one condition: that he should be allowed to approach the greatest composers in the country to get them to write the music for the films with which he was to be associated.

This condition is significant because it altered the entire course of film music. Up to that time the film producers had regarded the music as a very minor consideration, and generally employed musical "hacks" to provide nondescript stuff that could be pulled about anyhow, or to adapt selected passages from the classics and other published music

We shall see in a few moments what a remarkable change has taken place.

One of his earliest successes was " Wings of the Morning," in which the charming young lady who was later to become his wife appeared as a gipsy dancer. This, by the way, was the first British colour film. Then he was associated with such productions as " Don Juan," " Scarlet Pimpernel " and " The Ghost Goes West."

It was Muir Mathieson who had the privilege of directing the magnificent music which Arthur Bliss wrote for the film " Things to Come," adapted from the famous book, "The Shape of Things to Come" by H. G. Wells. For this, fourteen full orchestral recording sessions were necessary, and some of them lasted from ten o'clock in the morning until ten-thirty at night. The music has now outlived the film by several years: Mathieson has made several gramophone records of it and featured it in many of his broadcasts.

Another noteworthy film in which he was musical director was " Victoria the Great." The London Symphony Orchestra was engaged for this, together with the Life Guards' Band, members of the London College of Choristers, and many of the musicians who took part in the Coronation of King George VI and Queen Elizabeth in Westminster Abbey. The actual music used at the Coronation of Queen Victoria in 1838 was woven into the music by Anthony Collins, who also composed much of the original music used in the film. In reviewing this film, the ' New York Herald Tribune ' admitted that up to that time no American film had ever had such fine music as this great English production.

During 1935, Mathieson was invited to give a series of concerts with a section of the BBC Orchestra. Since then he has been on the air in a variety of orchestral programmes, notably those made up of music he has used in his films, including compositions by such people as Richard Addinsell, Sir Arnold Bax, Arthur Bliss, Benjamin Britten, William Walton and Dr. R. Vaughan Williams.

When Queen Mary visited the Denham studios in 1939, Muir Mathieson was conducting the three choirs used in " The Four Feathers." Her Majesty sat in semi-darkness for quite a while listening to the chanting of "native" music with tom-tom accompaniment.

" Sanders of the River " won the Venice Cup in the 1935 International Film Exhibition as the picture with the best musical accompaniment. Michael Spoliansky was the composer, and attributed much of the success of the music to Mathieson's brilliant conducting.

In recent years, Muir Mathieson has directed the music of such films as " Malta G.C." and " The Flemish Farm," for which the scores were written by Sir Arnold Bax and Dr. R. Vaughan Williams respectively. He has also been associated with the Ministry of Information productions, Army and R.A.F. Film Units and Crown Films.

*   *   *

When I commented upon the impressive list of distinguished composers who had written scores for him, he told me of some of the difficulties he had experienced in getting them to do film work. One, for instance, seemed quite horrified at first and would not consider the offer made by the company, but Mathieson went personally to his home and explained, among many other things, that the film offered a unique opportunity of getting the public interested in contemporary British music. At last the eminent composer acquiesced and is now very nearly as keen on film music as Mathieson is himself!

A composer has often to be persuaded to do quite a lot of research work to get material appropriate for the film upon which he is working. When Geoffrey Toye undertook the music for " Rembrandt," for instance, he had to make a special study of old Dutch songs of the period.

Muir Mathieson emphasises the great value of films to the young, struggling composer. Good work is always in demand—in fact it is sometimes a problem to find men capable of writing suitable music.

Mathieson has always advocated the commissioning of special music for each film. The adaptation of other music can never be recommended, for apart from the obvious difficulties encountered in trying to make it fit exactly to the film, there is always the danger of "association." By this I mean that the attention of the people in the audience might easily be distracted from the film because they recognize a tune in the music. The ideal film music is never obtrusive unless, of course, the producer wishes it to make some special effect; it should lend " pictorial " and emotional colour to the film without distracting the attention of the audience in any way.

I hope I have not created the impression that Mathieson is interested in nothing else but film music, for he is an able conductor of symphonic works, and on many occasions recently has broadcast with the BBC Northern Orchestra. He is interested in all types of orchestras from dance bands upwards.

He is most anxious that the leading symphony orchestras should include more works by British composers in their repertoire. The taste of the public must be built up gradually so that their ability to appreciate music does not lag too far behind the modern development of the art.

*   *   *

Muir Mathieson married Hermione Darnborough about eight years ago, soon after he had first met her at one of the "Hiawatha"

91

productions that I have already mentioned. She was then a ballerina with the Vic-Wells Company; now she finds her time fully occupied with their little daughter Muirne and their small son Ian.

Mathieson is a typical Scot, secretly rather proud of his unmistakable accent. His chief recreation nowadays is painting, but in peacetime, when he has just a little more leisure than at present, he enjoys motoring, fishing and riding.

MUIR MATHIESON

[*Anthony*

HERBERT MENGES

HERBERT MENGES

❦

WHEN I first met Herbert Menges I was beginning to get a little depressed by assurances from prominent musicians that as a nation we are not really interested in opera, so I did my best to provoke a counterblast to their pessimism. The provocation was hardly necessary, for although he recognized our operatic shortcomings, there was a note of indignation in his denial of public apathy. What was even more important was the evidence he gave me proving that opera was undoubtedly playing its part in the great renascence of music. But let me deal with the biographical side of this sketch first.

Herbert Menges was born at Hove on August 27th, 1902, the youngest of four children, of whom the eldest is Isolde, the well-known violinist. His father, George Menges, was of German descent, but his mother is English, and between them they ran an academy of music which provided their children with an excellent musical background. " My earliest recollection is of Isolde playing her fiddle," Menges told me; " she gave her first recital when she was three and a half."

He started to learn to play the violin as soon as he was old enough to hold the instrument properly, and at the age of four made his first public appearance at the Hove Town Hall. But as he grew up he was more attracted to the piano, and after taking lessons from Mathilda Verne and Arthur de Greef, went to the Royal College of Music for a three years' course. He declares that the greatest benefit he derived from this course was the instruction in composition he received from Vaughan Williams and Gustav Holst.

His first public engagement as a conductor was in 1925, and shortly afterwards he founded the Brighton Symphonic Players which in time became the Brighton Philharmonic Orchestra, one of the best musical organizations of its kind in the country.

Later, he founded the London String Players, toured with them and frequently broadcast, and in 1931 was appointed Musical Director of the Old Vic. This accounts for his association with the incidental music of so many of our serious plays. He wrote nearly all the music used for the Old Vic productions of Shakespeare, and also for many of John Gielgud's productions since " Richard of Bordeaux."

In October, 1941, Menges became joint conductor with Laurance Collingwood of the Sadler's Wells Opera Company. His experience has not been gained entirely in the theatre, however, for he has conducted most of the greater symphony orchestras, including the L.P.O., BBC and the Liverpool Philharmonic, from time to time.

One of the most important branches of the work Menges has done in London was in connection with the London Rehearsal Orchestra, which he founded in 1931 primarily to enable the younger and more enthusiastic professional musicians to come together to study new and difficult compositions. Although many of the members of this ensemble were regular players in the leading orchestras, there were also musicians who were temporarily out of touch with symphonic work, and advanced students seeking admission to the greater orchestras. Many eminent conductors gave their blessing to this important venture, and realized the value of such an organization as a training ground and " clearing house " for the younger players. Menges conducted the regular weekly rehearsals and was able to note the work of promising young musicians so that he could recommend them to orchestral managements from time to time. Many players, having found valuable experience with the London Rehearsal Orchestra, have since become regular members of leading symphony orchestras.

Attention has been drawn in the past to the unfairness of open competition for orchestral vacancies, because it has so often meant that a first-class man has been " let down " by a sudden spasm of nervous excitement, and the inferior player not so susceptible to " nerves " has been given the job. The London Rehearsal Orchestra, besides being a valuable educational organization, offered an alternative method of selection by which managements could follow the progress being made by the younger players and witness their work in consort with others. Occasional public rehearsals were held at which an audience was present by invitation. Plans are now being made to re-establish this orchestra as soon as conditions permit, and it is likely to be of great assistance to players returning from the forces.

*   *   *

Herbert Menges is very optimistic about opera in this country. He has noticed a steady increase in the enthusiasm with which the Sadler's Wells Company is received by all types of audiences. In the north, especially, they play to packed houses night after night.

The lack of suitable theatres is one of the primary causes of the limitations placed upon British opera, and the absence of suitable singers is due to there being no proper school of opera in England. He insists that we must organize on an adequate scale a new school devoted entirely to the training of professionals in opera, including instrumentalists and stage craftsmen.

Menges feels strongly the importance of opera sung in English, but he considers that there is no need to discourage either foreign opera companies visiting this country after the war or the performance of opera in its original language by English companies. Far from stifling English opera, such performances should act as a stimulus to improve our national opera.

In referring to criticisms of the Sadler's Wells performances, he told me that some people were saying that the orchestra is too loud. His answer was, first, that the accommodation for the orchestra in the majority of theatres is so ridiculously small that in most cases the orchestra pit has to be extended so that the players sit on the level of the stalls. This puts the singers at a great disadvantage, because it means that the orchestra is *between* them and the audience, instead of being in a sunken pit.

Secondly, Menges points out that few singers in England to-day have full-sized opera voices, and that although every effort is made to avoid " drowning " them, there is a limit to the degree to which the orchestra can be suppressed without spoiling the music.

Thirdly, the audience's demands to hear the words are often a trifle unreasonable. The same people who expect to hear every word the singer utters in English will gladly listen to an opera in German or Italian, and not care a hoot about the words because they do not understand them!

Finally, people in this country invariably judge opera from Gilbert and Sullivan standards. In light opera the composer often uses the orchestra merely to provide a general and more or less unobtrusive accompaniment, whereas in grand opera the orchestra plays such a highly important part that to keep it down and suffocate the musical climaxes would ruin the entire production. The emotion of the whole opera is prominently portrayed in the orchestral part of the music. Menges also points out that while the music is usually of a high quality, the words of translated opera are often puerile and of little æsthetic value.

In support of his arguments he drew my attention to a passage in the first act of " La Bohème " where Puccini indicates *fff* for the orchestra while the soloists are singing *f*.

Menges maintains that far too many people regard the orchestra merely as a means of providing a discreet background of accompaniment for the singers. The fact is, of course, that the singers and players are all part of *one* ensemble of which the conductor is the director, and he alone is responsible for the balance of all the music, vocal and instrumental. Under proper conditions there should be complete unity of all the executants.

When we went on to discuss English music generally, Menges said: "I can't help feeling that this country is too cold for music. It is not easy to get good work at a rehearsal if the company is compelled to perform in a cold concert hall or an icy theatre. Apart from the fact that intonation suffers, the physical effort is chilled." Menges believes that warmth is necessary to induce the expansive feeling that enables an artist to give of his best. For that reason he appreciates the value of good food and wine as warmth-producing essentials!

*   *   *

He was married in 1935 to Evelyn Stiebel, and they now have two sons, Nicholas aged five and Christopher aged three. Their home is in London. His chief recreations are reading and philately, but touring with an opera company and the fulfilment of other musical engagements does not allow much time for indulgence in either of them.

He is fairly tall, dark, and has a disposition that is slightly more serious than the average musician one meets to-day. At first I had the impression that he was a trifle aloof, but I soon discovered that this was due entirely to mutual shyness. His reticence disappeared quickly when I introduced the subject of the future of music in this country, because he feels very strongly that in planning the part that music must take in the general reconstruction after the war, we must give far greater attention to the filling of administrative posts. More discrimination must be used to see that knowledgeable men of wide experience with proved administrative and business ability are chosen to extend the organization of musical culture. In the past, English music has too long been dominated from the organ stool, with lamentable results.

MAURICE MILES

BOYD NEEL

MAURICE MILES

❧

FOR at least two or three centuries in the history of English music
the cathedral choirs of this country were regarded as the cradles
of our national music. In the past, so many of our great musicians
began as cathedral choirboys that I am a trifle disappointed to find that
few of the conductors I have met were initiated into the mysteries of
part-singing in these ancient ecclesiastical establishments.

I am not suggesting that cathedral choirs *always* provide an ideal
musical education, because so much depends upon the ability and
temperament of the organist; and my own experiences as a cathedral
singer have taught me that organists can reveal anything from pure
genius to sheer imbecility. But here and there one comes across musicians
of extraordinary ability whose careers have been built very solidly upon
the foundations laid in boyhood by the study of Palestrina, Byrd,
Gibbons, Boyce, Purcell, the Wesleys, and so forth; and on the whole
I think a musical education of this type is a valuable preliminary to
an academic training.

From all this you will probably have guessed that Maurice Miles
was once a cathedral choirboy. You are right. Born at Epsom in 1908
of musical parents who when he was quite small taught him to play
the piano, the violin and to sing, he won a choral scholarship to Wells
Cathedral. Here he learnt all about canticles and conkers, deans and
doughnuts, and came under the influence of Canon Davies, the organist.

There was nothing remarkable about his voice, and he never shone
with sufficient brightness as a solo boy to reduce the old ladies to tears
when he sought the wings of a dove, but his musicianship was excellent
and in due course he became "Senior Boy" (head chorister).

Miles played in a small local orchestra from the age of twelve, and
under the benevolent guidance of Canon Davies, who advised him to
adopt music as a career, he won a scholarship to the Royal Academy
of Music. He studied the violin there under Charles Woodhouse, singing under Frederick Keel, and the piano with Clifford Curzon. For
conducting, he was a pupil of Ernest Reed and Sir Henry Wood.

While he was still in his "teens" he was conducting a choral
society at Uxbridge. He was evidently not lacking in confidence, because

I

at one concert he gave a complete performance of " The Dream of Gerontius " (Elgar).

In 1930 he joined the staff of the BBC as an assistant in the Balance and Control Department and found that his work gave him valuable experience not only in score-reading, but in the art of listening intently. While he was at the BBC he went to Salzburg and had lessons in conducting with Clemens Krauss.

He resigned his appointment in 1936 to take up a dual job: as conductor of the Buxton Municipal Orchestra in summertime, and of the Bath Municipal Orchestra in winter. At Bath, particularly, he had plenty of scope, and made the most of it by organizing several very fine musical festivals.

In 1939 the spirit of adventure took him across the Atlantic. He visited Buenos Aires, where he conducted chamber and symphony orchestras; Monte Video to conduct the S.O.D.R.E. Orchestra in a series of concerts which enabled him to introduce a great deal of English music unknown in that part of the world; and Santiago, where he conducted the National Orchestra of Chile. While he was on his way home he heard that war had been declared.

Until he was called up in December, 1940, he was the conductor of the Erith Musical Society, and while he was in the army he ran a string orchestra of his own. During the past few years he has also appeared as a guest conductor of the London Philharmonic, London Symphony, Liverpool Philharmonic and BBC Symphony orchestras.

In October, 1943, the military authorities released Maurice Miles for special duties with the BBC, and since then he has been responsible for the music in the broadcasts to Latin America.

*   *   *

Musicians frequently marry members of their own profession, they often show preference for artists, and a few have been known to marry their secretaries, but Miles chose a lawyer for his bride! I ought to add, however, that Miss Eileen Wood, LL.B., whom he married in 1936, studied music in France and is by no means unskilled in her husband's art. They have two children, Anne, age seven, and Hugh, age two; and live at Edgware.

*   *   *

When I was talking to Maurice Miles about modern music, he declared that although the war had brought a new public who were more ready to hear new music than those who had been brought up on Beethoven and Tschaikovsky, there still remained an appalling neglect of our own contemporary composers. In music, as in many other things, one had to become fashionable to be successful.

He also pointed out that the lavish orchestrations of a great deal of modern music is a frequent cause of its disqualification by those who have to make up programmes for musical organizations which are not heavily subsidized. Expenses have to be watched continually, as there are few orchestras that can afford to augment their personnel with large numbers of additional players merely to perform some new work which would probably have a doubtful reception in any case.

Another contributory cause of the neglect of quite a large amount of contemporary music is the habit of some publishers of charging very high fees for the right to perform it. It is understood, of course, that music-printing is expensive, and that composers are entitled to receive a reasonable fee, but occasionally the charges are quite prohibitive, and consequently the proposal has to be abandoned.

Miles also deplores the fact that·there are so few opportunities for the younger conductors to get experience. He appreciates that a big name is of great value to the box-office, but fails to see how the smaller people are going to get known if they are never given a chance. In the past several wealthy conductors have solved the problem by " buying " concerts; that is, by engaging an orchestra and by promoting concerts entirely at their own expense. But in this manner it is possible to lose anything up to five hundred pounds on each performance, so what is to become of the impecunious young man who far from being able to indulge in such expensive luxuries, has to earn a living by his art? Whether the situation is quite as black as Mr. Miles and some of the other younger men paint it, I do not know, but I am convinced that there is little possibility of improvement until the musicians themselves take the matter in hand and establish a national organization for the business of concert giving. The National Association of Symphony Orchestras has started on the right lines, but it is not sufficiently comprehensive to be able to carry out the complete administration of musical entertainment. There is no reason why the musical profession should not be as efficiently organized as any other. Now is the time for musicians to adopt a far-sighted policy—particularly if they are to secure general subsidies for their art.

BOYD NEEL

❦

SEVERAL physicians have been known to abandon their profession to become authors—Somerset Maugham, Francis Brett Young and Warwick Deeping, to mention only a few—but as far as I am aware, Boyd Neel is the only doctor of medicine who has become a professional musician.

Born in Blackheath, Kent, in 1905, he was educated at the Royal Naval College, Dartmouth (though actually I think he spent most of his schooldays at Osborne House, Isle of Wight, where a section of the College was housed) and at Cambridge, where he took his degree. As a student he spent the greater part of his time in organizing and performing in the various musical activities carried on by the undergraduates, and he admits that he only just scraped through his examinations. After all, a man can't be expected to show a great deal of interest in biology or *materia medica* when he is taking a principal part in amateur opera, planning chamber concerts and doing a hundred and one other jobs connected with music. Nevertheless, he got his degree and went to St. George's Hospital for three years. Here, he saw the great work of healing in its true light and appreciated the urgency of it, so he relegated his music to a very inconspicuous place on his daily timetable, and put all his energy into his work. He went through every department of the hospital, and then worked as a general practitioner in the slums of London for five years.

Although the sense of performing a great social service gratified him, he had to be honest with himself and admit that he loathed medicine, and eventually he made up his mind to get out of it by seeking a livelihood in music. In those days of severe economic depressions, a musician's life was a precarious existence, and one cannot help admiring the courage of this young doctor.

So in 1933 he founded the Boyd Neel String Orchestra, a body of eighteen young professionals from the Royal College of Music and the Royal Academy of Music. He decided that if his first concert was a success he would carry on; if not, he would abandon the venture.

In choosing his personnel he was equally bold: he selected all young people on the threshold of their careers so that his project would be sustained by the enthusiasm and vitality of youth. Hundreds of applicants were heard, and ultimately six first violins, four seconds, three violas, three 'cellos and two basses were engaged. They rehearsed every Sunday morning for six months, and then in June, 1933, their first concert was given at the Aeolian Hall. Representatives of the BBC were present, and were so impressed that they did not hesitate in recommending the Orchestra for a series of regular engagements. Thus they began their long association with broadcasting, and this, of course, did a great deal to establish them.

After that first concert Boyd Neel gave up his medical career, and he has never regretted his decision. He felt confident because at that time there were no permanent small orchestras in this country: small ensembles were generally sections of the larger symphony orchestras. Moreover, the amount of music being played by string orchestras was small, and consequently, a large number of excellent compositions for strings were almost unknown to the general musical public. Boyd Neel believed that if he unearthed such treasures and gave excellent performances of them, he could vastly increase the demand for concerts of music for strings. He has succeeded, and in doing so has also contributed substantially to musical research.

In its first year the Boyd Neel Orchestra was offered a contract by the Decca Company, and began making that remarkably fine range of records which has now exceeded a hundred. Among them we find rare works of unusual interest and the entire Concerti Grossi for strings of Handel.

Another factor worth recording is that within a few months of its establishment, the Orchestra gave the first performance, a private one, ever to take place at the Glyndebourne Festival Theatre.

In 1937 Boyd Neel accepted an invitation to take his orchestra to give a concert of English music at the Salzburg Festival. This was most successful, and earned it the distinction of being the first foreign orchestra to play at that famous gathering. Furthermore, the extremely exacting audience there were particularly charmed when they discovered that the members of the Boyd Neel Orchestra were the youngest band of players they had ever heard at their Festival. Neel himself was only thirty-two at the time.

* * *

I have said so much about the Boyd Neel String Orchestra that I am afraid you will get the impression that its conductor never appears with any other body of musicians. This, of course, would not be correct,

101

for his experience during the past ten years has been most varied. He has conducted the BBC Orchestra, the Brussels Philharmonic Society, and a dozen other musical organisations. In 1939 he toured Portugal for the British Council.

Then came the war, and at first it looked as if six years' hard work would dissolve into nothing. The youth of many of the Boyd Neel players sent them quickly into the various services—including Frederick Grinke, the brilliant leader—and their conductor returned for a little while to his original profession—medicine.

As everybody now knows, it was soon discovered that music was as necessary in wartime as in the days of peace, so Boyd Neel reassembled his Orchestra, engaging substitutes for those who had been called up, and resumed his work. Not for one moment did he think that in a year or so he would be overwhelmed with work!

In April, 1943, he took on the additional duties of Music Adviser to the London Region for E.N.S.A., and became connected with the London Regional Committee that is responsible for education in the Services. This meant extra administrative work, the giving of dozens of lectures with gramophone records and soloists, and countless other engagements. His Orchestra became associated with C.E.M.A. and took an active part in the work of that organisation.

*   *   '*

Boyd Neel is a bachelor. He has no time for recreations except reading—when he can interest himself in anything from a detective story to a learned scientific treatise. Now and then he reads a medical book, not because he has any intention of practising as a doctor again, but because he likes to know what progress is being made in the eternal conquest of disease.

The absence of a State Opera in this country is a point upon which he feels very strongly. Every large city in Great Britain should have not only a permanent opera company, but also its own symphony orchestra. He insists that the symphony orchestras should be zoned, so that each performs the bulk of its concerts in its own region. Every orchestra could then make one national tour a year.

Boyd Neel believes that a Ministry of Culture or Fine Art would be a dangerous organization, and feels that general subsidies for music would probably result in the encouragement of mediocrity. The system adopted by C.E.M.A. under which limited guarantees are given against losses incurred on approved concerts seems to him to be the more satisfactory way of subsidizing music.

The photograph of the Boyd Neel Orchestra you see in this book was taken when they played at the Queen Charlotte's Hospital Celebration Concerts at the Queen's Hall. They gave a programme of eighteenth century music with Richard Tauber and Joan Hammond, all dressed in costumes of the period. The picture behind them is Gainsborough's famous portrait of Queen Charlotte, from the National Gallery. Hadyn's " Farewell " Symphony was played by candlelight, and as each player came to the end of his part, he got up, blew out his light and went quietly off the platform, making what has now become a ritual very much more picturesque.

SIDNEY NEWMAN

᚛᚜

A VERY tactful friend of mine has just informed me that having acquainted my readers with the musical life of Glasgow in my sketch of Warwick Braithwaite, I shall be getting into very hot water if I don't write something soon about Edinburgh, because Edinburgh . . . no, I mustn't say it: it would be simply asking for trouble!

Sidney Thomas Mayow Newman, M.A.(Oxon), F.R.C.O., is the Reid Professor of Music in the University of Edinburgh, and conductor of the Reid Symphony Orchestra. All that sounds terribly dignified, and I'm afraid it rather suggests an austere, scholarly old gentleman of eighty; so let me assure you right now that Newman is a lively young man with ideas as modern as anybody else in this book.

He was born at North Finchley in 1906, but from the age of four lived a little further out of London—at Elstree, until his father retired. Then the family returned to Nailsworth, Gloucestershire, which for several generations was the home of the families of both of Newman's parents.

He began learning to play the pianoforte and violin at the age of six, and five years after won a music scholarship to Clifton College, Bristol. During his seven years at that school he studied the piano and subsequently the organ under Dr. R. O. Beachcroft, and the violin under Maurice Alexander, a well-known Bristol-musician. The musical life of the school was rich in opportunities for a varied training, for music scholars were encouraged to take a responsible share in the giving of recitals, promotion of concerts and the accompaniment of services in the College Chapel.

Newman was still a schoolboy when he gained his first experience as a conductor. This was when he directed the school orchestra, of which he was an enthusiastic member. He also made the most of opportunities to play in the Bristol Symphony Orchestra, although at that time he was concerned primarily with the task of equipping himself for a career as an organist. Some idea of his ability may be gained by the fact that he took his Fellowship of the Royal College of Organists while he was still at school.

BOYD NEEL

from a sketch by Hilda Wiener

SIDNEY NEWMAN

In 1924 he proceeded to Christ Church. Oxford, as Organ Scholar of that College and sub-organist of the Cathedral. He served for two years as assistant to Dr. Henry Ley until the latter's appointment as Director of Music at Eton College, and then worked under Noel Ponsonby. At the University he read for degrees in music and arts, and graduated with first-class honours.

I have so often heard musicians speak disparagingly of Oxford as a training ground for their profession that I was most interested to find in Newman a strong advocate of the University. He believes that the musical training afforded at Oxford is to be specially valued for the wealth of varied experience and opportunities assured by the choral foundations of certain College chapels, and by the enterprise and artistry of the many musical societies, which, of course, have a diversity of aims and interests. Thus in his case, the studies pursued under such excellent and inspiring teachers as Sir Hugh Allen, Dr. Ernest Walker, Dr. William Harris, Dr. Thomas Wood, and others, were matched by a wide field of practical experience. There were times, for instance, when Newman temporarily had in his care the entire music of New and Magdalen College chapels.

Experience as a conductor of opera was provided when in 1927 the Oxford Opera Club produced Gluck's "Alceste." Incidentally, Newman's association with this elicited from that eminent critic Ernest Newman a disclaimer of any previous knowledge of one "who rejoiced in the honoured name." In more recent years, "the importance of being Ernest" has frequently proved somewhat inconvenient when casual readers of 'The Sunday Times' with no regard for what's in a Christian name, have done Sidney Newman the embarrassing honour of holding him accountable for the stimulating effusions of his illustrious namesake.

In the nineteen-twenties the Oxford Music Club and Union in the historic Holywell Music Room was indeed a flourishing society. There each week during term were to be heard the finest string quartets, ensemble artists and recitalists of that time. Concerts were also given by members of the club at which not infrequently the works of young Oxford composers received their first, and no doubt in some cases their last, performance. The earliest compositions of Lennox Berkeley were often heard there—and were lauded or torn to pieces according to the taste, sobriety, or maliciousness of those who happened to be present. There also one might chance upon some such irresponsible extravaganza as that which sought for novelty of effect by the calculated pulling of a chain off stage, at the moment of a dramatic *general pause!*

The caretaker of the Music Room was often made the butt of the members' wit. When a notice appeared directing the owner of a missing ring to "apply to the caretaker," somebody added the words " or to the Nibelung "; and it needed a tactful and lengthy discourse upon Wagnerian opera before the secretary could allay the suspicions of that humble custodian as to the point of the remark.

The Club also promoted the practice of ensemble playing, and every week some three or four chamber music groups were coached by Ernest Tomlinson, the viola player, who had succeeded Frank Bridge in this charge.

" It was during my term of office as President of the Club that I first met the late Sir Donald Tovey, whom fourteen years later I was to succeed as Reid Professor at Edinburgh," Newman told me. " To the younger generation in Oxford at that time Tovey was known only as a sort of legendary being whose recounted exploits regularly staggered the imagination. I thought it high time to produce the man himself. Before the concert, at which he was to play the Hammerklavier Sonata, the Goldberg Variations, the Scriabin 5th Sonata, etc., Tovey was to dine with me in hall at ' the House.' For probably the only occasion in his life, Tovey arrived half-an-hour before he was due, and confronted by the three doors which invariably perplex visitors to Oxford college rooms, chose the wrong one, and presented himself in my bedroom to discover me in nude amazement in the stage between bath and dressing. He regarded me with eyes beaming like a lighthouse (they always seemed to give out more than they took in), and then remarked casually: ' I see that I am not late. Do you know that remarkable book by Knud-Jeppesen. . . .' "

*   *   *

From Oxford, Sidney Newman went to the Royal College of Music, and was there during the greater part of the two following years (1928-30), while holding a senior scholarship from his College. He studied composition under R. O. Morris, orchestration under Gordon Jacob, conducting under Malcolm Sargent and Aylmer Buesst, violin with Ernest Tomlinson, and ensemble playing under Ivor James. The pianoforte and (except for a short period under Henry Ley) the organ he pursued on his own, and also found time for a good deal of reading of eighteenth-century musical æsthetics.

Then he went abroad for four to five months as a free-lance travelling student. Munich and Salzburg festivals were followed by six weeks in Vienna, visits to Prague, Dresden and Leipzig, and finally a month or so in Berlin. Almost every night of the week he was at a concert or the opera. Lucky man!

It was at a " Gewandhaus " rehearsal at Leipzig that he first met Bruno Walter, to whom he had an introduction. Tapping his portfolio the famous conductor said: " Come on in. I have just brought back from Russia a remarkable symphony by a young man you have never heard of, named Shostakovitch!" It was ten years before Newman heard that first symphony again.

When he returned to England he went back to the Royal College of Music for a couple of terms. Before he left Oxford he had already changed his views considerably regarding the kind of musical career he wanted to adopt, so it can be readily understood that after two years of varied experience, and after his interest in conducting and chamber music had been aroused, he felt disinclined to become an organist, although he always welcomed any opportunity of getting back to an organ stool to play Bach, Franck, Handel, and the best of Rheinberger, Parry, etc.

In 1930, Sidney Newman was appointed Lecturer in Music at Armstrong (later renamed " King's ") College, Newcastle-on-Tyne, in succession to Dr. W. G. Whittaker, who had been appointed to the Chair of Music at Glasgow. Newman also became the conductor of the Newcastle Bach Choir founded by Dr. Whittaker, which had achieved considerable fame in the nineteen-twenties not only by its performances of a very great number of the Bach Cantatas, Motets and other choral works, but also through its revival of such works as the Tallis Forty-part Motet, the Byrd Great Service, and others. This choir was no less enterprising in the field of contemporary music, in fact Newman found himself called upon to conduct anything from Palestrina to Vaughan Williams. Usually some six or more concerts were given in a year, and some remarkably fine works appeared in their progammes, including several that had been neglected by other choirs on account of their technical difficulty.

Armstrong College Choral and Orchestral Society, like all the other students' societies in this country, was inclined to have its ups and downs in those days, but it certainly did not lack enterprise. On one occasion, for instance, its members gave a concert performance of many scenes from Mussorgsky's " Boris Godounov " in the original version. It had at that time just been revived at Sadler's Wells.

For a number of years, too, Newman ran a flourishing students' madrigal society whose work covered a wide range of the finest English madrigals. He told me that Newcastle made a deep impression upon him because of its wealth of keen amateur musicians. The weekly Informal Music Recitals at the College were contributed by professionals and amateurs alike, who performed all types of music according to the particular scheme of the programmes. They did that astonishing set of nine four-part Fantasies by Purcell, for instance, the early quartets of Mozart, the Clavier Concertos of C. P. E. Bach, and the Clementi Sonatas; not to mention first performances of works by local composers, the highways of one or another of the classical or modern composers, and the by-ways of others. Professional chamber music concerts were promoted by the Newcastle Chamber Music Society. For many years Newman contributed the programme notes for their concerts, making so extravagant a demand on the printer's type and the audience's patience that he felt he justified Joachim's observation to Brahms that in this country the programmes often amount to a small book!

During his last year at Newcastle he was the conductor of a string orchestra of sixteen players known as the Newcastle String Players. They had been formed by Dr. S. L. L. Russell, and Newman helped them to continue their good work by giving with them a number of recitals and C.E.M.A. concerts in the Newcastle vicinity.

It would be impossible for me to detail all Professor Newman's other musical activities in that northern city, but I ought to refer briefly to his work as a pianist, because being severely restricted by the exceptionally small size of his hands, he has been obliged to confine his "public" repertoire to such composers as the Bachs, Mozart, Beethoven, Scarlatti and suchlike. It would, however, be very wrong to deduce from this fact that his taste is limited.

One last word about Newcastle. The last two or three rehearsals before each of the Bach Choir concerts were almost like miniature musical festivals in themselves, and Newman has very happy memories of the great assortment of personalities who helped to make everything so enjoyable. Enthusiasm ran very high and became most infectious. On one occasion his money went rolling all over the floor after he had made an almost superhuman effort to convince doubting fiddlers about Bach's intentions regarding a famous aria in the " St. Matthew Passion." At the end of the day there was invariably a jolly musical party " to wash down one good wine of music with another "; and there one might have met with anything from Harold Samuel's parlour trick of sitting on the floor and playing Bach fugues over his shoulders, to a Brahms String Sextet in full swing. There was at least one occasion when claret and clarinet quintets became inextricably mixed.

In 1940 Sidney Newman was appointed to the Reid Chair of Music at Edinburgh University in succession to the late Sir Donald Tovey. Associated with this is the Reid Symphony Orchestra, founded by Tovey in 1916, a professional orchestra of resident players, so Newman naturally became its conductor.

It must not be supposed, however, that the Orchestra's work is necessarily confined to the activities of the University. The position is that the Professor either conducts himself or appoints a deputy, and the rehearsals are attended by the music students as part of their course. For many years, eight concerts a season was the normal practice. During the last three years the number of concerts given has been twelve, eight and twenty-four respectively. Wartime conditions and regulations have raised increasingly difficult problems, but owing to the universal shortage of competent players, a clear-cut policy for the Orchestra as a body of resident professional players cannot be settled until after the war.

*   *   *

Newman believes that the amateur musicians are the backbone of English music—particularly in the provinces, and therefore their musical activities are just as important as professional concert-giving. Their work often reaches a very high standard, and one frequently finds in it a freshness and vitality that is too often a minus quality in professional work. For this reason, and because the amateurs invariably form the most enthusiastic and appreciative of audiences at professional concerts, their efforts should receive every possible encouragement.

Professor Newman feels strongly that the public must be taught not only to expect a high standard of performance in the concert hall, but what really constitutes this standard, because so many people seem to be unable to detect perfection in music: they are apt to be misled by technique and highly-coloured work, and consequently never learn to appreciate a really artistic performance. (I am reminded of a certain church choir in which the general opinion was that nothing was any good unless it was very loud and very slick.) The younger listeners of today are certainly becoming more critical, but we must see that their criticisms are based on the right standards.

He welcomes the various groups that promote ensemble playing, and notes with satisfaction their ever-widening interests, but he deplores the lack of organisations for the promotion of song. "People have no idea of the wealth of song that still has not yet been explored," he told me, "I feel that our musical life will not be healthy until the art of song is put in its proper place in this country."

109

Of the composers of today he is very hopeful, and he is glad to see that they are generally aware of the possibilities of writing music for instruments. He hopes that the established musical organizations will do more to acquaint the public with contemporary music, and to help our composers to understand the particular types of audiences for whom they are writing.

The twentieth-century composer, Newman declares, is subject to such diverse and long-range influences in the environment in which he lives and works that he tends to become eclectic, or to be so markedly original that his work is unintelligible to the ordinary people and of little use outside the contemporary music groups.

Newman also wishes that the orchestras and choirs that pride themselves on the amount of new music they perform would realize that it is not the *first* performance of a work that counts, but the second, third and fourth, because the general public rarely appreciate anything modern the first time they hear it.

* * *

When he is on holiday, Newman frequently takes a " 'bus-man's holiday" by visiting various chamber music circles. His chief recreation is walking, which is associated with a keen interest in old roads and tracks, bridges and churches, particularly when they can be explored with the aid of old maps. His enthusiasm for English verse was shared by the smaller ensembles, including the more unusual combinations of his wife, whom he married in 1940, and lost tragically three years later.

Since 1940 he has held a commission in the Territorial Army as a gunner, and has been assisting in the training of University cadets.

His compositions consist almost entirely of his early songs, but he has made a few excellent transcriptions, including one of the lesser known of the two Mozart Fantasias in F minor.

CLARENCE RAYBOULD

THERE must be very few people in this country who have never heard the announcement " The BBC Orchestra conducted by Clarence Raybould . . . ," so any sort of introduction from me would be superfluous.

He is fifty-eight, a native of Birmingham. At King Edward's School in that city he distinguished himself not in music but in languages, for in those days music rarely entered into the curricula of our secondary schools. He started to learn to play the piano at the age of six, and in twelve months made his first public appearance in a pupils' concert.

On leaving school he became a junior clerk at the Birmingham and Midland Institute, an educational establishment which provided classes in languages, commercial subjects, literature and music, and which later became affiliated to Birmingham University. At the end of his first six months they told him that he was not much good, and he would probably have left but for the fact that Granville Bantock had become interested in him. Bantock at that time was in charge of the Institute's musical activities and had observed the keenness with which Raybould attended the music classes after his daily work in the office. Consequently, on learning of Raybould's failure as a clerk, he offered him a little job as a sort of general factotum at ten shillings a week.

That was how Clarence Raybould got to his feet upon the first rung of the musical ladder. He acted as an accompanist, looked after the music and made himself generally useful. A free studentship enabled him to make rapid progress with his studies, and in but a little while he was playing either the French horn or the percussion in the orchestra.

Raybould's improving technique at the piano then made him decide to specialize in accompaniment, and he became the regular pianist at the students' fortnightly concerts. After a few years, he accepted a position on the Institute's teaching staff, and took classes in the rudiments of music, harmony, form and orchestration. He also began to accept public engagements as a pianist at local concerts. His first was at Walsall, where he received the princely fee of seven and sixpence for playing a Mendelssohn Trio at sight!

111

When the Chair of Music was established at Birmingham University, Elgar became the first professor, but was succeeded shortly afterwards by Sir Granville Bantock, who encouraged Raybould to study for a degree in music. The diligence with which he worked for it was rewarded by his earning the distinction of becoming the first Bachelor of Music of Birmingham University.

Raybould was also attracted to the organ in those days. He used to play at the Unitarian Church in which the Chamberlain family worshipped, and became a Fellow of the Royal College of Organists in 1912 or thereabouts.

In 1916 he joined the army. He became a private in the Artists Rifles, but was later commissioned in the Shropshire Light Infantry. He took part in many heavy engagements with the enemy in France but apart from slight gas poisoning towards the end of the war, he came to no harm. At the end of the war he resumed his musical activities. immediately, in fact he was still in uniform when he joined the Beecham Opera Company as an assistant conductor and coach. One of his greatest ambitions was fulfilled when Beecham occasionally allowed him to conduct complete performances. With Julius Harrison and Eugene Goossens, his co-assistants. he toured the provinces and gradually learned the Company's entire repertoire.

When the Beecham Opera Company dissolved, Raybould became one of the British National Opera Company's guest conductors, and spent the rest of his time in building up his reputation as an accompanist. Lionel Powell became interested in him, and because of his excellent knowledge of languages, arranged for him to accompany many of the distinguished foreign singers who visited this country.

In 1922 he was engaged to conduct "Lilac Time" at the Lyric Theatre, Shaftesbury Avenue, but after a while he gave it up because he could not endure the intolerable repetition day after day. For the next twelve months he conducted " The Beggar's Opera " at the Lyric, Hammersmith.

Raybould was playing at the Albert Hall one Sunday afternoon in 1924 when during the interval Lionel Powell confronted him and asked if he would be prepared to go to Australia *that week* on a tour as an accompanist and solo pianist! He blinked in astonishment for a moment, thought very quickly, and accepted the offer on the spot. Two or three days later he set out with Bratza, the eminent violinist, and Charles Hackett, the famous American tenor.

Two of his outstanding memories of that tour are of his visit to Sydney, where he received an invitation to lunch in the Commodore's

CLARENCE RAYBOULD

KATHLEEN RIDDICK

flagship (the ship's band greeted him with a selection from "Lilac Time"!) and of an evening in Melbourne when he sat down to play the piano and the pedals fell off!

Clarence Raybould then became interested in film music and was the first musician in this country to be engaged as a conductor for a sound film. At that time, however, he was still making the greater part of his income as a pianist and accompanist.

In 1933 Sir Landon Ronald invited him to take over the opera and orchestral classes at the Guildhall School of Music, and in the same year he received his first engagement with the BBC as a guest conductor. As time went on he did more and more work with the various BBC orchestras until in 1936 he was offered a position on the musical staff. This meant giving up his position at the Guildhall School of Music, but it led eventually to his appointment as Chief Assistant Conductor of the BBC Symphony Orchestra, the position he still holds. Now, of course, the bulk of his work is with the BBC, though he still conducts outside concerts occasionally.

By special arrangement with the BBC he went to Copenhagen, Oslo and Stockholm in 1937 to conduct a series of broadcast concerts of British music, and in the following year made a similar tour to Munich, Prague and Hamburg. His fluent French, German and Italian enabled him to converse freely with the members of all the orchestras he had to conduct—a great advantage, of course—though when he was in Prague he found difficulty in conveying his wishes to the first clarinet who seemed quite unable to understand requests made in any of these languages. Finally, the player stood up and said in the twangiest American: " Say, Mr. Raybould, I guess I don't unnerstand yer accent: why don't yuh speak plain English?" Apparently he had been born in Czechoslovakia, but had spent all his life in the United States.

Raybould went to Nantes in 1939 on behalf of the British Council to conduct an Anglo-French concert, and was genuinely surprised when the members of the Schola Cantorum there asked for Purcell's "Dido and Aeneas!" It was sung in French and was very well received.

He went with the BBC Symphony Orchestra to Bristol at the outbreak of hostilities in the same year, and conducted the first concert of the war. In less than twelve months he went to Stockholm and Oslo again by air to conduct a further series of concerts of British music. He left Oslo only a few days before the Germans marched in!

*   *   *

A genial personality without the slightest trace of affectation, Clarence Raybould is popular wherever musicians are gathered together.

He has strong views on musical matters and isn't afraid to express them. In the various discussions I had with him he expressed some concern over the fact that conducting is apparently becoming a cult with people who wish to bask in the limelight of musical eminence without bothering to make themselves practical musicians. One finds it in amateur as well as professional circles, and it is becoming a menace. It is so much more easy to adopt a supercilious manner and wave a stick about than it is to sit for hours at a piano perfecting one's execution of a Chopin Ballade. Not for one moment would Raybould wish to dissuade those who feel they have a flair for conducting, but he insists that no man should dare to attempt to conduct a professional orchestra unless he could at least take a choral rehearsal playing an accompaniment on the piano. He considers that as a rule a conductor should not be given professional engagements unless he could, if necessary, earn a living as a practical instrumentalist. Conducting is an art that cannot really be taught, and there are far too many young people being induced to take lessons or to attend conducting classes when they ought to be learning to be practical musicians. Moreover, we must see that young people don't get the foolish idea possessed by some people that conducting is an easy way to fame. As in any other form of serious musical activity, you have to sweat at it if you are going to be really successful.

Raybould believes that there was a decadent streak in composition between the two world wars, but he is now confident that our younger composers have begun to see the necessity for feeling, warmth and beauty in music, and that they will not be tempted to indulge in mere exhibitions of their cleverness. Although the modern tendency is towards complexity, Raybould feels that in most cases a new composition should be able to make a favourable impression in some way at its first hearing. He hates dullness in music.

He thinks that in their eagerness to criticize, many people are apt to overlook the tremendous advantages they now enjoy through radio. So much is taken for granted nowadays. For this reason, he particularly appreciates the many letters he receives from the most distant corners of the earth from people who are finding great joy in the BBC Overseas broadcasts.

An interesting point that came out in our talks was that from what he has learnt from his travels abroad, Raybould maintains that here in Britain we know far more about the music of other countries than they know about the music of their neighbours. This is all the more true in the case of contemporary music. Another point in our favour is that from his experiences abroad he has come to the conclusion that the standard of our orchestral playing is second to none.

He gets exasperated when people start talking about the high technique of certain jazz players and composers. The flashy bits of "swing" that people say are so brilliant are really most commonplace. There is nothing clever in them, and any capable " straight " musician could produce stuff like it without the slightest difficulty.

If you want to get Raybould really worked up, however, tackle him on the subject of the guying and " adaptation " of the classics for jazz purposes. The jolly smile disappears and a glint of goriest murder comes into his eyes. I shudder to think what would happen if he ever caught a jazz-merchant in the act!

That reminds me, too, that he is not at all happy about the way good music is so often hacked about for ballet dancing. Symphonies are most unsuitable for ballet, and the way they are chopped up comes very near to vandalism. There is plenty of good suitable music available, so why is there this passion for pulling about music that does not readily lend itself to the purpose? He told me that he once attended a rehearsal of a ballet using a Beethoven symphony. At the beginning of the Allegro movement, the director stopped the conductor and told him to take it much slower, because the dancing could not be done at the speed indicated by the composer!

.Raybould is a great admirer of the work of Walt Disney, and notes with great satisfaction that in the making of his films the utmost respect is shown for the music.

Finally, a word about the use of music in radio plays. He appreciates the necessity for music, but objects strongly to the use of odd chunks of the classics, especially when a few bars are "squirted in" as part of some "effect." From all points of view it would be far better if music were specially written for radio plays—as occasionally it is.

KATHLEEN RIDDICK

❧

So many people look upon conducting as an exclusively masculine career that I feel I must include a sketch of one of the very few women who are battling against the wall of prejudice. Whatever one's feelings are on this controversial subject, one cannot help admiring Miss Riddick for the remarkable effort she has made, and I am sure that there are very few who begrudge her the success she is now enjoying.

She was born in 1907, a native of Epsom, where her father, an enthusiastic amateur musician, conducted a local orchestra. Her mother was a professional pianist and gave every encouragement when as a child she showed marked ability at the piano. At the age of ten she started to learn to play the 'cello, and for some years afterwards made it her principal instrument.

One of her greatest joys as a girl was to attend her father's orchestral rehearsals, and her keen interest was rewarded when, soon after her sixteenth birthday, he allowed her to deputize for him during an illness. She had by that time already completed her first two years at the Guildhall School of Music, and was so obviously capable as a conductor that in a couple of years he let her take over the orchestra completely, so that he could play the double bass in it instead.

At the Guildhall School she did no conducting, chiefly because it was thought that the subject would be of no use to a woman. The 'cello was her principal study, with the piano a subsidiary. She frequently played in chamber music and made her first broadcast as a member of the Serre Trio soon after Broadcasting House was opened.

In 1932 she formed the Surrey String Players and got her first regular experience as a conductor. Dame Ethel Smyth became the Patron of this ensemble, and took a keen interest in its progress.

The first real encouragement Miss Riddick received from a male member of her profession was when she went to the Royal Manchester College of Music for a short conductor's course. Mr. R. J. Forbes, the Principal, advised her to specialize in conducting and suggested that she should go to Salzburg for a further course of training. This came as a complete surprise to her because she had grown quite accustomed to being told that a woman had no earthly chance of making any sort of progress as a conductor.

116

While she was in Manchester she had the privilege of conducting the Hallé Orchestra for a little while during the course, and received many favourable comments from its members afterwards, so she decided to take Mr. Forbes' advice and go to Salzburg to complete her training under such eminent conductors as Bruno Walter, Nikolai Malko and Paumgartner.

On her return to England in 1938 she found herself faced with the problem common to all conductors in the earlier stages of their careers: the absence of an adequate orchestra with which to work; so she founded the London Women's String Orchestra, the first all-professional women's orchestra this country had ever known. Of this there is a story to be told.

When she announced her intention of establishing this Orchestra, her friends with one accord began to dissuade her, because they felt sure that with no wealthy "backer" to guarantee the inevitable losses, such a venture would be doomed to failure. She persisted, however, and after lengthy auditions chose eighteen first-class professional players to whom she explained her scheme. These women, accustomed to working against the prejudices of audiences, conductors and concert-agents, supported her whole-heartedly. They booked the Aeolian Hall, London, and gave a first concert which was acclaimed by all the critics as an outstanding success. Representatives of the BBC were present, and received a very favourable impression.

But good press notices cannot be used to pay one's expenses, and after meeting her liabilities, Miss Riddick found herself quite unable to finance the plans she had made to proceed with the establishment of the Orchestra, She told her players quite frankly of the difficulties before her, and to her astonishment and delight, they all offered to subscribe towards the expenses of the next concert. This was a splendid start, and before very long they were booking provincial tours. They broadcast for the first time in April, 1939, but within six months the war had put a stop to everything as far as they were concerned.

*   *   *

In the general resurrection of music, Miss Riddick was one of the first to get back to work. After a while C.E.M.A. was established, and by making limited grants against losses, provided the London Women's String Orchestra with as much work as they could conveniently manage, including engagements to play in Durham, Gloucester, Canterbury and Rochester cathedrals. The Orchestra also gave several concerts at the National Gallery with Dame Myra Hess.

Few conductors show more consideration for contemporary composers than Miss Riddick: her programmes often contain an unusually large proportion of new music. At a concert given in May, 1940, for instance, we find first performances of works by Bohuslav Martinu, Arnold Cooke, Henk Badings, and Victor Yates. At another concert in September, 1943, with Leon Goossens, she gave the first performance of Rutland Boughton's Oboe Concerto No. 2, and of the " Fantasie for Strings " which Alec Rowley had specially composed for the London Women's String Orchestra.

The strength of prejudice has now made her change the name of the ensemble to " The Riddick String Orchestra," by the way, because the feminine title used hitherto was the cause of their losing several engagements!

They have played in many quite remote parts of the country in the course of their provincial tours. Miss Riddick will always remember how on one occasion she had to telephone the programme to the local parson so that he could get it printed in time for their arrival. On entering the village hall she discovered that they had been billed to play, among other things, a " Sweet in Sea."

*   *   *

Kathleen Riddick's standing as a conductor was appropriately recognised by the BBC when they invited her to conduct the BBC Orchestra on November 23rd, 1943: an honour of which she may justly feel proud. I ought to add, too, that she has frequently conducted the Croydon Symphony Orchestra, a semi-professional body formed by Coleridge-Taylor and conducted for many years by W. H. Reed.

Her chief demand is that in the musical profession women should be judged entirely upon their merits. Although so much is said about women's equality nowadays, she still finds a solid barrier of prejudice in most musical circles, particularly when appointments are being made. It certainly looks as if the mantle of the late Dame Ethel Smyth has fallen upon Miss Riddick, for she never ceases in her struggle for the proper recognition of women as musicians.

She was married in 1934 to Mr. George Bixley, an accomplished amateur viola player. Their home is at Epsom, Surrey, and they now have a baby daughter.

STANFORD ROBINSON

※

V ERY few people at the BBC ever speak of " Mr. Stanford Robinson ". he is just " Robbie,"—" a splendid fellow," " a perfect darling," " such a nice young man," " a jolly decent chap," or " rather a pet," according to the sex and disposition of the speaker.

I should imagine that plenty of people in Leeds are proud to claim that he was born in their city in 1904, the son of a well-known local organist. He was called " Stanford," by the way, after C. V. Stanford, one of his father's favourite composers. At the age of five he could already play the piano tolerably well, but much as he liked the instrument, he never wished to become a virtuoso: the piano did not give him sufficient scope. So he haunted the bandstands in all the public parks in Leeds enviously watching the pompous-looking conductors of the military bands. Symphony concerts in those days were a rarity.

When the family moved to London he was quick to take full advantage of the new opportunities he found there. By the time he was fifteen he had conducted an orchestral piece of his own composition in public and had assembled and trained an amateur orchestra which met in the Robinsons' drawing room every Wednesday evening to rehearse. Instead of objecting to the noise as most parents would have done, Robbie's people gave him every encouragement: his father bought a clarinet and learned to play it so that he could fill a yawning gap in the woodwind, and his mother provided them all with supper afterwards—a rash undertaking if there were many appetites as good as young Robinson's. What the neighbours thought of this amateur orchestra isn't our concern.

Stanford Robinson left school just at this time, after a slight difference of opinion with the headmaster: he was unable to see eye to eye with the scholastic gentleman on the subject of home-work. Resolving to make a career in music by fighting his way up from the bottom, he got a job as a cinema pianist, but soon passed on to better positions in one or two of the London hotel orchestras. Within three years he was at the Royal College of Music studying conducting under Sir Adrian Boult, who did a great deal to help him.

The experience he had gained with his amateur orchestra proved to be of the greatest value, for during his first term at the College he distinguished himself by conducting Gluck's opera Orpheus." Later, he surprised everybody by conducting " Hänsel and Gretel " entirely from memory and by getting many invitations to conduct performances of " The Beggar's Opera " at the Lyric Theatre, Hammersmith.

In 1924 came his golden opportunity—a chance to join the BBC. The position offered was not of any great importance, but he could see the vast possibilities that lay beyond; so he applied, and was engaged on a month's probation as an assistant to Stanton Jefferies, then the Director of Music. He still recalls his first day at Savoy Hill: " It was a Monday, and I arrived all bright and eager. . . . . I was shown into a room in which there was a desk with nice clean blotting paper, pen and ink. In the same room was K. A. Wright with his secretary, Dorothy Wood; and in an adjoining room sat Rex Palmer, the London Station Director.

" I sat down at my desk hopefully. Nothing happened. Somebody brought me a diary in which I wrote my name. At about eleven o'clock somebody brought me coffee, and at one o'clock, nothing having happened, I went out to lunch. I came back refreshed, and ready for instant action. Still there was nothing to do. Tea came at about four o'clock, but after that, nobody seemed to want me. There appeared to be nothing in broadcasting for me to do, and I was almost in despair when Dorothy Wood came to me at about 5.30 and asked if I was busy. Receiving an eager negative reply, she said ' Mr. Kenneth Wright would be awfully grateful if you would do a little job for him.' 'Delighted,' I said, 'What is it?' 'Would you be so kind as to ring up the booking office at Charing Cross and ask the price of a season ticket to Richmond?' That was my first day's work at the BBC. That was in 1924, of course, and things are very different to-day. However, by the end of the first week I was caught up in the toils of broadcasting, and I've never lost the thrill of it."

Although he conducted several programmes during his first few weeks, including one on St. Patrick's Day, March 17th, he was told at the end of the month that his services were no longer required as he was not of the " right type." Very crestfallen, he conveyed the news to Stanton Jefferies, who subsequently arranged that he should take over the job of engaging touring artists. This kept him on the staff. In those days, artists were booked for a week at a time and made a tour of all the BBC stations : Bournemouth, Cardiff, Birmingham, Manchester, Glasgow, Aberdeen and Newcastle; and it was Robinson's job to keep a series of artists constantly going around, and to fit them in at the convenience of the local station directors.

Then, as a side-line, they gave him the job of training the London Operatic Choir, a semi-professional body who used to swell the chorus at Covent Garden. This was the first choir to be used by the BBC for its studio productions. In the spring and summer of 1924 it rehearsed about once a week and appeared every six or eight weeks in either "studio opera" or musical comedies. By the end of the summer the demand for choruses in studio productions had grown so much that it was decided to form a professional BBC Chorus, and Stanford Robinson, being the last of a long line of Yorkshire choir-trainers, was made responsible for it, despite his youth.

The London Wireless Chorus, as it was then called, was formed by him in October, 1924, with about twenty voices. Robinson's first job was to rehearse them for their microphone début, a performance of "The Immortal Hour," but they did comparatively little until early in 1925, when they began rehearsing twice a week, and took part in the religious services broadcast from the studios. Their first big oratorio broadcast was a performance of " The Creation " in February of that year.

Then he gradually developed the Chorus with daily rehearsals, so that its work could be extended. One of its greatest operatic achievements was when augmented to eighty voices it sang under the conductorship of Albert Coates in a performance of " Kitesh " at Covent Garden. On July 5th, 1925, a small section of the Chorus sang a closing hymn to a Sunday programme, and this proved to be the forerunner of the Epilogue. During this year, eight singers were selected from the Chorus to specialize in the study of madrigals and part-songs, and thus were born the Wireless Singers, now known as the BBC Singers. " It was a wonderful team, and with some slight changes in personnel it worked with me for several years giving splendid performances of our great English heritage of choral music."

*　　*　　*

In his early days at the BBC, Stanford Robinson did a variety of odd jobs. On one occasion he deputized for an announcer, and owing to some sort of hitch he had to read a talk at sight. Not until he had got through the first couple of paragraphs did he realize that it was all about China and Taoist monks! He soon got into an appalling muddle with all the Chinese names, and afterwards this rather damped his ardour for " lending a hand," though he often arranged and announced programmes of new gramophone records.

In the autumn of 1925, October 23rd to be exact, Stanford Robinson conducted the orchestra in a broadcast entitled "The Disorderly Room," in which an almost unknown comedian featured. His name was—Tommy Handley!

Now, with his permission of course, I am going to let you peep into Robbie's private diary to see an entry made at the end of that year:

" Mon. 21st Dec.

I began to rehearse the Masked Carol Singers, a lot of West End socialites (?) who got together to go round the West End private houses and hotels to sing carols in aid of charity, each evening at a different house, finishing with supper. I had had so much caviare and champagne by Christmas Eve that I got gastritis and jaundice, and was away ill for nearly a month."

This probably accounted for:

" Wed. 23rd Dec.

I conducted a programme including 'Three Carols' by Peter Warlock. I was taken violently ill at the end of the second one, . . . rushed outside the studio while the announcer was introducing the third, . . . was sick . . . conducted the third, and then passed out and was taken home in a car."

*   *   *

On a memorable evening in 1927, Stanford Robinson was called upon at twenty-four hours' notice to conduct "Tannhäuser" for Percy Pitt, who had suddenly been taken ill. This led him into one of the tightest spots he has ever been in, for he had arranged to conduct the BBC Male Chorus that week at the Astoria Cinema (in Charing Cross Road) in a "scena" in which they had to appear as pirates and sing sea-shanties. One of these performances had to be fitted in during the interval between the broadcast of the first and second acts of "Tann-hauser," an arrangement made possible by having a taxi waiting for him. The chorus had a little more time in which to get back to the studio because they were not required immediately at the opening of Act II. On this particular evening, however, the stage show over-ran, and Robbie found the red light flashing madly when he got back to the studio. Shortly before the entry of the male chorus, not a single man had returned from the cinema, and poor old Robinson was almost frantic! It looked as if the opera would be a fiasco. Suddenly, about ten bars before the Knights of Thuringia had to enter, the studio door opened and in walked "a most awful-looking gang of cut-throats, still with their make-up on and wearing their costumes, doubtless having thought it more important that they should quench their piratical thirsts before the next performance. . . ." In a few seconds they were singing with knightly dignity "Hail, bright abode"—and Robbie breathed again.

The National Chorus was established in 1928, when the need for a full-sized choral society of its own made the BBC seek the help of two hundred and fifty keen amateur singers. A little publicity brought well over six thousand applications, and to Stanford Robinson and Ernest B. Wood (who was to be the Secretary of the Chorus) fell the task of choosing suitable voices: eighty sopranos, fifty-five contraltos, fifty tenors and sixty-five basses.

After extensive "weeding out," about a thousand possible candidates remained, all of whom had to be tested very carefully; so there started the greatest audition the BBC has ever held. The applicants were nearly all horribly nervous: some bleated timidly, others bawled their heads off, and quite a number took fright at the very door of the studio and fled!

Hour after hour Robinson and Wood sat there patiently giving them "marks" for quality, volume, resonance and steadiness; disqualifying people with wobbly voices and bad intonation, and gently dissuading those who couldn't read music but were quite sure that they could " pick it up by ear."

Ultimately, the final selection was made, and the chosen singers had to undertake to rehearse every Friday evening, to " work hard with concentration and enthusiasm," to remain in their own choral society or to join one of the other recognized choral bodies immediately, and to appear suitably dressed at the concerts. All this without payment of any kind; and then people say that we aren't a musical nation!

Stanford Robinson assembled them all for their first rehearsal in a hall near Covent Garden, and tried them out on Parry's "Blest Pair of Sirens." As he raised his baton he found himself wondering what his great assortment of voices drawn from all parts of London and the Home Counties would sound like, but in five minutes he was convinced that the National Chorus would become one of the finest choral societies the country had ever known. Their first performance was of a setting of " The Pilgrim's Progress " by Sir Granville Bantock.

* * *

Now let's look at Robbie's diary again:

" Mon. 13th Feb. (1928):
Sir Edward German conducted a performance of his own 'Merrie England.' We had many talks previously, and I came to know him very well. I remember on this occasion although he rehearsed everything very carefully, he spoilt much of it at the performance by getting excited and taking every-thing at quite a different *tempo* from that on which he had insisted at the rehearsals."

" Thurs. 10th May.
A chorus rehearsal of ' Oedipus Rex ' with Stravinsky. I was
astonished at his appearance, . . . with his little moustache
and spectacles. He was very punctilious about his music being
performed without what he called expression. We all found
this very difficult to do, and thought he was a bit mad in
wanting us to do it."

" Tues. 17th July:
I was roped in to conduct an orchestral session for Columbia
with Eva Turner at the small Central Hall. She recorded her
famous aria from 'Turandot,' and 'O mia Patria' ('Aida'). The
success of this session led to my being frequently engaged by
Columbia for a long time after this. They were busy re-
making their catalogue electrically, and I often conducted three
sessions a week. In this way I came to meet practically all
the well-known English singers and a great many Covent
Garden stars who made records while they were over here."

*   *   *

Do you remember the Bach Cantatas that at one time were broadcast on Sundays? Over a hundred of them were conducted by Stanford
Robinson, but despite the excellent standard of the performances, a
large section of the public complained bitterly about them. Actually,
the controversy was really about the dullness of the Sunday programmes,
and the Bach Cantatas were made the scapegoats: a great pity, because
in many people's minds the name of Bach became a synonym for
dullness.

In 1932 Stanford Robinson was made conductor of the BBC Theatre
Orchestra, which meant, of course, that he had to give up much of his
choral work. He increased the number of players in the Orchestra and
made it into a first-class ensemble. Rehearsals went on for hours on
end; nothing but everybody's best would satisfy him, and light music—
normally taken for granted and just given a " run through "—was
rehearsed in as much detail as if it were a symphony. For example,
Viennese waltzes were played so perfectly that when Julius Bürger of
Vienna came over to conduct his Strauss-Lanner potpourri, he exclaimed
in real astonishment " But you play waltzes exactly like a Viennese
orchestra!" Later, the son of a great French writer of waltzes said that
not since his father's death had he heard waltzes played as he wanted
them until he heard the BBC Theatre Orchestra under Stanford
Robinson.

When in 1934 Robbie married Miss Lorely Dyer, the members of
the Orchestra presented their conductor and his wife with a cocktail
cabinet and an extra-special goldfish to add to his aquarium. The bride-
groom, of course, had to make the observation that a cocktail cabinet

was very much like marriage: the trouble being not in the initial outlay but in the cost of its upkeep.

Over the following Christmas, Stanford Robinson trod heavily on one of Sir Thomas Beecham's pet corns by broadcasting an abridged version of " Hänsel and Gretel." The newspapers came out on New Year's Day in a rash of " slashing attacks " on the BBC, in which Sir Thomas described the performance as " a complete travesty, a monstrous perversion of the opera, and the most ineffable piece of impudence ever perpetrated." But if you, my patient reader, imagine that I am going to get involved in this controversy, I am afraid you are going to be disappointed. Needless to say, the newspapers had their fun out of it, and then proceeded to display their magnanimity by printing correspondence in defence of both sides of the argument.

In any case, this spot of bother did not prevent the BBC from choosing Stanford Robinson for the position of Director of Opera when in 1936 it planned a new operatic department with the aid of Sir Landon Ronald. In May of that year he was relieved of general duties at Broadcasting House so that he could make a study of opera in this country. Then in the following July they sent him abroad on a grand tour to study opera in Salzburg, Zurich, Paris, Turin, Rome, Milan, Naples, Bayreuth, Berlin, Vienna and Budapest.

The first full opera production by Stanford Robinson's new Music Productions Unit, as it was called, was broadcast in January, 1938. It was Massenet's " Manon," with Maggie Teyte, Heddle Nash, Roy Henderson and Denis Noble; a fine performance which ran for its scheduled two hours without interruption. (To be exact, 1 hour 59 minutes and 40 seconds; thereby establishing a standard for good timing, in which the Music Productions Unit still takes great pride.)

Afterwards, Robbie and the cast were invited out to a supper party to celebrate the event. Driving there in his car he was "gonged" by the "courtesy cops," and the following dialogue ensued:

1st Cop: " Excuse me, sir, but are you aware that you have been driving through the park at more than twenty miles an hour?

S.R.: " I am very sorry. I am afraid I hadn't realised it."

1st Cop: "And are you also aware that you have been driving through a built-up area at more than thirty miles an hour?"

S.R.: "I am very sorry. I hadn't realised it."

2nd Cop: "And is he aware that his car licence is out of date?"

S.R.: "I am very sorry, I know the new licence isn't on the car, but I have it at home."

1st Cop: " I suppose you haven't a driving licence, have you?"

S.R.: " Not here, I'm afraid."

1ST COP: " What about a certificate of insurance?"

S.R.: " I'm afraid I haven't got that either!"

2ND COP: " Well, I must say, you have made a thorough job of it. Have you any explanation?"

S.R.: " I have just been conducting my first big studio opera for the BBC, and I'm afraid I'm just a little bit excited."

1ST COP: " Well, all right, but don't let it happen again. Good-night."

*   *   *

I should like to give some details of the many operatic successes that Stanford Robinson has had since that time, but unfortunately my space is limited, and in any case a mere catalogue of different operas would not be very exciting. Moreover, the fact that Stanford Robinson has appeared frequently as a conductor at Covent Garden, Sadler's Wells and in the provinces proves that his reputation is not confined to studio work.

Early in 1939 his left eye was injured by a piece of grit, and a delicate operation had to be performed. Within a week he insisted upon conducting a Strauss programme that he had previously arranged, but his medical advisers refused to remove the shades from his eyes. So he got a friend to take him to Broadcasting House, and then conducted the entire programme blindfold!

A few days later he left by air to conduct in Stockholm the Broadcasting Symphony Orchestra. It took him several days to convince them that he could see normally with his left eye. He also visited Rome to conduct the E.I.A.R. (Broadcasting) Orchestra, and remembers with special pride the ovation he received from the players after he had conducted them in a Rossini overture. " Many of them left their seats and came up to the rostrum to shake me by the hand with cries of ' Brava, maestro, Bravissimo!' It was most touching. Later I conducted them in some English music, and their delight in it and enthusiasm for it was a joy to see."

When war broke out, Stanford Robinson's department was moved to Evesham, where the BBC had taken a large house and converted it for broadcasting. You will no doubt remember all the cracks about "Hogsnorton," and the stories about the staff cycling to work through country lanes, and so forth, because the newspapers found plenty of " copy " in the rustication of the BBC. After a while, as most people know, they left Evesham for "somewhere else in the country."

In more recent years, Robbie has had another string to his bow: the BBC Theatre Chorus, which has been extremely popular in the Forces programme.

Tall, dark, energetic, and needless to say, very good-looking, Stanford Robinson has a vigorous style of conducting. He believes there is a tremendous future for broadcast opera. " I am after the ordinary man," he says, "through the medium of broadcasting. You see, I personally am a product of broadcasting: the studio is a second home to me."

He has some revolutionary views about studio opera which do not always meet with the approval of some of the older members of his profession, but time alone will prove whether or not his ideas are sound. For instance, he maintains that it is necessary to amend the text sufficiently to make it self-explanatory with the minimum of narration; so that listeners, depending entirely upon the ear, will be able to follow what is happening—who is going off and who is coming on, and how the plot is developing.

Of course, if television develops quickly after the war and becomes universally popular, everything will be changed, and then there will be truly wonderful scope for broadcast opera, though as Robbie said rather ruefully when I discussed it with him, " It will introduce new complications which do not trouble us at present." I thought of stout sopranos and short tenors and changed the subject quickly.

Robinson wants to see the English language adopted generally in opera in this country, and he sees no reason why we should not become as appreciative of opera as they are in Italy.

He vigorously advocates the use of bigger orchestras for broadcasting, because many are still deficient in strings. The practice of using a large complement of wind instruments with a small string section, he tells me, is a relic of the early days of broadcasting when a large body of strings could not be broadcast effectively. This was chiefly because the use of a full-sized string section meant that the woodwind had to be moved too far away from the microphone to be effective; the " mikes " in those days not being sufficiently sensitive. Now, of course, the microphones have been vastly improved, so the difficulty does not arise. It is possible to broadcast a full-sized symphony orchestra without any serious danger of its balance being upset.

Another unfortunate legacy of the early days is the small type of studio. Small orchestras and small choirs required small studios; but now, much larger premises are needed, though because of the war it will probably be some time before they are provided. An interesting opinion that came out in our discussion was that the Queen's Hall and the St. George's Hall were both better for broadcasting than any studio in existence in this country!

Most of the " fit-up " studios being used by the BBC in the provinces to which the musical departments are (at the time of writing)

127

evacuated are too small for any great expansion of the orchestra at present. Moreover, with many of the younger men in the services, there is an acute shortage of first-rate players. Nevertheless, the tendency towards bigger orchestras is developing.

As we conversed on modern music, Stanford Robinson said he thought it was sad that so few works gave pleasure to both audience and performers. "The tragedy of it is that few of my contemporaries write symphonic music that can be enjoyed at its first hearing by the majority of musical people," he complained. "Even many of those who *do* listen to it seem to do so only out of a sense of duty: they feel they *ought* to give it a hearing, even if they gain little pleasure from it. But this problem is not merely one of the audience. Many an enterprising conductor can remember occasions when his orchestra has made it perfectly obvious to him at rehearsal that it neither likes nor understands the music over which he, through previous study, is enthusiastic. Of course, if the conductor himself is bored with it .

Robinson told me that he had been present at first performances of many modern works and had talked with the performers afterwards. "If that's modern music, I don't like it," "Awful stuff," "Couldn't make head nor tail of it " and " Let's hope it'll be the first and last performance " were typical of the remarks he had heard, particularly when the work had not been adequately rehearsed, for it is often only after much study that a conductor and his orchestra begin to enjoy a modern work. " How then can a layman enjoy it at first or second hearing?" Robinson asks, ". . . . and if he doesn't, how can he be persuaded to come and listen to it again and again until he does? There is the problem of modern music."

In lighter music, Robbie's chief complaint is that radio listeners listen too casually, otherwise they would not be continually writing to him requesting music that is already being performed with the utmost frequency. " People write asking why I never play any music by Strauss; yet this composer figures prominently in my programmes year after year. I can only conclude that these correspondents never bother to look at the 'Radio Times.' The whole trouble is that many people don't *plan* their listening: they still expect to be able to switch on their wireless at any time of the day and get precisely the sort of music they want."

Another interesting fact I gleaned during our talk was that there is infinitely more money in orchestrating popular music than in writing it! This seems extraordinary, but it is apparently true, because many of our best orchestrators *can* write music, but can't afford to do so.

STANFORD ROBINSON

[Howard Coster

MALCOLM SARGENT

There seems to be very little demand nowadays for new English musical shows in the theatres: revivals of such musical comedies as " The Maid of the Mountains " seem always to enjoy a preference. This tendency is worse in wartime, but Stanford Robinson thinks that the theatres will recover from it when peacetime conditions return, unless, of course, they are all to be dominated by business men whose *only* consideration is a certain and handsome profit.

*　　*　　*

Robbie's chief recreation in wartime is gardening. He is a keen horticulturist, and spends what little free time he gets on his allotment to produce the sort of vegetables that gladden the heart of every gardener. The easiest way to Robbie's heart is through a little practical advice on ridding his broad beans of blight.

In peacetime he is also an enthusiastic photographer, and never forgets to pack his camera whenever he goes abroad. And that reminds me that his dog, "Asti Spumanti," was named after the famous Italian champagne, for it was acquired shortly after the Robinsons returned from a holiday in Italy, and its antics reminded them of the sparkling vintage they had enjoyed in that country.

MALCOLM SARGENT

❧

A S a rule, I have to make one or two rather provocative statements before an orchestral conductor will talk freely at an interview. Before his players he may be a loquacious fellow, but put him alone with a writer for half an hour and he will generally require pumping. I say this because it explains my astonishment when Dr. Malcolm Sargent met me in the lounge of the Savoy. He swept in *con furioso*, jabbered away *molto vivace* for half an hour, and then suddenly swept out again, leaving in his wake a trail of swooning page boys. A distinct smell of scorch arose from the carpet as his retreating heels vanished from sight.

A native of the small South Lincolnshire town of Stamford, where his forbears had lived for five hundred years, he was born on April 29th, 1895, son of a keen amateur musician who was well known locally as a church organist. He became a choir boy, but singing did not attract him as much as the piano and organ, and throughout his time at Stamford School he longed to become an organist. So at quite an early age he took piano lessons from a local musician, who, as it happened, was responsible for his first appearance as a conductor.

His teacher was playing in the orchestra at a local performance of " The Gondoliers " and allowed Malcolm, then fourteen years of age, to be present at the rehearsals. The boy became acquainted with the music very quickly, and the golden opportunity occurred at the dress rehearsal when the conductor failed to appear. It was suggested very diffidently that perhaps " young Sargent " might carry on until the conductor arrived, so without further delay the schoolboy leapt up on to the rostrum, took up the baton and conducted the entire rehearsal with such ability that he became the talk of the town. In the same year he conducted the orchestra at a local pageant depicting the visit of Queen Elizabeth to Stamford, with equal success.

Continuing his studies to be an organist, he took the Associateship diploma of the Royal College of Organists in 1910, winning the Sawyer prize, and in the following year was articled to Dr. Keeton, the organist of Peterborough Cathedral. " I think those were the happiest years of my life," Dr. Sargent told me; ". . . for three years I was the assistant organist in that lovely Cathedral playing daily services, rehearsing with the fine choir, and studying under Dr. Keeton." Cathedral music moved him profoundly, and his most ambitious dream in those days was to become a cathedral organist with a magnificent organ and a professional choir of his own. I think there is little doubt that he would have achieved that ambition had not other opportunities led to even more attractive spheres of work.

He became a Bachelor of Music in 1914 and was appointed organist of Melton Mowbray Parish Church. As soon as he had settled in his new work he began to turn his attention to the general musical life of the town and surrounding districts. Within a few months he had organised several amateur operatic societies, musical societies and the like, and then extended his work to the city of Leicester, where he later founded the Leicester Symphony Orchestra.

*   *   *

After the Great War, during which he served in the 27th Durham Light Infantry, he took his doctorate and became a pupil of Moiseiwitsch. He also married Miss Eileen Harding Horne, of Drinkstone, Suffolk, in 1923. They have one son and a daughter.

The urge to compose began to take effect in those post-war days, and his "Impression on a Windy Day" came to the notice of Sir Henry Wood, who decided to perform it at one of his Promenade concerts, and invited Sargent to come to London to conduct it. After the work had been rehearsed and performed, Sir Henry could see a new career for Sargent, for in watching him handle the Queen's Hall Orchestra he had become convinced that the young Lincolnshire man was one of the most promising conductors in the country. In his typical fatherly way he urged Sargent to seek his fortune with the baton. Even the music critics declared that a brilliant young conductor had emerged from obscurity.

From that time his services were eagerly sought by choral societies and other musical organisations. The D'Oyly Carte Opera Company engaged him for two seasons in London, and it was in connection with this that the critics accused him of tampering with the orchestration. It was true that the orchestration he used was not that to which the public had become accustomed, but it happened to be the composer's original scoring! He had gone to a great deal of trouble to get the original orchestration, and it was no small credit to him to be able to show his critics just where their knowledge was lacking.

Then came engagements with the British National Opera Company, more requests from choral and operatic societies, an invitation to conduct the " Hiawatha" productions at the Royal Albert Hall, his appointment as conductor of the Llandudno orchestral season, and a dozen other offers. For three years he was associated with the Russian Ballet in London, and frequently appeared at Covent Garden.

One of the biggest contracts ever offered to him came from the management of a London cinema, who wanted him to play two ten-minute programmes a day for seven thousand pounds a year. To any young man this would have been a great temptation, but Sargent saw that if he started to play " popular " music in a cinema he would inevitably lose his prestige as a conductor of symphonic and other serious music, so he refused the offer.

Since 1926 he has been associated with The Gramophone Company Ltd. in the making of many records. His experience has also taken him into the world of films, for in 1931 he was chosen by British International Pictures to conduct their production of " Carmen."

*   *   *

The pace at which he was living and working was probably responsible for the breakdown which for a while stopped all his professional activity. His illness was a mystery to his medical advisers: he seemed to collapse for no specific reason apart from nervous strain, yet his condition became so serious that the possibility of recovery seemed doubtful. He was taken to Switzerland and for many weeks showed little sign of progress. Then he gradually regained strength and after a short period of convalescence his doctors allowed him to return to his work in London, but only on condition that he relaxed completely between rehearsals and concerts.

His musical tours abroad in the years that preceded the second world war took him as far afield as Jerusalem, where he conducted the Palestine Orchestra on several occasions, and Australia, where he gave a memorable series of concerts for the Australian Broadcasting Commission.

*   *   *

Since the outbreak of the present war Malcolm Sargent's greatest activity has been in taking music to the people who have suffered from aerial bombardment. He has toured Britain with most of our leading symphony orchestras and has given concerts in almost every city that has received the attention of the enemy.

When it became known that the Nazi propagandists were trying to woo the sympathy of the Swedish people by sending them their best symphony orchestras, the British Council asked Dr. Sargent if he would be prepared to fly to Stockholm to conduct a short series of concerts there. When he realised that this was an opportunity to assist in the promotion of good relations between our country and Sweden, and to introduce more British music to the Swedes, he accepted readily, even though it meant sacrificing a large number of engagements in this country.

132

He set out in a huge aeroplane that flew the greater part of the journey in the stratosphere—five miles above the earth's surface. It was a thrilling but decidedly chilly experience. Shortly before dawn they swept down from the clouds and saw the twinkling lights of a neutral country beneath them: they were approaching Stockholm.

Our " musical ambassador," as he was called, arrived just as the Berlin Philharmonic Orchestra were packing up after having given a concert in the city, and at his hotel he had the unique experience of sitting near Germans as they sat talking, with no great enthusiasm, about the war. He also remembers seeing a German troop train passing through one of the railway stations on its way to Finland. All the taxis, buses, cars and lorries were driven by gas produced in charcoal generators at their rear.

He found the Swedes a charming and friendly people. They entertained him lavishly and asked if everybody in England was as cheerful and confident as he, because they could not help noticing how very depressed the Germans were getting. Sargent was very impressed by the ease with which almost everybody spoke English: he discovered that it is taught in all the State schools in Sweden.

The Swedish orchestras were a delight to work with. They responded with an eagerness that left no doubt in his mind about their interest in English music. When he suggested that they should play William Walton's symphony, they said that they knew it so very well that they would prefer one of his more recent compositions! Their playing was of the highest quality—the perfect intonation of the woodwind was remarkable, and their excellent sight-reading enabled him to introduce several unfamiliar English works into his programmes.

At Gothenburg the Crown Prince and Prince Eugen attended Sargent's concerts, and the former declared that he had never heard the orchestra play better. The audiences cheered so much that it had to be explained to him that although much of the applause was for the performance and for English music generally, some of it was really for Winston Churchill!

He found that the new concert hall at Gothenburg was the answer to a musician's prayer. As far as acoustics and comfort are concerned, it is far nearer perfection than anything we have in this country.

The Swedish orchestras enjoy Government subsidies and give their concerts at prices within the means of everybody. Stockholm alone has two State Orchestras besides a State Ballet and Opera with fifty principals.

Of the English music he played in Sweden, Dr. Sargent found that the audiences preferred the works of Purcell, Delius, Vaughan Williams,

Benjamin Britten and Edmund Rubbra. Elgar's " Enigma Variations " drew tremendous applause whenever he played them.

While he was in Sweden, Sargent attended a luncheon at which he met most of that country's leading composers. In this way he learnt of many new Swedish compositions, which he has now studied with great interest. He is introducing several of them into the programmes he is now giving in Britain.

When he left, he received an invitation to make another visit as soon as he could conveniently do so, and to this was added a promise of eight concerts a month.

More recently, Malcolm Sargent has visited Portugal. Here, the members of the orchestra were overjoyed to find that he had arranged to introduce them to a dozen important works by British composers. At the rehearsals they used to express their delight by cheering him after every item that particularly pleased them!

*   *   *

Dr. Malcolm Sargent's vitality and seemingly limitless supply of energy is apparent more than ever in his conducting. Watch him during an *accelerando* passage when he is leading his orchestra up to a climax, and you get the impression of a fiery creature whipping up his fellows to burning fanaticism. Almost everything he does seems to be performed under nervous tension, yet he seems to thrive on it. He is remarkably successful with large choirs. When he is conducting the Royal Choral Society, for instance, or one of the big northern societies of which he is the conductor, he can hypnotize his singers into making a response that at times seems almost incredible.

His Saturday morning concerts for school children at the Central Hall, Westminster, have been an outstanding success. Through them, thousands of children have become inspired by great music, for not only have they heard it under ideal conditions, but they have also had it patiently explained to them in a manner that has caught their imagination.

Sargent believes that we need several more first-class orchestras in this country: there is room for at least eight in England alone. He favours subsidies for music because Britain must strive to make herself the centre of culture in the post-war world; otherwise she will disappear as far as art is concerned. The nation has become music-conscious during the past four years, and we must make the most of the great opportunities that this revival offers us.

ALEC SHERMAN

❧

I HAVE always found it interesting to watch the progress of our younger conductors as they make their way towards the front rank. Most of them have to struggle against heavy odds for years, unless they happen to be wealthy or possess very influential friends, because it is difficult to get adequate experience in professional symphonic work unless you can get an orchestra, and you can't get an orchestra until you have had plenty of experience, so . . . no, this isn't a conundrum, it's a simple statement of fact. There *are* just a few jobs that enterprising young men can get, but the scope they offer is often very limited, and in any case, there aren't half enough of them. Alec Sherman is one who seems to be overcoming his difficulties very well, and should have a good future before him.

He was born in London in 1907, and devoted the whole of his early life to the study of the violin. He was chosen for the BBC Symphony Orchestra when it was formed in 1930, and played in it for eight years under Sir Adrian Boult and the various distinguished guest conductors that were engaged from time to time. Having an acute sense of observation, he learnt from them the technique of conducting.

He had always been conscious of a desire to conduct, and confident in his ability to do so, left the Orchestra in 1938 to make a career for himself with a baton instead of a bow. It was anything but easy, because he had no immediate prospects of regular work, but he conducted the British Women's Symphony Orchestra for two seasons, and in 1941 founded an orchestra of his own: the New London Orchestra, a "Mozart-sized" ensemble of·about forty players. He was fortunate in getting mostly players who had specialized in chamber and solo work, and he soon had an ideal orchestra for the plans he had in mind. In but a few months they were giving excellent concerts in London, touring the provinces and broadcasting occasionally.

When Dame Myra Hess arranged to play the complete series of Mozart's Piano Concertos at the National Gallery, she chose Sherman and his New London Orchestra for this important work. One of these concerts was patronised by Her Majesty the Queen, who received Dame Myra and Mr. Sherman during the interval.

Alec Sherman has since conducted the BBC Symphony Orchestra—he is the first of its former members to do so, by the way—and also the London Philharmonic, London Symphony, Hallé and Liverpool Philharmonic Orchestras. In July, 1943, he became a conductor on the staff of the Sadler's Wells Ballet Company, to work with Constant Lambert; and in this new and interesting sphere of work he soon won the approval of the very discriminating audiences that patronise the Ballet at the New Theatre, London.

* * *

One of Mr. Sherman's most earnest desires is to see the principals of all the professional music organizations in the country gather together to plan concert-giving in an atmosphere of friendly co-operation. A start has already been made by the formation of the National Association of Symphony Orchestras, but he would like to see the work of this organization extended to cover the activities of all the smaller orchestras. He deplores the spirit of selfishness—and, let us be quite frank, even of spitefulness—that too often mars the relationship between musicians, for he believes that if they are to go forward and make the most of the great renascence of music we see to-day, they must all sink their personal interests and intrigues for the good of their art.

He welcomes C.E.M.A., with which his New London Orchestra is now co-operating, and hopes to see a great expansion of its activities in the future. Music needs some sort of State support, he thinks, although most of the concerts he has given have paid their way quite satisfactorily, but he does not wish to see his art come under Government control.

Having played under Toscanini, his admiration for him is absolutely unbounded, and he always tries to keep him in mind as a model of perfection. He believes that every conductor should, as part of his training, play in a professional orchestra for at least two or three years.

* * *

Alec Sherman is a bachelor. He is interested in sport and can play a good game of cricket. His other recreations are swimming, tennis and reading, not that his present engagements allow very much time for indulgence in any of them. His home is in London, where he lives with his brother, a doctor, who takes a great interest in music and assists in the management of the New London Orchestra.

ALEC SHERMAN

HEATHCOTE STATHAM

HEATHCOTE STATHAM

❦

UNTIL the present war, Dr. Heathcote Statham lived a comparatively quiet and unobtrusive life as organist of Norwich Cathedral, and it is only during the last two or three years that he has come into the limelight as a guest conductor of our greater symphony orchestras.

He was born towards the close of the nineteenth century in the Bloomsbury district of London. His father, who was an architect connected with 'The Builder,' was keenly interested in music and frequently took him to the organ recitals that used to be given at the Albert Hall on Sunday afternoons. No doubt these aroused his interest in music sufficiently to make him appreciate the great musical traditions of St. Michael's College, Tenbury, which has a choral establishment similar to the Cathedrals of the "old foundation," and after a few years there he went as a musical scholar to Gresham's School, Holt, Norfolk.

He was eighteen when he won an organ scholarship to Caius College, Cambridge, and studied under Dr. Charles Wood and Sir Charles Stanford for his degree in music. He tells me that he did nothing very remarkable at the University, though he was a member of the Music Club and occasionally played concertos with the College orchestra. A musical event prominent in his memories of Cambridge was the first performance of Vaughan Williams' "Sea Symphony," in which he played the percussion.

After graduating, he went to the Royal College of Music, and again came under Sir Charles Stanford, besides having the good fortune to work with Sir Walter Parratt.

His first appointment was as organist of Calcutta Cathedral. While he was in India he conducted several symphony and band concerts, which were chiefly patronised by European audiences, but he also attended various native gatherings for musical purposes. The Great War was in progress at the time, and he was a member of the Indian Defence Force, though he has no recollection of ever doing anything!

In 1919 he returned to England and became the organist of his former school at Tenbury. One of the greatest advantages of this job was the access to the famous music library collected by the College's eminent founder, Sir Frederick Gore Ouseley. It is one of the finest in the world. This enabled him to work for many months editing the anthems of John Blow (circa 1648-1708), besides writing various compositions for the organ and an operetta for boys' voices called " The New Master."

His next move was to Southampton, where he became organist of the Parish Church and conductor of the Southampton Philharmonic Society. Perhaps the highlight of his work in that southern town was a memorable performance of " The Dream of Gerontius."

When he was appointed organist and choirmaster of Norwich Cathedral he took over the conductorship of the Norwich Philharmonic Society, which can boast of having engaged at some time almost every artist of international fame for its concerts. In 1936 he also took charge of the Norwich Triennial Festival, the outstanding feature of the musical life of East Anglia, which dates back to 1770. He worked with Sir Thomas Beecham, and it is worth noting that this was the first time an organist of Norwich Cathedral had worked on equal terms with a world-famous conductor at this particular Festival.

It fell to Dr. Statham to prepare the great 1939 Festival, and as Sir Thomas Beecham was not available, Weingartner flew from Switzerland to take part in it. Alas! war threatened, and everything had to be cancelled.

Dr. Heathcote Statham's association with the London Symphony and London Philharmonic orchestras as a guest conductor began in 1940, when he took a performance of Moeran's Symphony in G minor at the Queen's Hall. Of this the ' Times ' said: " His exposition of an unfamiliar work was lucid, and he plainly knew every note of the well-packed score. Dr. Statham was extraordinarily successful in the two essentials of interpretation—breadth of view and regard for detail."

Since then he has toured with the L.P.O. and L.S.O. in various parts of the country, and has also appeared with them at concerts in London, notably those given at the Cambridge Theatre on Sunday afternoons.

*   *   *

He is particularly fond of conducting works of the modern English composers, but is disappointed to find that few of these compositions draw the public as they should. The chief difficulty, he thinks, is that many of these works are not easy for the average listener to appreciate at first hearing, and it is impossible to perform them frequently unless the orchestras are given substantial Government support. Nevertheless, he feels sure that modern English music will succeed in time, if only because the orchestras will not always be able to build their programmes on the more popular works of Beethoven and Tschaikowsky.

He is strongly in favour of a regional plan for symphony orchestras after the war. East Anglia, for instance, should certainly have its own symphony orchestra supported by Government subsidies, the rates of the various towns in the area, and private subscriptions. Such an orchestra would make Norwich its centre, and would give regular concerts in all the towns of East Anglia in turn.

Although he is a keen organist, Heathcote Statham is inclined to prefer conducting to any other form of musical activity. It is exciting and satisfying, he says, to be able to direct an orchestra made up entirely of first-class professionals. Of all the major works, he would rather conduct " The Dream of Gerontius " than anything else. " It is a great experience . . . it is like going through another world." Piano concertos also appeal strongly to him as a conductor, and he has a great admiration for the works of Benjamin Britten, Bloch and Vaughan Williams.

He was playing at a service in Norwich Cathedral one day in 1938 when the electrical mechanism of the organ fused, and in but a few minutes the whole instrument was burning. The service had to be abandoned, the choir making their exit during the psalms. It will perhaps be recalled that there was considerable controversy after this as to whether the organ should be rebuilt upon the screen, thereby dividing the nave from the choir, or put in a less conspicuous part of the building. The Dean and Chapter eventually decided in favour of the traditional position, and a new instrument—the second largest in the country—was installed just before the present war.

*   *   *

Dr. Heathcote Statham was married in 1928 to Mary Bourchier Wrey. His recreations are tennis, walking, going to concerts and cinemas, and playing chess "after a fashion." He is unlike the average orchestral conductor; he is inclined to be shy, nervous and very quietly spoken, yet one has only to see him on the rostrum to know that he is in every way the master of his orchestra. He is far more of a scholar than a showman.

GUY WARRACK

❦

L ET us now go north, over the border again, and meet Guy Warrack, joint conductor of the BBC Scottish Orchestra. He was born in 1900, a native of Edinburgh, and was educated at Winchester. His love of music developed quickly at school and although he assures me that he did nothing " noteworthy," I think it should be recorded that he frequently played the organ for the Chapel Services, organised House Choirs and other musical activities, and played the timpani in the School Orchestra.

His musical education was continued at Magdalen College, Oxford, under Sir Hugh Allen and Dr. Ernest Walker, and completed at the Royal College of Music, where he took composition with Gustav Holst and Vaughan Williams, and learnt conducting from Sir Adrian Boult. He won the Foli Prize and the Tagore Gold Medal. One of his most interesting recollections of Oxford, by the way, was of the visit paid to the University by Sibelius, when he was one of those appointed to entertain the great Finnish composer. On entering New College Chapel, Sibelius had to be asked rather firmly to stop smoking his cigar, and he showed his irritation in no uncertain manner!

Those early days were crowded with activity, for he was in demand both as a conductor and a timpanist. He once conducted the Albert Hall Orchestra in a performance of Act III of " Die Walküre " at the Royal College of Music in the morning, and on the same afternoon played the percussion in that orchestra at a Command Performance before King George V at the Coliseum. He also claims to be the only conductor who has conducted the " Meistersinger Overture " " three and a half times in two days " at the Albert Hall.

When he was twenty-five he joined the teaching staff of the Royal College of Music and became an examiner for the Associated Board of the Royal Schools of Music. He held both appointments for ten years. In 1926 the Oxford Orchestral Society chose him as their conductor, and in the ensuing years he also did excellent work in connection with the Oxford City Concerts for Children.

At about that time, too, he began a series of concerts in London with a chamber orchestra and produced several new British works by such composers as Constant Lambert, William Walton, Patrick Hadley,

140

Gavin Gordon, etc. He also performed many interesting revivals and arrangements of eighteenth century music.

Of his tours abroad, Mr. Warrack tells me that when he was in Rothenburg, Bavaria, he conducted an orchestra that possessed a very incompetent timpanist. The man made so many blunders during the rehearsal that at the concert Warrack was obliged to play the timpani himself and conduct at the same time!

For a year, 1927-8, he conducted the Royal Tunbridge Wells Symphony Orchestra and then became assistant conductor and chorus master for a season of opera given at the Royal Court Theatre under the direction of Sir Adrian Boult. Another point of interest that might be added at this juncture, is that Guy Warrack was conducting at the Lyric Theatre, Hammersmith, when Ellen Terry made her last appearance on the stage.

In 1934 he was appointed conductor of the Handel Society, but relinquished the post in the following year to take up his present position with the BBC in Glasgow. Since he first conducted the BBC Scottish Orchestra he has made over one thousand five hundred broadcasts, and has built up a repertoire of something like sixteen or seventeen hundred works. He is proud of having given many first performances of British compositions, and the first European performances of works by Aaron Copland, George Frederick Mackay, Daniel Gregory Mason, and other American composers. He has also revived many forgotten works by older composers of all nations.

Although he has conducted many orchestras in London and the provinces, he has not done very much in Scotland outside of the BBC, with the exception of one or two performances with the Reid Symphony Orchestra in Edinburgh.

He is inclined to think that the great musical revival is not quite as marked in Scotland as in England, though it has been his experience that there is always an audience for good concerts. In his opinion, the renascence of music is no mere war craze; it will continue in its effect, particularly as good music will probably be used more and more in the films.

Mr. Warrack objects to the type of ignorant musical journalism that one so often finds in the popular press: " purple patch " writing about the performances of celebrities, irresponsible criticism of the work of both composer and executant, and all the other types of humbug that tend to give the public a wrong sense of values. He also hates the invasion of political ideologies into the sphere of art. " Politics are boring enough in their own sphere without polluting others."

When I asked him if he thought the BBC music programmes were too scrappy, he replied: " I wouldn't know, as I so seldom hear any. In making programmes, however, all tastes have to be catered for, and this may result in a certain scrappiness."

Guy Warrack's second marriage, in 1933, was to Miss Valentine Clare Jeffery, who was trained as a dancer under Ninette de Valois, and who specialized in teaching dancing to children for several years. He has three children: John, born in 1928, now at Winchester, and learning to play the oboe; Julia Mary, born in 1930, who is learning dancing under Madame Nicolaeva-Legat; and Nigel, born in 1938.

He tells me that his recreations are " billiards and pure mathematics."

His compositions (all for orchestra) include:

Variations for Orchestra (1924)
Symphony in C minor (1932)
*" Jota "
" Fugal Blues "
Viennese Waltzes: * " Das Straussmädchen "
                  * " Der Mandelbaum "
Lullaby
Divertimento Pasticciato

*Also published as piano duets.

The more important of Guy Warrack's arrangements for orchestra are :

Suite from " Cupid and Death " (Locke and Gibbons)
" Musica Bellicosa " (XVIII century marches, etc.)
Overture: " Britannia " (Arne)
Overture: " Artaxerxes " (Arne)
Overture: " Diana, ossia Diana Vendicata " (J. C. Bach)
Sinphonia: " Belshazzar " (Handel)
Overture in D (Galuppi)
Six Scottish Dances (MacCunn)
Concerto No. 2 in D minor (Mudge: an eighteenth-century composer of whom little is known)
Four Pieces: " The Bohemian Forest " (Dvorak)

GEORGE WELDON

繋

I HAVE always had a notion that to talk to a Midland music lover about Manchester's Hallé Orchestra is about as dangerous as it is to praise one artist to another. The reason is not hard to find: Birmingham is a much larger city than Manchester, and any resident in the former will tell you that of course it is in every way superior to any city in Lancashire. I suspect that the rumour about Manchester's perpetual rainfall originated in Birmingham. But when it comes to music, the great Hallé tradition puts the Midland folk rather at a disadvantage, and those who are more discreet than I am carefully avoid the subject.

Birmingham, however, is not going to play second fiddle to Manchester indefinitely, and unless I am very much mistaken, we are going to hear a great deal more about the City of Birmingham Orchestra during the next few years. This is where George Weldon comes in, for to this young musician has fallen the task of putting our great Midland city in its right place on the musical map.

He is a native of Chichester, and although there were no musical traditions in his family, his parents discovered that he was stirred by music as soon as he emerged from the more troublesome stages of babyhood. He cannot remember a time when he was unable to play the piano.

He was educated at Sherborne School and did not conceal his joy when he discovered that his lameness precluded him from taking part in the majority of the sports and other activities that came under the heading of " physical training," because he was able to devote all the time thus saved to his musical studies. Apparently even this was insufficient: he remembers that as a punishment for spending time on music at the expense of his general education, he was once prevented from playing the piano for half a term. I think I ought to add, however, that if his lack of interest in the normal curriculum of the school caused any pedagogic bitterness, it was effectively neutralized by his willingness and outstanding ability to give any number of piano recitals at school concerts. Moreover, he was always on the spot when the services of an accompanist were required.

As soon as he left school he went to the Royal College of Music as quickly as a Southern Railway train could carry him. With Muir

Mathieson and a small crowd of other enthusiasts he studied conducting under Dr. Malcolm Sargent and Aylmer Buesst.

Much of his experience was gained with amateur choral, orchestral and operatic societies, and he has particularly happy memories of his work with the Tunbridge Wells Symphony Orchestra and the Newbury Orchestral Society, which, by the way, claims to be the oldest of its type in the country.

His first opportunity to conduct an entirely professional orchestra came when he was appointed as assistant to Julius Harrison, who was then the conductor of the Hastings Municipal Orchestra. He directed the orchestra for several weeks during 1937 when Julius Harrison was indisposed.

The outbreak of war in 1939 brought his work at Hastings to a close, and although he ran an orchestra of his own in that town for a while during 1940, the accompaniment provided by the Nazi airmen rather spoilt the effect, so he abandoned this venture and began touring the country with the London Symphony Orchestra. Then came the chance to conduct the R.C.M. Orchestra, which had previously been under the guidance of Dr. Malcolm Sargent, and to direct a season of the International Ballet, besides engagements with the London Philharmonic and National Symphony orchestras.

Weldon will never forget how at one concert which he was conducting at the Albert Hall, a cat suddenly appeared among the 'cellos, and then proceeded to walk right across the platform mewing a protest to the music being performed. Eventually it had to be chased through the audience to the back of the hall.

When the death of Mr. Leslie Heward robbed the City of Birmingham Orchestra of one of the most able conductors in England, the management decided to hold an open competition for the post. A number of conductors were each invited to take one of the Orchestra's concerts so that a choice could be made. That was how George Weldon received his appointment.

For several years the City of Birmingham Orchestra has been associated with the Midland Region of the BBC, and now, far-reaching plans are under consideration which would give the orchestra the status it deserves.

*　　　*　　　*

Weldon deplores the unimaginative programmes that are so often offered by British orchestras, and at all times he strives to introduce the best of the lesser-known music into his concerts. He believes that the demand for new music is steadily growing, although one still finds here and there an audience that looks upon unfamiliar music with

James Bacon & Sons Ltd.]

GUY WARRACK

[*Swarbrick*

GEORGE WELDON

distrust—especially if it is the work of a British composer! This unfortunate attitude towards contemporary British composers is perhaps the result of the more revolutionary ideas that some of them hold, but Weldon is convinced that the " new music " is now settling down and becoming more " logical."

He hopes to do far more concerts in the future for factory workers, so that the good work that E.N.S.A. is doing in wartime may be carried on into the peace. The value of children's concerts, too, cannot be over-estimated.

Weldon admits that he has a strong preference for Russian and English music: Elgar and Walton, especially, appeal strongly to him. He is afraid it will be a long time before the British public get out of the foolish habit of being " taken in " by foreign-sounding names: it seems almost impossible to convince the ordinary concert-goer that a pianist with a name such as Johann Schmidt is not necessarily a better musician than a man who calls himself simply John Smith.

*　　*　　*

George Weldon is a bachelor, and can think of no recreation more stimulating than a drive in a car capable of doing eighty or ninety miles an hour. In peacetime, his formula for dispelling worry was to get a powerful sports model and to let it rip on a good stretch of road. If you ever tread heavily upon one of his musical corns, you have only to change the subject quickly and begin talking about carburretors and superchargers, and before long he will admit that after all you probably were right—the horns *were* a bit sketchy in the middle of the second movement.

IAN WHYTE

§

THE BBC Director of Music for Scotland was born in 1901 near
Dunfermline, Fifeshire, the birthplace of Andrew Carnegie. He
could play the organ and piano when he was a boy, having received
lessons from his mother at a very early age. He can still remember
being given his mother's permission to play the organ in Dunfermline
Abbey when he was only ten or eleven.

He won a scholarship to the Carnegie School in Dunfermline and
stayed there until shortly before the end of the Great War. Another
scholarship—this time for the piano—brought him to London to study
at the Royal College of Music under Dr. R. Vaughan Williams and
the late Sir Charles Stanford. He has most happy memories of these
two eminent British composers; both fascinated him, though Vaughan
Williams seemed the more "pacific" of the two. Whyte believes that
we have yet to give them the recognition and appreciation they deserve.

His first appointment on leaving the College was as " Music
Henchman " to Lord Glentanar. This entailed residence at Aboyne, a
village near Glentanar House, and a variety of musical duties, including
the production of operas, ranging from Gilbert and Sullivan to Mozart's
" Seraglio " and " Magic Flute," with local talent, the conducting of
local choral societies, acting as organist, and so forth.

In 1924 he married Miss Agnes Mary McWhannel (he tells me that
this is a Scots' variation of McDonald). Their son Donald, born in
1926, shows promise as a sculptor, painter, engraver and wood-carver.

Ian Whyte was appointed Musical Director of Scotland in 1931, and
became conductor of the BBC Scottish Orchestra as soon as it was
formed. His taste in music is catholic, and he believes that music is
a message from God to man, the composer and executant being the
channels through which it must come. He has arranged over two
hundred old Scottish melodies for voice, string quartet, string orchestra
and full orchestra; and has many compositions to his credit, principally:

Symphony in One Movement
Symphony in Four Movements
Two Overtures: "The Treadmill" and "The Bassoon
    Factory"
Two Operettas: "The Forge" and "The Tale of the
    Shepherds"

Piano Quintet
Violin and Piano Sonatas
Ballet: "Goblin Ha"
"Sonnet 30" (Wordsworth), for chorus and strings.

*   *   *

Whyte is anxious to see the standard of orchestral playing in this country raised so that the great new audiences of to-day will become acquainted with music at its best. To bring this about, a State subsidy for all the professional orchestras is necessary. He does not favour Government control of music, and objects strongly to the use of his art for propaganda purposes, believing that music *is spiritual propaganda,* and that anything on a lower plane is unworthy.

When I asked him which of the more prominent conductors of to-day he admired, he replied: "Beecham for physical thrill; Boult for architecture and a good deal of spirituality; Barbirolli for energy—both physical and spiritual—and for orchestral tone building; but Toscanini— ' God's musician '—for all! Toscanini is the complete summit for me. I once went to the artists' door of the Queen's Hall to see if I could get a closer look at him. As I was placed, and because of passers-by, I had to stand aside to let him and his wife pass. I raised my hat . . . . and he raised his to me!"

Coming to the work of our contemporary composers, Whyte feels that there is a tendency to be "cerebral." He says: "Being one of them, I can speak for myself. It's easy to put notes down—and to be ' original ' —but harder to recognise them upon re-performance. I think some composers don't think the latter necessary as long as they sound good."

I asked if film music interested him. He replied " As mere background, no! As semi-background, no! As dramatic or lyrical linking, yes. It is in that way we shall have to evolve it."

On the question of broadcast opera, Ian Whyte is doubtful whether even the development of television after the war will solve the problem, because it will never be " the real thing." Radio, he feels, should be able to invent something new and " real " of its own.

Finally, here is his advice to those with aspirations to conduct: "(a) don't 'play' with 'temperament,' but concentrate upon learning every detail of your job, and (b) learn the score and don't think of yourself!"

LESLIE WOODGATE

✤

MY last musical portrait is of the Chorus Master of the BBC, Leslie Woodgate, a Londoner, born in 1902. He and his five brothers were all choirboys in London churches, and he confesses that the rather elaborate " flowery " music at Holy Trinity, Sloane Street, did much to arouse his interest in choral singing.

He was educated at Westminster and at the Royal College of Music. In his early youth he was attracted to the stage, and was only fourteen when he appeared as a dragon in the famous Christmas production, " Where the Rainbow Ends," to which Roger Quilter wrote the music. Another theatrical engagement he secured at about that time was the part of a newspaper boy in " The Luck of the Navy."

At the age of eighteen he was appointed Organist and Choirmaster of St. Andrew's Church, Park Walk, Chelsea, and also became private secretary of Roger Quilter. I have no doubt that his association with that distinguished composer caused him to start writing music in earnest, and it soon became evident that he possessed unusual ability in that direction. On his twenty-first birthday he received the most wonderful present that any young composer could wish for: a notification that he had been given the Carnegie Award, an honour that previously had gone exclusively to much older, established composers. He received it for two compositions for men's voices, strings, organ and piano: " The Hymn to the Virgin " and " The White Island."

It must also have been a great encouragement to him to find that other works of his were becoming quite well known. John Coates and Roland Hayes gave the first performance of several of his songs, and did much to make them popular with the general musical public.

Woodgate left the Royal College of Music in 1924, having held the George Carter Scholarship for organ and composition and having gained the A.R.C.M. for composition. He then sought further experience in a variety of musical activities.

He became associated with " Where the Rainbow Ends " again in 1928, but this time as musical director, and for the next ten years he conducted its incidental music at the Christmas performances. His other appointments have included the position of Organist and Choirmaster at the Alexandra Orphanage, and the Musical Directorship of the

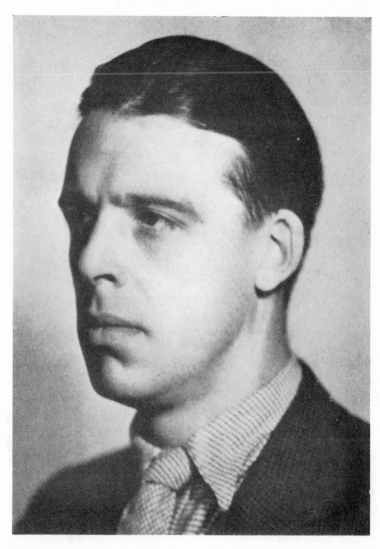

IAN WHYTE

LESLIE WOODGATE

L.N.E.R. Musical Society and of the Northampton Polytechnic. As an adjudicator he has appeared at musical festivals all over the country, notably at Blackpool, Morecambe, Skegness, Wallasey and Lewes.

Leslie Woodgate became the Chorus Master at the BBC on New Year's Day, 1934. His work includes the direction of the BBC Singers, the BBC Chorus and the BBC Choral Society, and the success which he has achieved with these bodies has earned him the reputation of being one of the most able choral conductors in the country. It is worth recording that when Toscanini was in this country he chose Leslie Woodgate to act as his chorus master, and spoke very highly of his ability when he returned to America.

Even now in wartime, Woodgate still keeps in touch with various independent provincial organisations as far as his duties with the BBC permit. During the past two or three years he has conducted several concerts given by the Huddersfield Glee and Madrigal Society and by the Leicester Philharmonic Society.

* * *

He was married in 1928 to Miss Lena Mason, who until 1940 was one of the first violins in the BBC Symphony Orchestra. They met as students at the Royal College of Music, by the way. Their home is at Wembley Park, and they have a son aged nine, Crispian Roger—named after Roger Quilter—who is now a probationer in the choir of Christ Church Cathedral, Oxford.

Woodgate's recreations are tennis and poetry. In the latter, his taste is catholic with a preference for the lyric. He tells me, too, that he adores cats and dogs.

While I am mentioning these more personal details I ought to add that one of his brothers, John Duncan, did a great deal of broadcasting as a baritone before he joined the army; and that Florence Woodgate, the actress, is Leslie Woodgate's niece.

* * *

I met Woodgate at the BBC Club in Chandos Street. We dived down into the snack bar in the basement and sat drinking tea while I tried to draw him out on controversial points in music.

Above all, he thinks it is deplorable that so many children are growing up hearing nothing but " synthetic " music nowadays, that is, music reproduced by the radio, gramophone or cinema mechanism. " They are getting an entirely wrong impression of the tone of the various orchestral instruments: the reproduction is invariably distorted." To correct this, he urges the provision of a much greater number of children's concerts, and more recitals in the schools. Woodgate is very anxious about the education of today. He believes that one of our greatest tasks is to help the younger generation to appreciate good art, literature and music, so that the noxious effect of the cinema is counteracted.

Contrary to the opinions of some of the other authorities on choral music, he declares that there is no sign whatever of a decline in choral singing. The war has upset the plans of many of our choral societies, depleting their numbers of tenors and bases, but the enthusiasm remains, and in the north especially, choral singing will be as strongly supported as ever when peace returns.

Contrasting the north and south of England, he says that the chief difference in the choirs lies in the fact that in the north they have marvellous voices and enjoy singing, whereas in the south the voices are not quite so good, and the people have to be *encouraged* to sing. If it is any consolation to the southern choirs, I would add that he has found that the subtleties in their singing are more effective than in the north, where the heartiness is apt to be too predominant at times.

In Wales, the singing is excellent, but he thinks that many of the choirs are inclined to lack good musical taste. This, however, is slowly being improved by the rising generation of Welsh composers and musicians, and Woodgate is confident that there will arise a new school of Welsh music worthy of that country's wonderful traditions in music.

He is a firm believer in modern music. The contemporary British composer is doing great work for the culture of our country: not all of the compositions of today can be regarded as successful, of course, but their general influence is good. These works are not lacking in emotion, as so many people seem to imagine, but their emotion is different from that revealed in the compositions of the romantics. It is much more restrained, and consequently it is apt to be overlooked by those who are impatient in their judgment of modern music. We must remember that restrained emotion is far more likely to endure than emotion that gushes out unimpeded.

Modern music demands much more effort on the part of the listener, because the composer of to-day does not wear his heart on his sleeve. Listening nowadays requires the use of the brain, as well as of the emotions. Most of us are thirty or forty years behind many of our modern composers, and as a result we find that their work is unintelligible. In twenty years' time our children will listen to Stravinsky and Bartók as easily as we listen to Bach.

Woodgate's only criticism of our modern composers is that so many of them seem to be unable to get away from cynicism. We are all inclined to be cynical—the two world wars are responsible for that—but this should not encroach upon music, because it obscures completely the true feelings of the composer. Despite this tendency, which will probably disappear when the present strife subsides, the young composers of to-day are going forward, and he believes that they have a great future.

Finally, Woodgate contends that all musicians should have some knowledge of the other arts: they need take no great active part in them, but they should be able to appreciate beauty in other forms than music, because in these forms should be the source of much of their inspiration.

THE LIFE OF SIR HENRY

AN APPRECIATION BY SIR ADRIAN BOULT:

" ON FRIDAY, the 28th of July [1944] Sir Henry Wood, besides conducting an Aria for Miss Joan Hammond and a Concerto for Mr. Maurice Cole, gave us a performance of Beethoven's 7th Symphony which will not easily be forgotten. It swept us along with all the torrential energy of that immortal work, and any stranger who was listening at home might well have thought that the performance was in the charge of some brilliant young conductor in his early forties. Those of us who were privileged to be there were thrilled once again by our old friend's perennial energy and perennial youth, and could never have believed that this was his own last homage to Beethoven.

" In this jubilee year, when so many tributes have poured in from all over the civilized world, it has been a moving experience for many of us to read all that has been said of Henry Wood by friends and colleagues everywhere. Two of his many qualities stand out again and again from these writings : his amazing breadth of sympathy with every progressive school and every honest composer; and his selfless service to all music, including as it did his unassuming readiness to let composer or artist take all the laurels at a public performance.

" Indefatigable worker as he was, he must surely have been well content to ring the curtain down on this notable broadcast, though all his friends, and particularly I know those in the Orchestra, were longing to see him back for the actual fiftieth birthday of the Proms on August 10th. That was not to be, and so we must let our own memories take us back to the countless hours of musical instruction and of familiar delight in Queen's Hall.

" We look forward to the new Henry Wood Hall, and hope that our subscriptions will make it a worthy memorial, and thus show our gratitude that the English musical world has been so immensely blessed by the work and life of Henry Wood.

ADRIAN C. BOULT."

J. WOOD 1869 - 1944

I.

Henry J. Wood was born in Oxford Street, London, on March 3rd, 1869. Strictly speaking, his father was an optician, but most of the business done in his shop was the sale not of spectacles, but of the model steam engines which he so skilfully constructed. It is also worth noting that his father was not the type of business man whose thoughts were centred upon nothing but money-making: he was a gentleman of cultured tastes in literature, art and music; he played the 'cello and possessed a fine tenor voice, which he used to good effect in the choir of St. Sepulchre's, Holborn, and in the Sacred Harmonic Society. His wife, too, was devoted to music, and had an excellent soprano voice.

So Henry Wood was blessed with parents who gave him every possible encouragement in learning the arts he loved. He had no schooling until he reached the age of nine, when he was sent to a small educational establishment in Argyle Street. He stayed there until he was fifteen, and although he showed no outstanding ability in the general subjects of the curriculum, he won every prize the school could offer for art and music. Later he went for a while to the St. John's Wood Art School, where he once met Whistler.

His love of art developed quickly when for six weeks after an illness he was sent to Crickheath Hall, near Oswestry, to recuperate. In that quiet pastoral country he spent most of his time in exercising his unusual ability to sketch. His skill as a painter must often have made his parents favour his adoption of art as a career, but fortunately for us he decided in favour of music, though I have no doubt that had he devoted his life to art he would have become one of our greatest painters. He was still only a boy when he was offered ten pounds for one of his sketches.

Although his artistic inclinations were revealed early in life, I must emphasize that he was a typical English schoolboy. He loved engines and mechanical contrivances of all types, he constructed electrical equipment for the entertainment of his friends, and among other pets, kept white mice and guinea pigs!

While he was still very young, he used to go with his father to St. Sepulchre's on Sunday mornings and sit in the organ loft listening enraptured to the fine Renatus Harris organ. To his great joy, he was given permission to practice on it when he reached the age of ten.

Normally, the pumping of this instrument required the services of two or three men, but Henry could employ only one: a typical old Cockney, who had to refresh himself at regular intervals at the " Saracen's Head " nearby.

He was only ten years old when he was authorized to play for the Wednesday evening services at St. Mary's Aldermanbury. His feet could scarcely reach the pedals, and to play even a sketchy base he had to perch himself precariously on the extreme edge of the bench. A kindly uncle used to be present on these occasions, and as the youthful organist received no official fee for his services, it was his custom to slip half-a-crown into Henry's hand at the end of each service. This money was carefully saved to buy new organ music.

Sir Henry's sense of absolute pitch was acquired very early in life from his father's habit of tapping glasses and cups on the table at meal times and asking him to say what note they sounded. His father believed whole-heartedly in the value of cultural activities, and took him to everything of outstanding interest in London: drama, opera, concerts, exhibitions—anything that would interest an intelligent lad.

He was always encouraged to make music at home. In the room allotted to him for use as a studio he held little chamber concerts with his friends. Enthusiasm at these informal gatherings ran so high that they rarely finished before midnight.

In 1883, when he was only fourteen, he was asked to give two or three organ recitals a week at the Fisheries Exhibition: an exciting opportunity which gave him a chance to play most of his favourite pieces, including excerpts from " Judas Maccabaeus " and " Samson " (Handel) and Mendelssohn's " Wedding March."

He became a pupil of Ebenezer and Louis Prout, who persuaded his father to send him to the Royal Academy of Music when he was sixteen. Here he studied the piano under Macfarren, the organ under Charles Steggall, composition with Prout and singing from Garcia.

Several of his own compositions were performed at the Academy while he was there, and on July 9th, 1890, two of his songs, "The sea hath its pearls" and "When on my couch I am lying," were sung by Ben Grove at the Royal Academy Public Concert in St. James's Hall.

His greatest ambition at that time was to become a teacher of singing. He possessed an excellent voice himself and took lessons from every professor he could find. It is also worth noting that Edward German was one of his contemporaries at the Academy.

In his autobiography, " My Life of Music," it is recorded that he *ran away* from the Royal Academy of Music. This was because he was so annoyed when a very inexperienced student was put on to conduct an organ concerto in which he was playing the solo part. He had worked for weeks on it to bring it to perfection, but everything was spoilt because the student-conductor was quite incapable of keeping the orchestra together.

However, Henry Wood received two bronze and two silver medals while he was studying there. I need hardly add, too, that being a kindly soul, he soon forgave those who had upset him, and his relations with that institution were always of the happiest after that time.

He had not been established very long as a teacher of singing before he found that he had as many pupils as he could manage, in fact, he was earning a handsome income by the time he was nineteen. He accepted the conductorship of several of the smaller choral and orchestral societies in the London area, and the first concert for which he received a fee as a conductor was given by a society at Clapton on January 1st, 1888. Sir Henry has always remembered that date, becausefifty years afterwards he celebrated his Jubilee as a conductor. The Bayswater Orchestral Society also provided him with some of his earliest experience as a musical director, and this enabled him to found the Hackney Orchestral Society.

The only noteworthy church appointment he ever held was that of organist and choirmaster of St. John's, Fulham, where he received sixty pounds a year. It was at this church that he once absent-mindedly played a funeral march at a wedding!

*　　　*　　　*

His father always followed his career with great interest and provided the necessary financial assistance to enable him to go on musical pilgrimages to Germany, Bavaria, France, Belgium and America. His friends must surely have envied his good fortune in possessing a parent who sent him to America expressly to hear the Boston Symphony Orchestra. He never forgot the first time he heard that famous orchestra play the " Eroica." It was " simply entrancing."

His first visit to Bayreuth was made in 1886. Later pilgrimages brought him in touch with most of the famous Wagnerian conductors including Mottl, Weingartner, Levi, and others, from whom he gained much of the knowledge that enabled him to distinguish himself as an authority on Wagner.

Quite early in his career he met Sir Arthur Sullivan, and quickly became a close friend of that eminent composer. He recalled in his autobiography how hurt Sullivan was when he found that the theatre audience chattered noisily while the orchestra was playing the overture to " The Yeomen of the Guard."

One day Henry Wood saw an advertisement for a conductor who was required to tour with a " Grand English Opera Company." Before applying for the post, he went with his mother to one of the company's performances in London and found that the orchestra consisted of a handful of players and a conductor who tried to compensate for the lack of instruments by filling in the gaps in the music with his left hand on a decrepit piano.

Nevertheless, he applied for the job because he felt that the chorus had possibilities, and thought the experience would be valuable. He was accepted at a commencing salary of two pounds a week and soon found himself at Charing Cross with a chorus of forty, a travelling orchestra of half-a-dozen, ten principals, a stage manager and the usual staff, bound for Ramsgate. In later years he often looked back and chuckled over his experiences with that extraordinary company, but at the time it was a source of constant anxiety to him, though he certainly succeeded in pulling them through their performances somehow.

He had many amusing experiences. In his autobiography he told how in one Lancashire town the stage carpenter had to adapt a wooden cow to represent a horse. The contours of the animal did not allow him to make much of a success of the job and on the first night the gallery crowd began bawling:

" Taak it 'ome! Thaat were't no 'orse! Thaat's a bloody cow!"

By the end of the first season Henry Wood felt that he was on the verge of a nervous breakdown and had to ask to be released from his contract.

*   *   *.

Back in London, he went into partnership with Gustav Garcia, who was running an operatic school in Berners Street, and secured an engagement to conduct a three months' tour of the Carl Rosa Opera Company. This time he had a far better orchestra and a fine company of highly trained singers, including Marie Roze.

His reputation as an operatic conductor was established when he directed Tschaikovsky's " Eugène Onegin " during a three months' engagement in London with the Imperial Opera Company of St. Petersbourg. It was at this time that he met Granville Bantock and Bernard Shaw.

II.

SHORTLY after the opening of the new Queen's Hall, which at that time was almost unknown, Mr. Robert Newman took Henry Wood into the arena, which had been cleared of seats, and asked him what he thought of the idea of having Promenade concerts. Wood took a quick

The Late SIR HENRY J. WOOD

HENRY J. WOOD in 1890

glance around and replied that he thought it would be a grand success.

Newman immediately took him out to lunch at Pagani's, and explained that he wanted the public to come to love good music. He proposed to do this by running nightly concerts; improving the people's tastes gradually by starting with quite popular programmes and introducing better items here and there until it became possible to do entire programmes of the finest music.

In February, 1895, he called on Wood and told him that he had decided to give the Promenade concerts a trial for a ten weeks' season. A permanent Queen's Hall Orchestra would have to be formed and would Henry be its conductor?

Sir Henry always remembered the tremendous thrill he felt at that moment when he visualized himself conducting his *own* symphony orchestra. Newman had great faith in him and believed that in time he would become a brilliant conductor. Up to that time all the celebrated conductors in England had been foreigners, but in Wood he saw a young man who could achieve eminence without disguising his identity, as many English musicians did in those days, by assuming a foreign-sounding name.

Much of the money for the first season was put up by Dr. George Cathcart, the ear and throat specialist, who offered financial assistance to Newman on two conditions: first, that the Continental low pitch was to be used so that there would be less strain upon the singers' voices; and secondly, that Henry Wood was to be the conductor. Dr. Cathcart was a great admirer of Wagner, and believed that Wood was the only Englishman who really understood his works and could conduct them properly.

The high English pitch had been the subject of much controversy, but up to that time it had been maintained because the wind instruments (and particularly, of course, the organs in the concert halls) were tuned up to it. Newman had always advocated the high pitch, but with a little persuasion from Wood he acquiesced and accepted Dr. Cathcart's offer, which was therefore directly responsible for the inauguration of the first Promenade season.

When all the arrangements had been completed, Wood set out to engage his orchestra, choosing chiefly the younger and more talented members of other London orchestras. Mr. Fry Parker was the leader for the first season, but was succeeded by Arthur Payne, who retained the position for many years.

It is interesting to note that the majority of the players of the wind instruments refused to buy new ones because they did not believe that the Continental pitch would be generally adopted in England. This meant that Dr. Cathcart had to buy most of the instruments himself (Henry Wood chose them personally at Victor Mahillon's establishment in Paris) and lend them to the players. But by the end of the first season most of the players had revised their opinions and bought their new instruments from Dr. Cathcart.

On the opening night, August 10th, 1895, Henry Wood received a colossal welcome from a packed house. There were eighty players in the orchestra, and prices ranged from one shilling in the promenade to five shillings in the grand circle, with season tickets from one guinea to five guineas.

Sir Henry kindly gave me permission to reprint the original programme, which, as you will see, is very different from the sort we get to-day:

OVERTURE	" Rienzi "	Wagner
SONG	Prologue (" I Pagliacci ")	Leoncavallo
	MR. FFRANGCON DAVIES	
(A)	" Havanera "	Chabrier
(B)	Polonaise in A	Chopin
	(orchestrated by Glazounov)	
SONG	Swiss Song	Eckert
	MADAME MARIE DUMA	
FLUTE SOLOS	(a) Idylle	Benjamin
	(b) Valse from Suite	Godard
	MR. A. FRANSELLA	
SONG	" Thou hast come "	Kennington
	MR. IVOR McKAY	
Chromatic Concert Valses " Eulenspiègel "		Cyril Kistler
	(First performance in England)	
SONG	" My Heart, thy sweet Voice "	Saint-Saens
	MRS. VAN DER VERE GREEN	
GAVOTTE	from " Mignon "	Ambroise Thomas
SONG	Vulcan's Songs (" Philemon and	Gounod
	Baucis ")	
	MR. W. A. PETERKIN	
Hungarian Rhapsody in D minor and G major		
(No. 2)		Liszt

INTERVAL OF FIFTEEN MINUTES

GRAND SELECTION	" Carmen "	Bizet
	(arranged by Cellier)	
SONG	" Largo al Factotum "	Rossini
	MR. FFRANGCON DAVIES	

OVERTURE	" Mignon "	Ambroise Thomas
SOLO CORNET	" Serenade " MR. HOWARD REYNOLDS	Schubert
SONG	" My Mother bids me bind my hair " MADAME MARIE DUMA	Haydn
SOLO BASSOON	" Lucy Long " MR. E. F. JAMES	
SONG	" Dear Heart " MR. IVOR McKAY	Tito Mattei
" The Uhlans' Call "		Eilenberg
SONG	" The Soldier's Song " MR. W. A. PETERKIN	Mascheroni
VALSE	" Amoretten Tanze "	Gungl
GRAND MARCH	" Les Enfants de la Garde " (First performance)	Schloesser

When we compare this with the wonderful programmes to which we are now accustomed, we see what Sir Henry did to educate the public during his fifty years of conducting.

It will be observed that even in this first programme there were two items performed for the first time in England. Thus the " Prom " tradition of introducing new works originated at the very start of the series. This practice proved to be very popular and successful, because there was always an attractive number of popular items to " carry " the novelties. By it, millions of people discovered that their notions about the dullness of " high-brow " music were all unfounded, and that there was plenty of good modern music for those who cared sufficiently to acquire a taste for it.

At the end of the first season it was decided that unknown artists must always be given an audition before they were engaged, as many influential people had attempted to push in performers who were definitely below the average standard of proficiency required of professionals. Sir Henry kept the notes he made at these auditions year after year, and they reveal that many of our most celebrated executants made their début at Promenade concerts.

Very often Sir Henry would sit patiently listening to an endless succession of quite hopeless people so that he could be certain that nobody with talent or possibilities had been overlooked.

*   *   *

In his second Promenade season Henry Wood introduced Tschaikovsky's " Casse Noisette Suite " to the public. This was given so great an ovation that he was compelled to repeat three of its movements, but I wonder if his audience knew then that it would become such a favourite as it is to-day? On the other hand, Rimsky-Korsakoff's " Scheherazade," which is also very popular to-day, was received quite coldly when Wood first performed it.

An interesting fact is that Sir Henry's first acquaintance with the Tschaikovsky " Overture 1812 " was when he heard it played in a public house at Victoria! The Band of the Coldstream Guards was rehearsing it, and he was invited to be present. The Overture delighted him, and he immediately ordered a full set of orchestral parts so that it could be put on at a Promenade concert.

It must not be imagined that in the early days of the " Proms " everything went smoothly for Henry Wood. On the contrary, Newman lost quite a lot of money during the first six years, and this must certainly have caused Wood some anxiety. His insistence on punctuality at rehearsals, too, was resented by many of the older players, who had the most dilatory habits. He was always a great disciplinarian and never tolerated the slovenliness and indifference one finds in a certain type of orchestral musician. After one rehearsal he happened to overhear one of his players ask a colleague: " I wonder where Newman picked up this brat Wood?"

At the end of the 1901 season, Newman found that the financial burden of running the Queen's Hall Orchestra was too much of a responsibility for one man to bear, so Sir Edgar Speyer formed a small syndicate to take over the entire organisation.

One day, Princess Olga Ouroussoff visited Wood's studio and asked to be given singing lessons. Sir Henry discovered that she had a true Russian soprano voice, and from that time took a keen interest in her musical career. More than that, he married her in July, 1898!

Princess Olga, who was also an accomplished linguist, appeared afterwards in many of Sir Henry's concerts. She was first heard at the Promenade concerts in 1901, when she sang " Elizabeth's Prayer " from " Tannhäuser."

*   *   *

Wood had the honour of taking his Queen's Hall Orchestra to Windsor Castle on November 24th, 1898, to give a Command Performance before Queen Victoria. The Queen chose the following programme:

> Good Friday Music; Prelude Act. III (" Die Meistersinger ");
> Overture, " Hansel and Gretel "; " Le Rouet d'Omphale ";
> " Symphony Pathétique " (third and fourth movements);
> " Siegfried Idyll "; Vorspiel (" Parsifal "); and the Overture
> from " Die Meistersinger."

At the conclusion, Her Majesty requested that they should play " The Ride of the Valkyries." Sir Henry immediately produced the music and gave a magnificent performance, but in their enthusiasm the brass forgot the limited dimensions of the Long Gallery, with the result that they almost blew the Royal audience out of the building. Nevertheless, the Queen was delighted, and warmly commended Sir Henry when he was presented to her by the Lord Chamberlain afterwards. Her Majesty presented him with a beautiful baton inscribed with the Crown and the initials V.R.I.

In 1899 Wood shared with the French conductor, Lamourex, the privilege of conducting the concerts of the London Musical Festival. For this, his own orchestra joined with the ensemble that Lamourex brought from Paris for the occasion.

Another outstanding date in Sir Henry's memory was February 2nd, 1902, when King Edward and Queen Alexandra attended one of his celebrated Sunday afternoon concerts.

With Princess Olga and Dr. Cathcart he went on a short visit to America in 1903. They were deeply touched when on their arrival at New York, Andrew Carnegie came on board to welcome them; but this was only the beginning of the enthusiastic reception that American music lovers had planned for them. Every possible kindness and consideration was shown to them, and Sir Henry received many tempting offers from people who wanted him to spend several months in the United States every year to conduct some of the famous American orchestras.

The Director of the Metropolitan Opera House in New York offered him fourteen pounds an hour to teach singing in his school of music, but there was a stipulation that lessons were to be only twenty minutes in length and three to the hour. Even if Sir Henry had been interested in the offer he would have refused on account of this condition, because he always maintained that no lesson should be of less than forty minutes' duration. He reminded the Director that the American mode of high-speed living could not be applied to art.

*　　　*　　　*

His enthusiasm for introducing new music to his audiences was not always appreciated. When in 1912 he conducted the first performance of Schönberg's " Five Orchestral Pieces," for instance, the audience showed their impatience and disapproval by hissing. As a contrast to this, when he first gave them Elgar's " Pomp and Circumstance " marches, they would not allow him to proceed with the programme until he had played the one in D-major three times!

When " Finlandia " was introduced to the London public by Sir Henry in 1906, it created a furore of applause. Another public favourite,

"Solemn Melody" (Sir Walford Davies), was first played at the Queen's Hall on September 8th, 1909.

I wonder how many of my readers know the origin of the famous "Fantasia on British Sea-songs" that has now become the traditional closing item on the last night of every Promenade season?

Shortly before the Trafalgar Day Centenary in 1905, Robert Newman thought it would be a good idea to celebrate the occasion with a special concert, so he asked Henry Wood to make up a programme of items all of which were to be about the sea. This he did, but it was felt that a really popular climax would be required, so Sir Henry collected all the sea-songs he could find and just in time for the concert, arranged the Fantasia as we now know it. He never thought for one moment that it would become such a favourite. Some years ago he decided to omit it, but his post on the following morning was so full of letters of protest that he resolved never to make such an experiment again.

ALTHOUGH the Promenade concerts always took up a great deal of Sir Henry's time, he probably did more than any other eminent conductor to promote music in the provinces. The present war forced him to abandon this work, but for years he was the conductor of the Hull Philharmonic Society, and in Nottingham he founded the City Orchestra in 1897. For many years he was associated with the Norwich Musical Festival, the Wolverhampton Musical Festival, and similar concerts in Birmingham, Cardiff, Manchester, Liverpool and Leicester. He became the musical director of the Sheffield Amateur Music Society in 1904.

All this provincial work taxed his physical strength to the utmost, for it meant that not only did he spend whole days in conducting rehearsals and concerts, but that his small amount of leisure was taken up in travelling.

* * *

The foundation of the London Symphony Orchestra in 1904 was the result of Robert Newman's rule forbidding members of the Queen's Hall Orchestra to send deputies. Abuse of the deputy system had by that time given Wood so much trouble and disappointment that Newman's action was the only solution. About forty members of the orchestra resigned, and formed themselves into the London Symphony Orchestra with Richter as their conductor.

* * *

In 1907 Wood invited Max Reger to lunch during that composer's visit to this country. Knowing his partiality for beer at meal-times,

Wood ordered two dozen bottles. He recalled in "My Life of Music" that Reger consumed *most* of the beer provided, and then had four glasses of whisky and soda after the meal. That afternoon he drove down to the German Club with the intention, Sir Henry said, of getting a drink.

During a rehearsal at the Hippodrome at Exeter, the management calmly informed Wood that there was a sea-lion in a tank under the stage. The animal was apt to bark for food, so throughout the concert a man had to feed it with fish to keep it quiet. During the softer passages the orchestra could hear the sea-lion splashing about and quite expected it to raise its voice in an effort to take part in the concert. What was even more disconcerting, however, was the appalling smell of the animal's prolonged luncheon.

Debussy's first visit to the Queen's Hall on February 1st, 1908, was so successful that Newman invited him to return in the following year. On this second visit a most unusual thing happened. After carefully rehearsing the orchestra, Sir Henry invited him to conduct his own works, but at the concert Debussy lost himself completely during the second of his Nocturnes, and, deciding to stop the orchestra and start again, he tapped the desk. To his amazement the orchestra *refused to stop!*

Sir Henry attributed this to the fact that they knew they were all playing correctly, and had they stopped, the audience would have thought that the fault was theirs. Between ourselves, Sir Henry didn't blame them!

*　　　*　　　*

Tragedy broke into Sir Henry's life towards the close of 1909 when Princess Olga died after a short but painful illness. For some time he found the greatest difficulty in continuing his work, but the kindness of his friends and the thought that the Princess would have wished him to find consolation in his music enabled him to carry on alone.

IV.

HENRY J. WOOD was knighted by King George V on February 23rd, 1911. This honour set a seal upon his great work of bringing joy to millions and of helping them to learn and love all that is good in music.

In the following May he gave the first performance of Elgar's Symphony No. 2 in E flat (dedicated to the memory of King Edward VII). Although the composer received three or four recalls, he felt convinced that the public did not like the symphony and went away very sad and disappointed. Sir Henry did his utmost to impress upon him that this work would receive its due appreciation when the public got to know it better, but he would not be consoled. Time has proved, of course, that Sir Henry was right.

*   *   *

Diverting from the subject of music for a moment, it is worthy of note that in 1911 there was an exhibition of Sir Henry's paintings at the Piccadilly Arcade Gallery for the benefit of the Queen's Hall Orchestra Endowment Fund. Fifty of his sketches in oil were on view.

*   *   *

Sir Henry at some time performed most of Dame Ethel Smyth's compositions. On one occasion when she was conducting one of her own works at a Promenade concert she mounted the rostrum, picked up Sir Henry's baton, and, deciding that it was much too long, calmly snapped it in two. She then threw one half away and proceeded to conduct with the other! I need hardly add that Sir Henry had a sense of humour.

Dame Ethel's rehearsals were rarely without some amusing incident. She had a habit of stopping the orchestra to refer to Sir Henry, who would usually sit in some obscure corner of the hall. She would then call out, " Henry, where are you? Hen . . RY!"

The introduction of women players into our orchestras has for many years been a controversial subject, but Sir Henry was always in favour of giving women with real talent a fair chance. He introduced six ladies into his orchestra on October 18th, 1913, as an experiment, and never regretted the venture. His many years of experience taught him that in most cases competent women were quite as good as men and had a habit of repaying recognition of their ability with excellent work. It should be noted, however, that Sir Henry never allowed women to undercut male players: he always insisted that they must be paid equal money for equal work.

At the outbreak of the Great War, Sir Henry found himself in difficulties with the more narrow-minded people, who demanded that no German music should be included in his programmes. Eventually, with the aid of Robert Newman's tact, he succeeded in quelling the agitators.

As the demand for the performance of the National Anthems of the Allies increased he re-scored several of them, including our own, which he transposed from B flat to G so that the people could more easily join in the singing of it.

By the way, Solomon made his first appearance at the " Proms " on 24th August, 1914—a child of only eleven years, dressed in a silk shirt and short knickers. His performance of Beethoven's Piano Concerto No. 2 was described by Sir Henry as " amazing."

164

As the war dragged on Sir Edgar Speyer and Lady Speyer, who were of German birth, were obliged to go to America (after they had spent thirty thousand pounds of their private fortune in providing music for the British people) and Messrs. Chappell's took over the Queen's Hall Orchestra. Owing to a legal technicality concerning its title, it had to be renamed " The New Queen's Hall Orchestra." Sir Henry retained the conductorship, of course.

On Good Friday, 1917, he gave a " Parsifal " concert in the presence of Queen Alexandra. This coincided with America's entry into the war, so he re-scored " The Star-spangled Banner " for the occasion.

Some idea of the public's appreciation of his efforts to keep the flag of music flying in wartime may be gathered from the fact that early in 1918 he received a tempting offer to go to America to conduct the Boston Symphony Orchestra for a whole season every year. Somehow, the news of this leaked out and it was mentioned in the newspapers. Immediately a terrific deluge of telegrams, telephone messages and letters swept upon him from music lovers, who were alarmed at the very idea of his leaving Britain. Deputations beseeched him to stay at home to continue his great work, and although it had always been his most ambitious dream to conduct so superb an orchestra, he decided that he could not forsake his own people. His decision was announced on June 1st, and when he went to conduct a concert on the following day he received an amazing ovation.

But that was not the end of the matter. Mr. A. J. Balfour requested Sir Henry to meet him at the Foreign Office, and asked him to reconsider the offer because the Government were anxious to further this country's friendship with America. Sir Henry could not be entreated, however; he explained that the musical public of Britain needed him and that on this account he felt it would be impossible to leave London at that time.

*   *   *

The twenty-fifth season of the " Proms " was marked by another Royal visit. King George and Queen Mary attended with Sir Edward Elgar (then Master of the King's Music) and heard a fine programme, which concluded with the " Fantasia on British Sea-songs." After the concert the King congratulated him and remarked that "Rule Britannia" was "a jolly fine tune."

In 1926 Sir Henry went to America again and conducted some of the famous Hollywood Bowl Concerts. The Bowl is a natural amphitheatre capable of accommodating a vast audience: a perfect setting for symphony concerts on a grand scale. One evening while he was there he found Charlie Chaplin in the audience and was pleasantly surprised to find that the great film star was keenly interested in British music.

In the same year Robert Newman was taken ill suddenly, and died after a short illness. This was a great blow to Sir Henry, who in one stroke lost not only a good friend, but also an extremely capable manager. Newman's assistant, W. W. Thompson, took charge and soon proved himself to be highly efficient.

* * *

Sir Henry's first broadcast was on January 20th, 1927, from the People's Palace. In the same year the BBC took over the Promenade concerts; the first one under the new régime being given on August 13th, 1927. Sir Henry welcomed the new arrangements because they freed him from the obligation of always having to put the box-office first in the consideration of programmes. Moreover he was then able to call daily rehearsals and preliminary rehearsals on four days before the opening concert, resulting in a higher standard of performance and making the introduction of difficult new works a more simple matter.

W. W. Thompson retained his management, by the way, as the BBC were quick to appreciate his ability and experience in dealing with the more temperamental members of the musical profession. The orchestra was merged into the newly-formed BBC Symphony Orchestra in 1930, a year which Sir Henry always remembered as the first in which he was able to present Mahler's colossal Eighth Symphony. This ' Symphony of a Thousand,' as it is called, was written for a thousand performers, including a chorus of four hundred and an orchestra of one hundred and thirty.

In the same year he visited South Africa and conducted the City Orchestra of Cape Town at four concerts before a most enthusiastic audience. After that, his musical holidays took him to such places as Costa Rica, Trinidad, Hamburg, Copenhagen, Boston, Mass., Montreal and Quebec—to mention only a few.

* * *

The pseudonym " Klenovsky " was adopted by Sir Henry in 1929 when he wanted to present his own transcription of Bach's Toccata and Fugue in D minor. In the past the critics had been rather abusive about Sir Henry's scoring, so he decided to pull their legs publicly. Had his own name appeared against this item, they would have been no more kind than on previous occasions, but as it was performed as a Russian transcription, it was acclaimed as a brilliant success. In but a short time the truth leaked out, much to the annoyance of certain people.

V.

SIR HENRY celebrated his fifty years of professional conducting on January 1st, 1938. When he went to rehearse the BBC orchestra at

Maida Vale that morning he was greeted by tremendous cheers from the orchestra and a delightful little speech from Paul Beard, the leader. Sir Henry's own way of celebrating this was to hold a grand Jubilee Concert in the Albert Hall on October 5th, and to offer all the proceeds to endow beds in London hospitals for orchestral musicians.

The following is an extract from the programme:

Conductor
SIR HENRY WOOD

Pianoforte
RACHMANINOFF

Singers

Sopranos
ISOBEL BAILLIE
STILES-ALLEN
ELSIE SUDDABY
EVA TURNER

Contraltos
MARGARET BALFOUR
MURIEL BRUNSKILL
ASTRA DESMOND
MARY JARRED

Tenors
PARRY JONES
HEDDLE NASH
FRANK TITTERTON
WALTER WIDDOP

Baritones and Basses
NORMAN ALLIN
ROBERT EASTON
ROY HENDERSON
HAROLD WILLIAMS

The BBC Choral Society
The Philharmonic Choir
The Royal Choral Society
The BBC Symphony Orchestra
Leader: Paul Beard
The London Symphony Orchestra
Leaders: W. H. Reed and George Stratton
The London Philharmonic Orchestra
Leader: David McCallum
The Queen's Hall Orchestra
Leader: George Stratton

Organists
Stanley Marchant   Berkeley Mason
Arnold Greir

THE NATIONAL ANTHEM
Audience, Chorus, Orchestra and Organ

Evening Hymn   " O Gladsome Light "   Sullivan
from " The Golden Legend "
Overture   " Egmont "   Beethoven

167

Concerto No. 2, in C minor   Rachmaninoff
for Pianoforte and Orchestra
Solo pianoforte—Rachmaninoff

Sanctus from The Mass in B Minor   Bach

" London Pageant "   Bax

" Serenade to Music "   Vaughan Williams
for sixteen Solo Singers and Orchestra
(Specially written for this occasion)

" The Ride of the Valkyries," from " Die Walküre " Wagner

The " Hailstone " Chorus from " Israel in Egypt "   Handel

March, " Pomp and Circumstance," No. 1 in D   Elgar

All the performers gave their services and the handsome illustrated programmes were presented by Hubert J. Foss and Messrs. Henderson and Spalding, Ltd. Over nine thousand pounds was raised, and this enabled Sir Henry to give nine beds.

*   *   *

Before I pass on to the next part of this sketch I ought to record that he was honoured with the degree of Doctor of Music by three English universities: Manchester (1923), Oxford (1926) and Cambridge (1935).

*   *   *

The outbreak of war in 1939 brought his work to a sudden stop— but only for a little while. His beloved Queen's Hall—his musical home—was completely destroyed in one of the great aerial attacks upon London during the early part of the war, but even this did not deter him. With the support of the BBC he continued his Promenade concerts in the Albert Hall with all his former energy and enthusiasm, inviting Sir Adrian Boult and Basil Cameron to assist him.

Immediately after the loss of the Queen's Hall, Sir Henry set his heart upon providing London's music with a new home after the war, so his friends decided to inaugurate a " Sir Henry Wood Jubilee Fund " to raise enough money for this purpose as a tribute to him and to celebrate his fiftieth Promenade season. A committee was appointed under the chairmanship of Lord Horder, consisting of the following members: Viscount Allendale, Sir Adrian Boult, Mr. Leslie Boosey, Mr. Edric Cundell, Sir George Dyson, Mr. Harold Holt, Lord Keynes, Lord Latham, Sir Stanley Marchant, Mr. Benno Moiseiwitsch, Mr. B. E. Nicolls, Mr. W. W. Thompson and Lord Howard de Walden.

Mr. W. W. Thompson, the manager of the Promenade concerts, was appointed Secretary, and Lord Howard de Walden kindly offered to act as Treasurer.

Approximately eight thousand pounds went to this fund as the proceeds of the concert held at the Albert Hall on March 25th, 1944, to celebrate Sir Henry's seventy-fifth birthday. This was a red-letter day in London's musical calendar. The BBC Symphony Orchestra, the London Symphony Orchestra and the London Philharmonic Orchestra combined to make one huge ensemble, which was conducted in turn by Sir Henry, Sir Adrian Boult and Basil Cameron. The Queen, Princess Elizabeth and Princess Margaret were present, and during the interval Her Majesty received Sir Henry, congratulating him upon his wonderful life of music.

The programme was:

Overture: " The Flying Dutchman "	Wagner
Brandenburg Concerto No. 3	Bach
Symphonic Poem: " Don Juan "	Strauss
Piano Concerto No. 3 in C minor	Beethoven
(Solo pianist: Solomon)	
Introduction and Allegro for strings	Elgar
Scherzo and Finale (Symphony No. 5) in C minor	Beethoven
" The Ride of the Valkyries "	Wagner

A short speech was made by Viscount Camrose, paying tribute to Sir Henry's work and inaugurating a nation-wide appeal for contributions to the Fund.

A few weeks previously there had been a great gathering of musical and literary personalities at the Royal Academy of Music when Mr. Leslie Boosey, Chairman of the Performing Right Society, handed Sir Henry an album of over seventeen hundred signatures and a cheque for a thousand guineas, which, of course, also went to the Jubilee Fund.

Another celebration was the luncheon at the Savoy Hotel organised by the Musicians' Benevolent Fund in honour of Sir Henry. Special verses written by John Masefield and a fanfare composed for the event by Arthur Bliss added a touch of originality to the occasion.

*   *   *

Shortly afterwards, music-lovers read with delight in the Birthday Honours List that Sir Henry had been made a Companion of Honour, and as many as could crowd into the Albert Hall on Saturday, June 10th, gave him a tremendous ovation at the first concert of the Jubilee Season. The programme was:

The National Anthem

Overture: " Roman Carnival "	Berlioz
The Prize Song (" The Mastersingers ") ...	Wagner
Piano Concerto in A minor	Grieg
" On hearing the first cuckoo in Spring " ...	Delius
Overture-Fantasia: " Romeo and Juliet " ...	Tschaikovsky
Organ Concerto No. 7 in B flat (Set 2, No. 1)...	Handel

For this fiftieth season, three orchestras were to have shared the work: the BBC, London Philharmonic and London Symphony Orchestras, but in the middle of June the Germans began attacking London with flying bombs, and the Promenade season had to be abandoned. Much of the music that Sir Henry had chosen for his programmes, however, was broadcast by the BBC.

*   *   *

Early in August an acute attack of jaundice prevented Sir Henry from attending the special Anniversary Concert that had been arranged for the 10th of that month. Anxiety concerning his health was widespread, but the announcement of his death at Hitchin, on August 19th came as a shock to music-lovers all over the country. Thus, at a time when the whole of Britain was becoming more and more excited over the liberation of France by the Allied armies, our great conductor passed to his rest.

VI.

WHEN I visited Sir Henry in his flat near Regents Park to discuss this book, I was impressed, above all, by his high-spirited vitality, which led me to believe that at the age of seventy-five he was enjoying better health than plenty of men twenty years his junior. I found him planning his fiftieth promenade season with enthusiasm and confidence that could scarcely have been surpassed even in his youth.

We started to talk about the tremendous revival of interest in music that is now taking place. He was convinced that it was no mere craze; the young, especially, had learnt to appreciate good music, and found that they needed it in their daily lives. The support given to the Promenade concerts during the past few years had proved this conclusively. Sir Henry thought that much of the credit was due to the schools, which in recent years had looked upon music as an essential feature in the education of children. He said he would like to see an extension of the practice of allowing school children to attend orchestral rehearsals, for they learnt so much on these occasions.

" Will this musical renascence bring about a revival of opera in this country?" I asked.

Sir Henry thought for a moment and then replied: " I cannot help feeling that as a nation the English are not operatically inclined. Beecham ought to have established opera for all time, but did not succeed. We have very few suitable singers and no adequate accommodation."

Sir Henry said he was in favour of State subsidies for music because he wanted to see our great orchestras freed from the necessity of having

170

to consider the box-office when programmes were being chosen. He wanted the best orchestras to give the best music at concerts within the means of everybody. This could only be done with the aid of subsidies, because such concerts could rarely be made to pay. The continual repetition of favourite items at many of the symphony concerts to-day, he told me, was a sign that the promoters were afraid of losing money by venturing upon new works. Subsidies would come in time, in fact grants were already being made by C.E.M.A. for special concerts, chiefly those given to the Forces and factory workers.

" Do you think we might have a Ministry of Culture?" I asked.

" No! We don't want our culture to be controlled by civil servants. Music would get into a groove. All our musical organizations must retain their own individuality and freedom, and the acceptance of grants must not bring them under official control. We want more recognition of the educational value of music and more opportunities to encourage music-making in the schools."

" Would you like to see a State Orchestra in this country, apart from the BBC Symphony Orchestra?"

" I think we have enough orchestras already," Sir Henry replied. " The BBC Symphony Orchestra, the London Symphony Orchestra and the London Philharmonic Orchestra and the Hallé provide all the symphony concerts we require, but I should like to see them getting more rehearsals. At present all our orchestras, with the exception of the BBC, are giving far too many concerts with inadequate rehearsals. They are obliged to do so to make enough money to meet their expenses. The greatest advantage of a Government subsidy would be in the removal of this obligation."

Sir Henry always had at heart the welfare of his players, and he deplored the strenuous lives some of them lead in their anxiety to compensate themselves now for the lean years that preceded the present war. He thought that many of them were trying to do far too much. He believed that to play well, a musician must be able to enjoy a period of rest and recreation of some sort every day. No member of a regular orchestra should exhaust himself by taking on too many outside engagements: it was not fair to the orchestra. The best solution, he thought, was to pay the players sufficiently well to enable them to dispense with outside work altogether.

*   *   *

Sir Henry Wood did more than any other conductor of his day to raise the salary of the orchestral musician, yet he himself was never interested in money. In Newman's time he worked for fees that most prominent conductors would have regarded with scorn. His generosity towards impecunious musical organisations was typical of a man who put his love of music before everything else. He would patiently rehearse a choral society for hours without even the slightest recollection of the fee he had agreed to charge.

He told me he believed that the standard of orchestral playing in this country had improved tremendously during the past twenty or thirty years. The younger players, especially, seemed to take great pride in being highly efficient, and he thought that some of our singers would do well to emulate them.

Sir Henry was keen to encourage the young composer who showed real signs of creative ability. Unlike many of our older musicians, he had a fresh modern perception which enabled him to judge a new work without prejudice. His taste was never jaded. If he thought a work had genuine merit, he would perform it even if he personally disliked it. It was always his wish that each member of the audience should form his or her own opinion of a composition, and he disliked all insincerity, cults, intellectual snobbishness and fashionable affectations in music.

A few months before his death, he told me that he did not agree with those who asserted that by touring the provinces the national orchestras competed unfairly with the local symphony orchestras. On the contrary, he believed that the leading orchestras set a standard, and fired the enthusiasm of music-lovers in the smaller towns. Without this stimulus, he thought that the local orchestras would get slack and revert to the old notion that anything was good enough for the provinces.

For much the same reason, Sir Henry was in favour of inviting foreign orchestras to this country in peacetime. Apart from the great work of spreading the doctrine that culture is international, these orchestras helped to promote goodwill between the nations. But he wished that more English orchestras had been invited to tour the Continent. In the past, he had noted, foreign orchestras were keen enough to come over here, but rarely invited ours in return. He said he hoped that after the war one or two of the famous Russian orchestras would come over here for a while, for the Soviets were quite keen to exchange orchestras occasionally. He also thought that we should try to encourage more interchange of artists.

Sir Henry had great faith in the modern English composer. He believed that we have some very promising young men, and that the work of our more established composers—Vaughan Williams especially—would go the rounds of the world and establish itself for all time.

The chief fault he found in the younger conductor of to-day was his impatience and unwillingness to learn with amateur orchestras and choral societies. These organizations, he declared, provided an excellent training-ground because the conductor would encounter every fault imaginable, and in many cases would have to be a very good musician to keep the ensemble together at all. Sir Henry insisted that the art of conducting could be learnt only in front of an orchestra. If possible, all conductors should try to get some experience in opera, for in this type of work the musical director had to keep every single instrument playing exactly to his beat, otherwise when the principal soprano wished to hold a quaver for three and a half beats, there was bound to be a catastrophe! This sort of experience was despised by some of our younger conductors of to-day: they were too eager to start earning big money as soon as they left College.

It would be almost impossible to include in this sketch all Sir Henry's criticisms of the modern singer, but one point he emphasized in our discussion was that many singers nowadays did not seem to know the difference between a recitative and an aria, for in the former they rarely allowed the natural rhythm of the words to predominate.

We talked for some time about America, which he thought would continue to make rapid progress as a musical centre because their orchestras were so magnificent. The personnel of the average American orchestra generally represented every nation of any size in the world, but this never appeared to be in any way detrimental to the work of the ensemble.

Music in the Empire, he thought, was in a much less happy position, and he recommended that we should send our orchestras on Empire tours after the war. Australia and New Zealand were particularly in need of good music.

When we discussed film music, Sir Henry told me that he felt more happy about it now that the better orchestras were being engaged for this important work. Some of the films produced recently had used excellent music, but he thought that the reproduction in most of the cinemas was truly dreadful.

Somehow, the question of quarter-tones cropped up when we were talking about the future of music, and Sir Henry said he felt very doubtful about their use in symphonic music, though the composers of the future might make use of them frequently for special effects. When I suggested that large sections of the public would never be able to understand music at all if quarter tones were employed, he said: " Perhaps so, but you must remember that the ear can get used to anything. The music of Wagner and Strauss horrified people at one time."

However, Sir Henry did not exclude the possibility that the future might bring startling changes: there might be a new notation altogether. But the use of quarter tones at present would only turn the public away from the concerts, and he doubted whether many of our present-day instrumentalists could play such music. Good intonation was not easy to obtain at the best of times: with quarter tones it would become a nightmare.

When we came to the subject of broadcast music, Sir Henry said that on the whole the BBC did very well considering the time-limits imposed upon them and the multifarious subjects that had to be crowded into the programmes. He told me that on one occasion he asked Newman, who had been criticizing his Promenade programmes, to make out what he considered to be an ideal week's programme of " perfect Promenade music." Newman made several attempts, but eventually gave up in despair!

VII.

It was probably because of his vast repertoire that Sir Henry never conducted from memory. He was one of the most reliable conductors that the world of music has ever known: his stick never failed to give the indication the players required. His left hand did comparatively little: it was reserved almost exclusively for indications that could not be given by the baton.

He was always extremely conscientious, and spent an enormous amount of time personally correcting and editing parts. Everything was done methodically and with the utmost care, and until 1937 he personally supervised the tuning of every instrument before the concert Rehearsals and concerts were always worked out to a timetable.

He was not temperamentally " nervy," and never worried about anything. As one would expect, he inspired his players with a feeling of confidence, and despite his strictness, they invariably had a feeling of deep affection for him. They even forgave his use of a hand-bell to stop them at rehearsals!

Sir Henry loved his native London, and always enjoyed a morning spent in its shops. It grieved him to see its war-scars, and above all, to contemplate the ruins of his beloved old Queen's Hall. But he was not depressed. He talked to me like an enthusiastic youngster about the concert hall that will now be his memorial. " I should like to see a sort of Empire Meeting Hall; a fine structure that could belong to London. It would have to be *free*—that is, not tied to any society or syndicate. It would be the people's hall for the people's music, and I should like it to have two or three lesser halls for chamber music, lectures and discussions. It would also require a park for at least a thousand cars."

He thought that the site of the old Queen's Hall would be convenient, but doubted whether it could be made large enough. He had in mind a site near Regent's Park that would be ideal, but he realized that much would depend upon the general plans for the rebuilding of London after the war. The only point upon which he felt strongly regarding the site was that it should be *central* and within easy reach of the Underground and main line railway stations.

So there I will conclude. We may rest assured that the erection of this new concert hall was one of his greatest ambitions, and it is the duty of all music-lovers to see that this is made a memorial worthy of him.

[APPENDIX]

THE BBC SYMPHONY ORCHESTRA

T HE story of the BBC Symphony Orchestra is inseparably bound up with the life of Sir Adrian Boult, and most of it will be found in my sketch of him. There are, however, a few details which I have not yet recorded.

When war was declared in 1939, the Orchestra was sent to Bristol, and most of its concerts were given in the Colston Hall. It was reduced from one hundred and nineteen to ninety-two players, because it had already been agreed that the members under thirty-five years of age should be released for national service. Of the ninety-two left, a further forty-one have since volunteered for the forces, so that only fifty-one of its original members are left. Temporary players have, of course, been engaged to fill its ranks.

I think I ought to explain here the difference between " The BBC Symphony Orchestra " and " The BBC Orchestra," because this is a question that has been puzzling listeners for some considerable time. When it is announced that a programme is being played by " The BBC Orchestra " it means that either section B or C is being used. When Paul Beard leads it is generally the former, about sixty-five players; when Marie Wilson is the leader it is generally the latter, a much smaller ensemble of anything from thirty to forty players.

Sir Adrian has recently sent a " News-Letter " to all the members of the Orchestra engaged on national service, and he has kindly given me permission to quote from it. He explains that after the Orchestra had worked in Bristol for about two years it was moved to a place " . . . about fifty miles due north of London, and not very far from Cambridge, so that we are able to get over there five or six times during the winter and give concerts there on Saturday afternoons."

During its sojourn in Bristol, the Orchestra experienced many air-raids. During one of them, Paul Beard was blown off his bicycle, and in another Albert E. Cockerill and his wife were killed instantaneously by a direct hit.

First Violins—Leader: Paul Beard [BBC

Second Violins—Principal: Barry Squire (right) [BBC

Violas—Principal: Philip Sainton (left)

Cellos—Principal: Ambrose Gauntlett (left)

Flutes—Principal : Gerald Jackson [BBC

BBC]
Double Bass—Prin.: Eugene Cruft   Harp—Sidonie Goossens [BBC

THE BBC SYMPHONY ORCHESTRA

Oboes—Principal: Horace Green

CONDUCTOR: SIR ADRIAN BOULT

Clarinets—Principal : Frederick Thurston

Double Bassoon—Principal: Archie Camden

Horns—Principal: Aubrey Brain

Trumpets—Principal : Ernest Hall

Trombones—Principal : Sidney Langston

Tuba—W. Scannell

Tympani—Principal: E. Gillegin

" We were very proud to hear that two of our colleagues now on fire service, Mr. Terence MacDonagh and Mr. William de Mont, were given British Empire Medals for conspicuous bravery in a London fire. They came to see us one night at the Proms; and another frequent visitor is Squadron-Leader Bernard Shore, whose travelling duties sometimes bring him to our present base.

" Besides regular concerts in our base and visits to Leicester, Northampton, Rugby, Cambridge, Kettering, etc., we have visited London on a number of occasions. We have given a short series of Summer Concerts in the Albert Hall for the last two years.

" I think we all specially enjoyed Sir Henry Wood's Jubilee Concert. It was a great occasion, and the Hall was absolutely over-flowing. In addition we were able (quite literally even on that enormous platform) to rub shoulders with a great many old friends of the London Philharmonic and London Symphony orchestras, whom we had not seen for a long time. After the Concert, Lord Camrose provided all three Orchestras with an excellent tea.

" We have also successfully tackled the difficulties of wartime travel, and visited South Wales on two occasions for a week each, once with the full Orchestra and a second time with Section C, led by Marie Wilson, when we made our base at Aberdare, and co-operated almost every day with one of the many excellent choirs scattered about that neighbourhood.

" We also had three particularly enjoyable weeks with the Services, at Aldershot with the Army, Portsmouth with the Navy, and with the Royal Air Force at a depôt in South Wales. We were very proud to break the record takings of the Garrison Theatre, Aldershot, by one and ninepence—it had previously been held by Gracie Fields!

" The Navy entertained us in grand style. By the use of acres of the best bunting they transformed their gymnasium into an ideal concert hall holding twelve hundred people, and we all remember a marvellous party in the splendid Wardroom of the Barracks after our last concert.

" The R.A.F. week was marked by a particularly enterprising programme, including the Walton Symphony, and a visit from John Barbirolli.

" We have recently been back to Bristol, where we gave two Public Concerts and visited a number of places around, playing almost entirely to American troops. American hospitality lived up to its reputation, and the total weight of the BBC Orchestra rose considerably during the week!"

THE LONDON PHILHARMONIC ORCHESTRA

THE LONDON PHILHARMONIC ORCHESTRA was founded in 1932 by Sir Thomas Beecham and a group of wealthy friends who associated themselves with his ideals. He had been feeling very concerned about the standard of orchestral playing in this country, and had decided that the only way to get the sort of orchestra he wanted was to assemble an entirely new one personally.

He was adamant in his demand for an orchestra with permanent, unchanging personnel that could be moulded in the manner he desired, and therefore, the old system which allowed players to send inferior deputies as frequently as they liked had to be drastically reformed. He searched all over the country for players whose one ambition was to excel in orchestral work; men who, if necessary, were prepared to sacrifice personal considerations in the interest of the orchestra as a whole.

Many of the players he chose were young men: brilliant instrumentalists, but with only a limited amount of orchestral experience behind them, so to compensate for this, he also selected a substantial number of older and more experienced men to work with them. Thus he obtained the energy and verve of youth together with the steadiness and reliability of experience.

The first concert given by the London Philharmonic Orchestra was on October 7th, 1932. The programme opened with the famous " Carnaval Romain " Overture by Berlioz, and the audience were so amazed at the vitality and colour portrayed that ordinary clapping could not express their great appreciation: most of them cheered heartily, and quite a number stood upon their seats to do so!

In but a few weeks the new Orchestra was taking a leading part in the musical life of London. It was appearing with the Royal Philharmonic Society and the Royal Choral Society, besides figuring prominently in the International Seasons of Grand Opera at Covent Garden and the autumn season of Russian Ballet. Of the provincial towns, Leeds, Sheffield and Norwich were the first to engage it for their musical festivals.

One of the advantages of having an orchestra of his own was that Sir Thomas was able to specialize to some extent in the music of Delius and Sibelius, and he did a great deal to introduce the work of these two great modern composers to the general public. At Covent Garden, too, he was responsible for the first performances of many works almost unknown at that time.

In 1935 the L.P.O. made its first visit abroad. This was to Brussels, where two concerts were given in connection with an International Exhibition. In the following year a most successful tour of eight important musical cities in Germany extended the Orchestra's reputation far into the heart of Europe, and in 1937 the L.P.O. was able to visit Paris and give a concert for which every seat was sold.

When the war clouds began to gather in 1938 and 1939, many of the wealthier patrons of the Orchestra began to lose interest in it, and as Sir Thomas had never allowed financial considerations to affect his artistic policy, it is not surprising that these two factors brought the Orchestra into financial difficulties.

The 1939 Opera Season left the management with a serious deficit and when the declaration of war prevented the Russian Ballet from visiting this country, the Orchestra found itself faced with ruin. Mr. Thomas Russell, the Secretary, in his booklet "London Philharmonic," writes: "With the failure of the opera season and the non-arrival of the Russian Ballet, the historic building in Covent Garden reached the lowest point in its chequered career. The home of opera for centuries, where the voices of Patti, Melba and de Reszke had delighted generations of concert-goers, and where Weber and Wagner had made musical history, sank to become a dance hall. The indecent haste with which the transformation took place was an indication of the complete abdication of the recognised leaders of our pre-war cultural life. Musical life in London suffered severely from this misuse of a great building. But our attention was fully occupied by the announcement of the voluntary liquidation of the Company which had been governing the Orchestra."

Sir Thomas Beecham spoke so eloquently at the liquidators' meeting that all the trade creditors withdrew at the end of it without a word of protest and made no further attempts to press their claims. Moreover, when two members of the Orchestra put forward a scheme whereby the ensemble would become self-governing, he promised them all possible support and offered to defray the expenses of forming a new company.

On the following morning, the new company was formed, and only active members of the Orchestra were allowed to become shareholders or directors, though Sir Thomas was still recognized as the official conductor. In those dreary early days of the war the Committee met again and again to put the Orchestra on its feet. They had no money, no office staff, no home, and not even a sheet of official notepaper. When at last a short tour was arranged, it was anything but easy to raise enough money to provide the transport.

The first concert was given in Cardiff on October 1st, 1939, the forerunner of the magnificent series of provincial concerts that are now part of the Orchestra's normal routine. But at the end of the first three months, the financial position was as grave as ever, and Sir Thomas had to make a public appeal for assistance. The result was most encouraging, but then followed a sequence of tragedies that again emptied the coffers: a financially disastrous Bach Festival, an Anglo-French Festival which took place in the very week that France collapsed, and the first of the air-raids. It looked as if the end had come.

Then Mr. J. B. Priestley heard of their plight, and suggested that the Orchestra with three conductors and a soloist should take part in a " Musical Manifesto " at which he would make a special appeal. He also promised to bear personally any financial loss that might be incurred. Sir Adrian Boult, Basil Cameron, Dr. Malcolm Sargent and Miss Eileen Joyce lent their assistance, and it was a great success.

This brought an offer from Mr. Jack Hylton, who was prepared to undertake the financial responsibility of sending the Orchestra on a tour of the provincial theatres and music halls so that they could play popular symphony concerts to an entirely new section of the public. They began in Glasgow on August 12th, 1940, but alas! on that very day the air-raids on Britain were intensified. Some people naturally presumed that the public would no longer wish to attend symphony concerts, but they overlooked the fact that the mood of the people was changing rapidly. A new defiance was in the air; a determination that the Nazis should not rob us of our culture inspired music-lovers to continue their support in spite of personal danger, and with this encouragement the L.P.O. continued to visit all the blitzed towns of Britain regardless of danger, lack of accommodation, the shortage of food in certain areas, the blackout and the inconveniences caused by dislocated railway communications.

But another blow was yet to fall. On the night of Saturday, May 10th, 1941, the Queen's Hall was destroyed, and with it the instruments belonging to many members of the L.P.O., for a rehearsal was to have been held there on the following day. However, even this did not break the spirit of the players. New instruments were obtained almost miraculously, the next concert transferred to the Duke's Hall of the Royal Academy of Music, and the good work continued.

From that time, the Orchestra has prospered. The demand for good music has increased continually; and now, the chief difficulty is to find the time to visit all the towns that are clamouring for symphony concerts.

Efforts are now being made to establish the Orchestra on a more secure basis than it has ever enjoyed in the past, and if the Government can increase the grant now being paid through C.E.M.A., there is every reason to believe that the future of this famous body of musicians will be assured.

THE LONDON SYMPHONY ORCHESTRA

YOU will remember reading in my sketch of Sir Henry Wood that about fifty members of the Queen's Hall Orchestra broke away from it when they were forbidden to send deputies, and formed themselves into the London Symphony Orchestra. They became a co-operative body, and gave their first concert under Dr. Hans Richter, who had been their constant adviser and friend during the difficult transitional period.

From the start they adopted a policy of giving their concerts under guest conductors—a practice which has often been criticized—believing that it was better for both audience and orchestra. It certainly brought a great many famous names into association with the L.S.O. We find that the early concerts were directed by such distinguished men as Nikisch, Steinbach, Colonne, Elgar and Henschel, and it is worth recording that they all spoke very highly of the skill and adaptability of the players—particularly the strings.

Then followed concerts with Wassili Safonoff, the famous Russian conductor, a provincial tour under Elgar, and engagements for the season of German opera at Covent Garden. On June, 1907, a special concert was given to commemorate the completion of Richter's thirty years' work in England.

In 1912 the London Symphony Orchestra visited America and Canada. They played in New York and the larger towns of the East and Middle West, and then went on to Toronto, Ottawa and Montreal, returning finally for a farewell concert in New York.

During the Great War, Sir Thomas Beecham gave them valuable assistance, although comparatively few concerts could be given. In 1919, Albert Coates came on the scene and conducted for two or three seasons, during which Prokofieff came and played one of his own Piano Concertos.

The L.S.O. weathered all the trials that beset musical organizations in the difficult years between the two World Wars, adding to its lists of conductors such famous names as Goossens, Koussevitsky, Wein-gartner, Furtwängler, Sokoloff and Bruno Walter.

It was one of the first orchestras to resume public concerts after the outbreak of the present war. In October, 1939, when almost all other musical activity in England had ceased, they gave a concert at the Queen's Hall under Sir Henry Wood. This was followed by seven more in the ensuing months, and when the Promenade season came round, the Orchestra was engaged to take the place of the evacuated BBC Symphony Orchestra. During one of these concerts there was a severe air-raid, and the Orchestra played practically the whole night in the Queen's Hall to entertain those members of the audience who were unable to go home.

Since then the L.S.O. has toured all over the country, and in addition to its normal routine of concert-giving has performed on dozens of occasions before huge audiences of factory workers and members of the Allied forces. It is now operating in association with C.E.M.A. under that organization's latest scheme which embraces the larger orchestras.

THE HALLÉ ORCHESTRA

THE story of the Hallé Orchestra begins not in Manchester, as one would imagine, but in Germany; for it was there that Charles Hallé was born in 1819. At the age of seven he was giving public recitals as a pianist, and by the time he reached early manhood he was sufficiently accomplished to move to Paris and make a handsome income. The revolution of 1848 drove him to London, where he lived for two or three years before he accepted an invitation to live in Manchester.

In the great cotton city he found enough pupils to enable him to earn a living, so he decided to settle down there and cultivate the rather crude love of music he found in the Lancashire folk around him. Choral music appealed most strongly to them, but their taste was not good, for they had become accustomed to music that was decidedly second-rate, chiefly because they had never been introduced to anything better. There was, however, a nucleus of cultured musicians, and with their assistance he began to introduce symphonic music as he had known it in Paris.

The great Art Treasures Exhibition of 1857 brought him his first opportunity to launch out on a large scale. He formed a full-sized symphony orchestra of the best musicians he could find, and gave several excellent concerts which fired the enthusiasm and imagination of the people. Thus encouraged, he decided to inaugurate a series of orchestral concerts to be known as the Hallé Concerts. The first series opened in January, 1858, and although at the end the net profit was only half-a-crown, he was determined to continue them each year. This he did with outstanding success, and they became a national institution. The Hallé Orchestra became famous, and some idea of their progressive policy may be gained from the fact that as Brahms completed each of his symphonies, Hallé was waiting to put them into his programmes.

Charles Hallé was knighted in 1888 in recognition of his great services to music, but even then he did not rest upon his laurels, for he had yet another ambition to fulfil: the establishment of a College of Music in Manchester for the benefit of the students in the north. This was accomplished in 1893, and he became the first Principal of The Royal Manchester College of Music.

When Hallé died in 1895 at the age of seventy-six, three prominent Manchester citizens, determined that his good work should be continued, took over the responsibility of running the Hallé Concerts and maintained them until the Hallé Concerts Society was formed in 1899. The Society is, of course, still in existence. Its members all give an irrevocable undertaking to act as guarantors to the extent of a hundred pounds each, and it is due entirely to their generosity that the Concerts have been continued year after year, because at the end of some seasons during the less prosperous years there were serious deficits.

As soon as it became established, the Society sought a worthy successor to Hallé. They acted boldly, and sent an invitation to one of the greatest conductors of the day, Dr. Hans Richter, explaining their constitution, objects and difficulties. In the fashionable musical circles the invitation was regarded more as a joke than anything else: nobody thought for one moment that Richter would leave his pleasant environment and condescend to work in a North of England town that was supposed to consist of little else than grimy cotton mills, and to be populated chiefly by uncultured factory workers! But Richter thought very highly of Hallé's great work and knew something of the good-hearted Lancashire people, so to the astonishment of all, he accepted the invitation.

His association with the Hallé Orchestra is now part of the musical history of Britain. It was he who established the music of Wagner in the north, and helped to introduce the work of Elgar to the people. At the same time, he was devoted to the classics, and upon them built the great reputation of his orchestra. It is worth noting, too, that he was always concerned about the personal welfare of his players, and must have been one of the first conductors in the world to suggest a pension scheme for the members of an orchestra.

Richter was succeeded in turn by Michael Bolling, Sir Thomas Beecham, Sir Hamilton Harty, Dr. Malcolm Sargent and John Barbirolli; all of whom have maintained the fine traditions of the Society, even during the hard times of economic depression when heavy financial losses were sustained: losses which would have forced many musical societies to exploit " popular " music for all it was worth.

It was during one of the " slump " periods that the number of concerts given by the Society was so drastically reduced that the players found it impossible to live on the fees they received. There was little to be done because the northern towns simply could not offer the Orchestra more engagements, and as the situation became more critical, the Committee, after careful consideration, decided to accept an offer made by The British Broadcasting Corporation to engage a nucleus of the Hallé Orchestra, including the principals, and to use them in the BBC Northern Orchestra on the condition that they were to be released for all the Hallé Concerts. It was an arrangement fraught with difficulties, but it worked, and the Hallé Orchestra was kept in being throughout the years of anxiety that ruined hundreds of other professional musicians.

When the outbreak of the present war heralded the great revival of interest in music, the Hallé Orchestra received overwhelming demands for concerts: probably more than ever before in its history. There was but one course open for the Society: to reconstitute the entire Orchestra on an entirely new basis. With the welfare of the players in mind and with the intention of making it an ideal ensemble capable of fulfilling all the demands made upon it, the Committee decided to pay all the players a regular salary.

Then arose the question of engaging an eminent conductor able to devote the whole of his time to the work. Dr. Malcolm Sargent, who had been conducting most of the Society's concerts in the past, was unable to undertake the task, so it was decided to send a telegram to John Barbirolli, who was then working in America.

As the reader now knows, Barbirolli accepted this invitation and returned to assemble one of the finest orchestras the country has ever known. He gathered together all the most accomplished of its former members, he searched everywhere for promising young players, and in one month welded them into one body with some of the personnel

THE LONDON PHILHARMONIC ORCHESTRA

THE LIVERPOOL PHILHARMONIC ORCHESTRA

THE HALLÉ

THE SCOTTISH

ORCHESTRA

ORCHESTRA

THE CITY OF BIRMINGHAM ORCHESTRA

THE BOYD NEEL STRING ORCHESTRA

that had been engaged by the BBC. How he did it in but a few weeks, nobody knows—when I asked him myself he just laughed and said that much of the credit was due to his wife who acts as his secretary.

I think it must have been the thrill of reviving the glory of a noble tradition that inspired the Orchestra in those first few months: it certainly provided the impetus that enabled them to work with almost superhuman energy during the early rehearsals.

Today, the Hallé is once again leading the musical life of the north. The Society is financially independent, though valuable help has been given by The Carnegie Trust, The Pilgrim Trust and C.E.M.A. Furthermore, the Corporation of Manchester has come forward with a grant on certain conditions, during the past two years.

It must be emphazised, however, that the Society has no intention of allowing any supporting body to take any part in its financial control, or to influence its musical policy. The executive Committee is chosen only from members of the Society.

The only thing that seriously troubles the Hallé Society now is its lack of a musical home. The great Free Trade Hall, in which all the concerts were given since the days of Charles Hallé, was destroyed in an air-raid during the early part of the war. There are now very few suitable halls in Manchester, and many of the concerts have to be given in local cinemas, which certainly cannot be regarded as ideal! But the music-lovers of Manchester are not depressed: they are determined that as soon as conditions permit, their city will have a concert hall worthy of its great musical traditions.

THE SCOTTISH ORCHESTRA

IN 1891 a limited company was formed in Glasgow with the object of promoting orchestral music in Scotland by maintaining a first-class symphony orchestra for the purpose. I think I am right in saying that in those days Scotland possessed no regular professional orchestra of full symphonic dimensions. In any case, the task of organising such an ensemble was not an easy one, and it was 1893 before the complete body of eighty players was assembled, with permanent accommodation in Glasgow. George Henschel accepted the conductorship, and Maurice Sons was chosen as the leader.

The Orchestra made rapid progress, and soon became associated with all the leading choral societies north of the border. Henschel resigned in 1895 and was succeeded by Wilhelm Kes, who in turn made way for Max Bruch in 1898.

At the opening of the twentieth century, Frederic Cowen was appointed conductor, and held the post until 1910. Subsequent conductors were Mlynarski, Sir Landon Ronald, Julius Harrison, Talich, Richard Strauss, Fritz Steinbach, Edouard Colonne, Hans Richter, Sir Henry J. Wood and Albert van Raalte—though some of these cannot be regarded as more than guest conductors for a season. John Barbirolli was appointed in 1933 and continued in office until he went to America. Then George Szell took over for about two years until Warwick Braithwaite accepted the position.

The Scottish Orchestra has undoubtedly fulfilled its mission faithfully: it has a wonderful record of concert giving in Scotland, and has also visited London and various cities in the North of England, including Leeds, Newcastle and Huddersfield.

Mr. Warwick Braithwaite tells me that the Orchestra is now supported by a gift from Glasgow Corporation of five thousand pounds and an equal sum from Sir Daniel Stevenson. A further four thousand five hundred pounds is guaranteed by generous patrons in the City of Glasgow alone, and other contributions come from Aberdeen, Dundee, Inverness and Dumbarton.

The recent extension of the season in which the Orchestra plays has been enthusiastically welcomed by many thousands of music-lovers, and there is now a general demand for a permanent Orchestra to play all the year round. "Lord Inverclyde is in favour of this," Mr. Braithwaite tells me, " and has taken it up in public and suggested that the whole of Scotland should contribute towards the upkeep of the Orchestra. If this comes off, Scotland will come into line with Liverpool, Manchester, the L.P.O. and L.S.O."

THE CITY OF BIRMINGHAM ORCHESTRA

Soon after the end of the Great War, the need for an established City Orchestra was keenly felt in Birmingham. Within the last hundred years the City had seen the promotion of innumerable orchestral enterprises within its boundaries, but most of them had encountered insuperable difficulties—generally of a financial nature—and had eventually collapsed. So a Committee was set up under the chairmanship of the late Mr. Neville Chamberlain, then the Lord Mayor of Birmingham, to investigate the possibility of placing orchestral music on a more solid foundation than it had hitherto enjoyed.

It was not an easy task. Seaside resorts and spa towns had their light municipal orchestras because they had to consider the entertainment of their visitors, but up to that time no industrial city in Britain had thought of establishing an orchestra which would be subsidized from the rates. There was a certain amount of opposition from those who looked upon the proposal as merely another means of squandering the ratepayers' money, but Mr. Chamberlain and the others who had associated themselves with the scheme at last succeeded in convincing the Corporation that the formation of a good municipal orchestra would be a legitimate educational undertaking, and that it would be of enormous value in the cultural life of the City.

Thus, in 1920, the City of Birmingham Orchestra was founded, with Appleby Matthews, a prominent local musician, as its conductor. The management was entrusted to a private committee, two of whom were to be members of the City Council.

The early years of the Orchestra's life were not without vicissitudes but gradually it became stabilized, and when Dr. (now Sir) Adrian Boult took charge in 1924 it entered upon a period of prosperity and high artistic achievement. Mr. Chamberlain continued to take an enthusiastic interest in it, though of course when he became absorbed in national politics he had less time to devote to it than in the days when he was concerned primarily with municipal affairs.

When Dr. Adrian Boult became the Director of Music to the BBC in 1930, the committee were indeed fortunate in securing the services of Leslie Heward, young conductor of outstanding ability, whose name will for ever be associated with music in the Midlands. His death in May, 1943, brought sorrow into the hearts of music-lovers all over the country. In the programme of the Memorial Concert given in the Town Hall, Birmingham, on June 11th, 1943, by the City Orchestra, with Sir Adrian Boult and Dame Myra Hess, Professor Victor Hely-Hutchinson wrote the following tribute, which I reprint with his kind permission.

"Leslie Heward was one of the most variously gifted of men; in music, though he chose the career of a conductor, he could have risen to equal heights as a composer or pianist; besides this, he was a brilliant talker, a ready and able writer, and no mean draughtsman. As his amazing musicianship was infused with that ease and lightness of touch which are the accompaniments of true power, so his personal relations were all informed by a glorious sense of humour, which was the reverse side of an intense seriousness and single-mindedness as regards his art.

"Had it not been for this single-mindedness, he would certainly have achieved wide recognition earlier, for he sedulously avoided anything like self-advertisement or exhibitionism, nor did he ever go a step out of his way to try and cultivate those social contacts which can sometimes do so much to speed up a conductor's career. But social success, which he could have achieved brilliantly if he had cared to, simply did not interest him; he would have regarded it as a distraction from his work. He preferred his music and the society of his own friends; and few can ever have inspired a deeper affection among those who enjoyed his friendship.

" It is a tragedy that now, when real recognition had at last come to him, when his wonderful genius had reached full fruition, and at a time when orchestral music is more widely and deeply appreciated in England than ever before, he should have been taken from us. He was only forty-five, and in the course of nature we might have hoped that he would be a leader of music for another generation; in artistic steadfastness, perfection of accomplishment and catholicity of musical taste, there could scarcely be a finer one. As it is, he has passed from us at the height of his powers, and none of those who knew him will ever think of him, in his zest for life and music, as anything but a young man.

" So we must lay him to rest with the words which are carved on Schubert's gravestone: ' Music has here entombed a rich treasure, but still fairer hopes.' "

*   *   *

After a number of concerts given with guest conductors, George Weldon was chosen as musical director.

The City of Birmingham Orchestra has always been a full symphony orchestra, although the number of its strings has varied from time to time. At present there are forty. It has visited Burton, Banbury, Bristol, Bromsgrove, Cheltenham, Derby, Gloucester, Hanley, Hereford, Kendal (Westmorland Festival), Kidderminster, Leamington, Malvern, Newport, Newtown, Oxford, Rugby, Shrewsbury, Stratford-on-Avon, Worcester, Wolverhampton, Walsall, Warwick, West Bromwich and a dozen other smaller towns. Many successful concerts have also been given in famous public schools, including Malvern, Repton, Rugby, Oundle, Cheltenham, Eton, Clifton, Wellington and Shrewsbury.

The value of taking music to the schools has always been fully appreciated, and as soon as the Orchestra can be established on a full-time basis this side of the work will be developed considerably. All the secondary and grammar schools in Birmingham have been visited, and, in addition, excellent work has been done by sending quartets and trios drawn from the personnel of the Orchestra.